FETISHISM AND CURIOSITY

Laura Mulvey

INDIANA UNIVERSITY PRESS
Bloomington and Indianapolis

BRITISH FILM INSTITUTE
bfi

BFI PUBLISHING

First published in 1996 by the
British Film Institute
21 Stephen Street, London W1P 2LN
and the
Indiana University Press
601 North Morton Street, Bloomington, Indiana 47404

The British Film Institute exists to promote appreciation, protection and
development of moving image culture in and throughout the whole of the
United Kingdom. Its activities include the National Film and Television Archive;
the National Film Theatre; the London Film Festival; the Museum of the Moving
Image; the production and distribution of film and video; funding and support for
regional activities; Library and Information Services; Stills, Posters and Designs;
Research; Publishing and Education; and the monthly *Sight and Sound* magazine.

British Library Cataloguing in Publication Data
A catalogue record for this book is available from the British Library

ISBN   0-85170-5480
       0-85170-5472 pbk

US Cataloguing data available from the Library of Congress
A CIP catalog record for this book is available from the Library of Congress

ISBN   0-253-33211–7 (clothbound)
ISBN   0-253-21019–4 (paperbound)

Cover design: Romas Foord
Cover image: Les Vampires. Hartfort, 1916 (from *Les Affiches du Cinéma Français*
by Jean-Louis Capitaine)

Typeset by
D R Bungay Associates, Burghfield, Berks

Printed in Great Britain by
St Edmundsbury Press Ltd, Bury St Edmunds, Suffolk

For my son, Chad Wollen,
with love and gratitude for
the extent of his enthusiasms –
most especially, movies and Marxist theory.

Contents

Acknowledgments

Introduction has been adapted from 'Some Thoughts on the Theory of Fetishism in the Context of Contemporary Culture', *October* no. 65, Summer 1993.

Chapters 1 and 2 have been developed from 'It Will Be a Magnificent Obsession. The Melodrama's Role in the Development of Contemporary Film Theory' in Jacky Bratton, Jim Cook, Christine Gledhill (eds), *Melodrama. Stage Picture Screen* (London: BFI, 1994). I would like to thank Christine Gledhill for inviting me to the conference on which the book is based.

Chapter 3 is based on a lecture entitled 'Cinema and Sexuality' given as one of a series in honour of the centenary of cinema at the Museu da Imagem e do Som, Sao Paolo. I would like to thank Ismail Xavier for inviting me to contribute to this event.

Chapter 4 has been adapted from 'Pandora. Topographies of the Mask and Curiosity', first published in Beatriz Colomina (ed.), *Space and Sexuality* (Princeton: Princeton Architectural Press, 1992). I would like to thank Beatriz Colomina for inviting me to the conference from which this volume is drawn.

Chapter 5 was first published as 'A Phantasmagoria of the Female Body. The Work of Cindy Sherman' in *New Left Review* July/August 1991.

Chapter 6 was first published as 'The Hole and the Zero. The Janus Face of the Feminine in Godard' in Colin MacCabe and Raymond Bellour (eds), *Jean-Luc Godard: Son + Image* (New York: Museum of Modern Art, 1992).

Chapter 7 has been adapted from my book *Citizen Kane* (BFI Film Classics; London: BFI Publishing, 1992).

Chapter 8 was first published as 'Xala: Ousmane Sembene 1976. The Carapace That Failed' in *Third Text* nos 16 and 17, Autumn/Winter 1991.

Chapter 9 also appears as 'The Pre-Oedipal Father; the Gothicism of *Blue Velvet*', in A. Lloyd Smith and V. Sage (eds), *Modern Gothic: A Reader* (Manchester: Manchester University Press 1996).

Postscript is reprinted with kind permission of Phaidon Press. It originally appeared as 'Changing Objects, Preserving Time' in *Jimmie Durham* (London: Phaidon Press, 1995).

I would like to acknowledge the generosity of the following:
The Society of the Humanities, Cornell University, for a Senior Fellowship, Fall Semester 1990; The Regents of the University of California for a Regents' Professorship at the University of California, Davis, Spring Quarter 1992; The Department of Women's Studies, The Ohio State University, for a Visiting Professorship, Fall Semester 1992.

I would like to thank:
Jonathan Culler, Director of the Society of the Humanities at Cornell, and all the administrative staff at the A.D White House, for their kindness and hospitality; also, the Fellows of the academic year 1990–1, especially Jonathan Nagate, for viewing and discussing *Xala* with me.

Irit Rogof, for suggesting and supporting my appointment as Regents' Professor, Sabrina Barton and Phil Barish for extraordinary help during my stay at University of California, Davis, and everyone who attended my seminar there.

Judith Mayne, for inviting me to Ohio State, and Christina Lane for her help with my administrative and academic work.

My colleagues at the British Film Institute, especially Paul Willemen for his patience during the many exacting moments he spent editing this book as well as his lively engagement with its contents, and Colin MacCabe for continuing, over the last ten years, to encourage me to publish my work.

My sister, Rosamund Howe, officially for her exemplary copy-editing, but also for many other acts of help and support.

Preface

The essays in this collection were written over the last five years. Although they are presented in thematic groupings rather than in the strictly chronological order of their writing, the sequence roughly corresponds to shifts in my ideas or, rather, to the inflection of my preoccupations. The Introduction represents an attempt to give an overview of the notions of fetishism deployed throughout the book. While writing most of these essays, I thought of fetishism as a psychological and social structure that disavowed knowledge in favour of belief. At the same time, I was interested in considering curiosity, a desire to know, as a counterpoint to the blindspots of fetishism. By degrees, I came to realise that the psychoanalytic concept of fetishism, because it could maintain knowledge and belief simultaneously, was more open to processes of decoding than other symptoms of unconsciousness. Its symptoms appear reified as things that attract the gaze but also provoke curiosity. Rather than seeing fetishism and curiosity as irreconcilably polarised, I tried to find a more dialectical relation between them.

The cinema is the main, but not the only, cultural area under consideration in this book. And my ideas are explicitly influenced by feminism, even if issues of femininity are not, for instance in the last few chapters, obviously under discussion.[1] More and more, I have tried to bring together questions of history with the theories that have formed my way of thinking. Part One is about Hollywood cinema of the studio system and so remains within the framework of most of my earlier writing about cinema. The chapters in Part One very obviously go back over ground that I have covered before, such as the Hollywood melodrama, Douglas Sirk, woman as spectacle in Hollywood cinema, and so on. But here I have also attempted to provide a historical dimension to my discussion of these familiar topics.

My use of the term 'history' here is too monolithic. Chapter 1, 'Americanitis', is explicitly autobiographical and traces the imbrication of my intellectual development with successive waves of British film theory. Chapter 3 is only a 'sketch towards a mapping' of familiar questions of spectatorship and femininity onto a more historical framework. It suggests that, while the iconography 'woman as spectacle' persists throughout the Hollywood cinema, the meaning and address of the icon may alter significantly according to inflections within the social, economic and even political dimensions.

My new concern with questions of history is partly a grateful response to the research into the history of the Hollywood industry that is taking place, primarily in the United States. However, I can only respond to, rather than participate in, these important discoveries and, even more importantly, nuances given to our understanding of film history. As my work with film theory only very gradually acquired an academic context, I have remained an 'essayist' and, I would say with no intended self-denigration, a dilettante. This book reflects the strengths and the weaknesses of my intellectual formation, and I hope that it will be read in this light.

In the process of editing these essays, most of which have been published previously in more or less different forms, I found that certain themes kept recurring almost to the point of repetition. I have left the repetitions, particularly in Part Two, seeing them as a thread of ideas which, as they accumulate, bear witness to a struggle to articulate images of femininity which I find both fascinating and difficult. In this section, I shift from the deciphering spectator, who is not so distantly related to Barthes's 'reader' and who responds to the semiotic regime developed so particularly by Hollywood, towards the 'rebus' of the fetishised female body. I found that I returned over and over again to the way that this body materialises as an imaginary spatial relation, a phantasmatic topography. Julia Kristeva's perception of the abject body, particularly as reformulated in Barbara Creed's work on the horror film, helped me to find a figure for the space into which the fetish collapses.

Part Three examines two films which explicitly refuse to displace abjection onto a fetishised female figure while carefully working through the psychic process of disavowal from a male point of view. I argue that through this refusal, the films demand a spectator who deciphers *politically*, as the refusal of fetishism is linked, in both cases analysed, to recognisable political crises. In *Citizen Kane*, Susan quite simply cannot sustain the status of fetish object, but after her attempted suicide she equally simply refuses to be 'abject'. Susan's behaviour is, in Freud's terms, normal. She leaves Kane to bear the burden of his own fetishism and abjection. Similarly in *Xala*, when the Western fetish objects collapse around El Hadji, the film inexorably and almost unbearably returns to the male body in the final scene of ritualised abjection. But no political solution, or even context, is available to *Blue Velvet*, the subject of Chapter 9 and one of the most darkly revealing films of the all-American psyche trapped in the excess of its own success.

'Postscript' on the artist Jimmie Durham closes the book in order to provide a reverse image of the Introduction. It was with relief that I found myself absorbed in a work of cultural production that made full use of irony as an aspect of oppositional art. Irony dismantles the surface certainties of fetishism and it dispels abjection as daylight does a vampire. The state of abjection is essentially anti-intellectual, beyond thought, and is related to the state of cultural breakdown experienced by colonised people. Durham's use of irony breaks both the binary opposition of colonised and coloniser and the negative aesthetics of the twentieth-century avant-garde so that his art opens up a dialectic which, once again, demands an active, ironic, spectator.

One implicit assumption running through the collection is that economic relations are changing in the world today. This is not to imply that apocalyptic change will convulse the world with the coming of the millennium. Quite clearly, however, the communications and entertainment industries, gathering momentum for over a century, have come to play a central part in late capitalist economies. With these considerations in mind, Marx returns onto the agenda of cultural criticism with renewed, and significantly altered, force, particularly the Marx who said: 'The hand-mill gives you society with the feudal lord; the steammill, society with the industrial capitalist. The same men who establish their social relations in conformity with their material productivity, produce also principles, ideas and categories, in conformity with their social relations.'[2] This Marx would no doubt have reflected with interest on the Rupert Murdoch phenomenon. For most of my intellectual life, such simple correlations would have fallen into the category of vulgar Marxism. Nowadays, the gap of determination between economic structures and culture seems to be narrowing.

This book, however, is not about the future and hardly even the present. The fetishisms in this book meet on the cinema screen, which for quite some time has not been a dominant mode of cultural production or the leading entertainment industry. Two broad themes recur within the more explicit topics under discussion. First of all, I am interested in understanding the ideologies and mode of address that belong to 'the societies of the spectacle' as structures of the psyche. Quite simply, if a society's collective consciousness includes its sexuality, it must also contain an element of collective unconsciousness. In order to avoid the connotations that belong to the concept 'collective unconscious', I have preferred to use the term 'social unconscious' (or sometimes 'collective fantasy'). I have not built on the Freudian aspect of Althusser's theory of ideology, but concentrated rather on the way that feminist theory has constructed collective fantasy into a 'symptomology' through an analysis of popular culture, particularly the cinema. Sexuality moulds these symptoms in two ways. On an overt level, twentieth-century commodity culture has flaunted sex. On another level, such erotic images disavow those aspects of a society's sexuality that are hidden and disturbing. In this sense, the obvious discourse of sexuality appears as a symptom, literally, in the case of the cinema, screening its repressions.

Although the 'screen' metaphor is temptingly evocative, it is important to remember that symptoms only emerge into the world transformed by displacement and condensation. The images that then appear, on the screen for instance, are coded. The second theme of the book revolves around the way curiosity might be transformed into a political process of deciphering images. And these images call out for the help of psychoanalytic theory to decipher them. My use of psychoanalytic theory is not sophisticated and is more in the spirit of 'dollar-book Freud' than 'Lacanian Freud'. It corresponds, that is, to the inscription of psychic elements into the works of popular culture that I analyse and it attempts to 'make visible' rather than to 'read in'. However, the process of reading is also one of enjoyment and excitement and, I think, relates closely to 'pleasures of the mind's eye', such as the riddles that Oedipus contemptuously dismissed when he defeated the Sphinx. My interest in a deciphering reading that appeals to curiosity also leads back to the cinema. The cinema combines word and image in the manner of a rebus and all cinema spectatorship has to be, to some extent, a decoding of meaning. Hollywood cinema, most of all, encrypts meanings into its formal properties, most particularly, of course, through a highly stylised use of *mise en scène*.

My approach to cinema is directed at its 'curious' nature, not at its 'realist' nature. Rather than its ability to reflect the world, I am interested in its ability to materialise both fantasy and the fantastic. The cinema is, therefore, phantasmagoria, illusion and a symptom of the social unconscious. It is precisely these elements that are fun to decipher, for any audience: for the detached 'Brechtian' spectator as well as for the feminist critic. In this book I have concentrated particularly on the forms of encryptment that affect images of femininity and fetishism.

Returning to fetishism: it is the most semiotic of perversions. It does not want its forms to be overlooked but to be gloried in. This is, of course, a ruse to distract the eye and the mind from something that needs to be covered up. And this is also its weakness. The more the fetish exhibits itself, the more the presence of a traumatic past event is signified. The 'presence' can only be understood through a process of decoding because the 'covered' material has necessarily been distorted into the symptom. The fetish is on the cusp of consciousness, acknowledging its own processes of concealment and signalling the presence of, if not the ultimate meaning of, a historical event. The fetish is a metaphor for the displacement of meaning behind representation in history, but fetishisms are also integral to the very process of the displacement of meaning behind representation. My interest here is to argue that the real world exists within its representations. Just as simulacra seem to be poised to take over the world, it is all the more important to attempt to decipher them.

The Gulf War did happen, in spite of what Baudrillard may claim.[3] Its picturing at the time, and the way its picturing was staged on television, are integral parts of its historical truth as well as being symptomatic of world history's narrative. At the same time, behind the once upon a time spectacle lies the incontrovertible reality of intense human suffering. And over the human tragedy, like a nuclear cloud, hang the difficult to decipher complexities of international politics and economics. The last four chapters in this book are about work which deals directly with the difficulty of reading history. At the same time, Welles, Sembene and Durham, two film-makers and one visual artist, show that history does leave its marks in coded traces and that the purpose of political imagery is not to reveal a given message, but to exemplify the deciphering of politics.

Feminist politics, when picking up the pieces in the aftermath of the crisis of the 1960s Left, played an important part in putting Freud on the political agenda alongside Marx: 'Marx and Freud'. For my political generation, feminist and post-60s, the combination of names has an almost incantatory ring and the desire to negotiate between the two sets of ideas has, like the search for the philosopher's stone, been at once inspiring and frustrating. Feminism's appropriation of psychoanalytic theory, in the first instance to develop a politics of images, unbalanced the potential alchemical mix in the direction of Freud. Now the sphere of the economic and the social, coded as the sphere of Marx, is forcing itself once again to the fore just as, paradoxically, the Marx-inspired regimes of Eastern Europe have crumbled. In Britain and the United States the economic and social crises generated by the right-wing regimes of the 80s are still escalating so that emptiness and bitterness now haunt the culture of consumption and the society of the spectacle. The 'images' issue is no longer only a feminist issue, or only a psychoanalytic issue, as advanced capitalism consolidates its world power through the entertainment and communications industries. Collapsing communism paradoxically received its *coup de grâce* from an aspiration to the culture of consumption in which com-modity fetishism plays a large part (however much capitalism itself, recession-ridden at this particular moment, may have its back against the wall). It was almost as though, in addition to the obvious and real political and economic problems that assailed the Soviet Union, the society acknow-ledged its own 'abjection' and the power of the enemy's fetish.

Now, psychoanalytic theory needs Marx, as echoes of the 30s, the fascism and nationalism that drove Freud into exile, resound around Europe. At the same time, as world politics moves into reverse mode, remaining Marxists will have to pay heed to the monstrous presence of the irrational in politics that appears increasingly to be stronger than the progressive movement of history.

As the concept of fetishism appears in the work of both Marx and Freud it could, on the face of it, provide the alchemical link between the two. Both used the term ironically, throwing back at their own societies the term used to encapsulate primitive, irrational, beliefs that were associated with Africa. The rationality of European thought, the term implies, might have purged society of superstitious beliefs in irrational phenomena and the interference of the supernatural in human affairs. But bourgeois economics and its psyche were still permeated by irrationalities of other kinds. Enlightenment still had further ground to retrieve. For Marx, a fundamental change in capitalist economic structures was a first prerequisite. While Freud clearly considered that psychoanalysis extended the rational to human irrationality, he also came up against its ultimate intractability.

Both Freud and Marx use the concept of fetishism in an attempt to explain a refusal, or blockage, of the mind, or a phobic inability of the psyche, to understand a symbolic system of value, one within the social and the other within the psychoanalytic sphere. However, the differences between the two invocations of fetishism are as, or more, significant than their similarities. One, the Marxist, is derived from a problem of inscription. How, that is, does the sign of value come to be marked onto a commodity? It is in and around the difficulty of establishing the exchange value of actual objects produced under capitalism that commodity fetishism flourishes, while the Freudian fetish, on the other hand, flourishes as phantasmatic inscription. It ascribes excessive value to objects considered to be valueless by the social consensus. How, that is, does an object acquire sexual value as the substitute for something else, the maternal penis that never existed in the first place, perceived as missing, an absence? In one case, the sign of value fails to inscribe itself on an actual object; in the other, value is over-inscribed onto a site of imagined lack, through a substitute object.

The discussion that follows is an experiment. It is an attempt to consider the way in which, in spite of their differences, the two concepts of fetishism raise certain semiotic problems; and then to consider ways in which a semiotics of fetishism might suggest a means of conceptualising a social or sexual reality within a theoretical framework. Lacan used the term 'Real' to represent those conditions of being that create the human subject but are totally inaccessible to human consciousness. That is to say, its matter can never be translated into either Imaginary or Symbolic systems of representation or signification. Although Lacan's point is of the greatest significance, it may be tempting to collapse the difficulty of articulating processes of history and the psyche with the impossibility of articulating the Real. In this chapter, I put forward a limited argument about varying structures of fetishisms which might constitute a 'symptomology' across social and psychic formations.

There are two main aspects to this argument. The first is to do with the particular structure of the Freudian fetish; the second is to do with the condensation between commodity and spectacle within capitalist economies. Fetishisms, like the grain of sand in the oyster that produces the pearl, create social and sexual constructions of things at intractable points that trouble the social or sexual psyche. If these constructs can be identified and understood to be symptomatic, their signifiers mark the delicate points where society and its consciousness lose touch. These are points where relations between people are liable to become relations between things.

The cultural analyst, while trying to draw attention to these 'points' and make them visible, may only be able to begin to reach them when new economic and social conditions come into existence, rendering the dying fetishisms easier to grasp. For instance, as I argue that the fetishisms, identified by Freud and Marx, merge (in their difference rather than their similarity) on the cinema screen, this may be possible because the cinema is no longer the entertainment industry's dominant medium. My experiment is directed backwards, at cultural forms to which history gives visibility as though the mind could only grasp their significance in the vanishing perspective of time. The process of disavowal (Freud) and estrangement (Marx) produces an over-valuation of things, and the over-valuation flows onto and affects an aesthetic and semiotic of things. I want to use C.S. Peirce's triad, the index, the icon and the symbol, as the starting point for a discussion of fetishism within the context of contemporary semiotic theory.

For Marx, the value of a commodity resides in the labour power of its producer. If this labour power could ever possibly inscribe itself indexically on the commodity it produces ... if it could leave a tangible mark of the time and skill taken in production, there would be no problem. But the index, the sign based on a direct imprint, fails. Value has to be established by exchange. Marx shows how value can be marked by the equation of different commodities of equal value. One commodity acts as a mirror, reflecting and thus expressing the value of the other or, indeed, as many others as it takes for the equivalence to balance. This stage is analogous to the Peircian icon. Slavoj Zizek[1] has pointed out that since this process assumes value to be a natural and pre-existing property of the commodity, it is analogous to Lacan's analysis of the mirror phase as a misunderstanding of identity. While value may be inscribed through this reflective process, it depends on the literal presence of the goods. It depends on a barter that has to be repeated as often as exchange takes place. Complex economic systems, with wide-scale production, exchange and circulation, developed a means of expressing equivalence through a generalised sign system: money. Money exchange takes place on the level of the symbol and the expression of value acquires the abstract and flexible quality of language. Not only does money, as the sign of value, detach itself from the literalness of object exchange but it also facilitates the final erasure of labour power as the primary source of value. The referent, as it were, shifts, away from the production process towards circulation and the market, where the commodity emerges and circulates with an apparently autonomous value attached to it. In Marx's terms, this appearance of self-generating value gives rise to commodity fetishism, or the disavowal of the source of its value in labour power. This process entails a fantasy disavowal. A commodity's market success depends on the erasure of the marks of production, any trace of indexicality, the grime of the factory, the mass moulding of the machine, and most of all, the exploitation of the worker. Instead, the commodity presents the market with a seductive sheen, as it competes to be desired. While money appears as a sophisticated, abstract and symbolic means of exchange, capitalism resurrects the commodity as image. Marx, writing in the 1860s, the decade which saw the first visible appearances of commodity culture,[2] says in some of the most-quoted sentences of *Capital*:

> In order to find an analogy, we must have recourse to the mist-enveloped regions of the religious world. In that world, the productions of the human brain appear as independent beings endowed with life, and entering into relations both with one another and the human race. So it is in the world of commodities with the products of men's hands. This I call the Fetishism which attaches itself to the products of labour, as soon as they are produced as commodities, and which is therefore inseparable from the production of commodities.[3]

Here is a perfect paradigm of the disavowal of knowledge in favour of belief. An abstract value system is grafted onto an imaginary investment in things, disavowing not only the origin of value but the process of symbolisation that brought it into circulation.

Commodity fetishism triumphs as spectacle. As spectacle, the object becomes image and belief, and is secured by an erotic, rather than a religious, aura. In her book *The Dialectics of Seeing: Walter Benjamin and the Arcades Project*, Susan Buck-Morss describes his perception of its primal staging:

> For Benjamin ... the key to the new urban phantasmagoria was not so much the commodity-in-the-market as the commodity-on-display, where exchange value no less than use value lost practical meaning, and purely representational value came to the fore. Everything desirable, from sex to social status, could be transformed into commodities as fetishes-on-display that held the crowd enthralled even when possession was beyond their reach.[4]

Producers become consumers. And the invisibility of the workers' labour is just as essential for the commodity's desirability as the visibility of the artisan's labour is for a craft object. Any indexical trace of the producer or the production process is wiped out, in a strange re-enactment of the failure of the workers' labour power to stamp itself on its products as value. Any ghostly presence of labour that might haunt the commodity is cancelled by the absolute pristine newness and the never-touched-by-hand packaging that envelops it. And the great intellectual achievement of capitalism, the organisation of an economic system as a symbolic system, can continue in its own interests.

The fetishism of the commodity is made up of spectacle and significance. That is, the 'sign value', as Baudrillard puts it, itself made out of highly connotative associations, stimulating desire that can be realised as market-driven demand. Its 'significance' is not the significance of production or its meaning in economic terms. Displacement comes into play, therefore, on two levels. The first, economic, disavows labour power and the second, semiotic, projects connotations of desirability. There is nothing intrinsically fetishistic, as it were, about the commodity in Marx's theory: to establish value would always be a complex process in a sophisticated system of circulation and exchange, and it may always be difficult to decipher the place of labour power as the source of value. Fetishism of the commodity, however, is a political symptom particular to capitalism and those societies that come under its sway. Commodity fetishism also bears witness to the persistent allure that images and things have for the human imagination and the pleasure to be gained from belief in phantasmagorias and imaginary systems of representation. Objects and images, in their spectacular manifestations, are central to the process of disavowal, soaking up semiotic significance and setting up elisions of affect. Most of all, they are easily sexualised.

In his short essay written in 1927,[5] just after he had dissected religious belief in *The Future of an Illusion*, Freud used the term 'fetishism' to evoke a consequence of castration anxiety. The psychic sequence of events that follow are enacted through the processes of disavowal, substitution and marking. The fetish object acts as a 'sign' in that it substitutes for the thing thought to be missing, the maternal penis. The substitute also functions as a mask, covering over and disavowing the traumatic sight of absence, especially if the 'absence' sets off associations with the wounded, bleeding body. The psyche constructs a phantasmatic topography, a surface, or carapace, which hides ugliness and anxiety with beauty and desire. This intricate confusion of the semiotic and the topographical, so important to the workings of the unconscious, has yet another facet. The fetish object also commemorates. It is a sign left by the original moment of castration anxiety and is also a mark of mourning for the lost object. The fetish as sign includes, therefore, even in its fixated belief in the female penis, a residual knowledge of its origin. The fetish object fixes and freezes the historic event outside rational memory and individual chronology. But the fetish still stays in touch with its original traumatic real and retains a potential access to its own historical story.

Thomas Richards argues that the first public celebration of commodity culture appeared in Victorian England at an overdetermined moment in history. He notes the way that the Great Exhibition implicitly displaced the recent 'social unrest of the 1830s and 40s':

The way it went about correcting history was to obscure it. The little cards, so hard to read, that accompanied each exhibited article rarely told their readers where or when the article was invented, much less who used it and for what purposes. Unlike a museum, the Exhibition made it very difficult to pinpoint the origins of individual objects. Instead, the space of the Exhibition revised the past by making it wholly present. ... By encapsulating the past in the glossy shell of the present, the Exhibition both commemorated the past and annihilated it.[6]

It is almost as though the Prince Consort had decided to distract the world from the political debates and upheavals that had culminated in the defeated revolutions of 1848. The exhibition of 1851 offered the people a new form of utopian aspiration and a new mode of social existence, as relations between people dissolved into relations between things and relations between things materialised into the society of the spectacle.

It is well known that the fetish very often attracts the gaze. In popular imagination, it glitters. It has to hold the fetishist's eyes fixed on the seduction of belief to guard against the encroachment of knowledge. This investment in surface appearance enhances the phantasmatic space of the fetish and sets up a structure in which object fixation can easily translate into image. While according to Marx the symbolic system of money is essential for the commodity's production and circulation, the Freudian fetish is constructed precisely to disavow the symbolic system at stake in sexual difference. And while the Freudian fetish includes a trace of indexicality in its function as 'memorial', the consumer of commodities is not known to whisper 'I know, but all the same ...'. However, the power of sexual fetishism can, enabled perhaps by homologous topographical structures, both split between spectacle and disavowal, overflow onto and enhance the commodity.

* * *

In the shift to consumer capitalism, modern commerce engages in a curiously double enterprise. On the one hand, a process of rationalisation; the transformation of selling into an industry. The department stores are organised like factories, with hundreds of workers, shareholding companies, vast turnovers, and careful calculation of continual strategies of expansion. On the other hand, the transformation of industry into a shop window ... the transformation of merchandise into a spectacle in fact suggests an analogy with an industry that developed a good fifty years after the first department stores: the cinema. In this case the pleasure of looking, just looking, is itself the commodity for which money is paid. The image is all, and the the spectator's interest is not engaged by the productive organisation which goes to construct the illusion before his/her eyes. In the way it appears, the Hollywood 'dream factory' necessarily suppresses its mechanical laboured parts.[7]

The cinema from its earliest days has fascinated its audiences as a spectacle, and one that engages belief in the face of rational knowledge. The cinema was the product of many pre-existing strands, including popular entertainment and scientific experiment. One strand, the one that is relevant to the argument here, links back to the skill and showmanship of phantasmagoric projections that had been used to raise spirits and ghosts for credulous audiences. Athanasius Kircher, who created the original camera obscura in the 17th century, used his projections to inform and enlighten his audiences. He would explain that the illusions he created were simply the products of a machine and the fantastic images that appeared could not, therefore, emanate from the supernatural world of spirit manifestations. As a Jesuit, he represented a Counter-Reformation Catholicism, which, responding to Protestant pressures for a more abstract concept of the deity and a purification of Christianity, stripped away the popular myths and rites of medieval religion. In this 'decline of magic', in Keith Thomas's words, folkloric beliefs in the spirit world, whether pre- or early Christian or the less orthodox of traditional Catholicism, were ripe for 'demystification'.[8] Kircher's camera obscura was poised between the old world, the primitive devices that raised devils, ghosts and other terrors, and the new, the machines that entertained with visual tricks, illusions and story telling.

The cinematic illusion, however, has continued to flourish on pleasure in belief, or rather, on the human mind's ability and desire to 'know' and to 'suspend disbelief' simultaneously. From this perspective, the cinema accuses the rational world, once again, of a credulity that belongs to the origin of the term 'fetishism'. In order to evoke 'the conversion of social relations into things' (the commodification of social relations through capitalist command over wage labour and land rents), Marx uses these metaphors:

> It is an enchanted, perverted, topsy-turvy world, in which Monsieur le Capital and Madame la Terre do their ghost-walking as social characters and at the same time directly as mere things. It is the great merit of classical economy to have destroyed this false appearance and illusion ... this personification of things and conversion of production relations into entities, this religion of everyday life.[9]

Reading this passage, it impossible not to feel that Marx was optimistic to hope that classical economy had finally banished ghosts and illusions, and succeeded in enlightening the world. It is almost as though his metaphors prefigure the (as yet uninvented) cinema machine, lying in wait to bring a new form of commodification and credulity to the people.

Fetishism, broadly speaking, involves the attribution of self-sufficiency and autonomous powers to a manifestly 'man'-derived object. It is, therefore, dependent on the ability to disavow what is known and replace it with belief and the suspension of disbelief. On the other hand, the fetish is always haunted by the fragility of the mechanisms that sustain it. Fetishes are supremely culturally specific. So, as Eisenstein showed so clearly in the gods sequence of *October*, one man's divine may be another man's lump of wood. Knowledge hovers implacably in the wings of consciousness. In Octave Mannoni's famous phrase, the fetishist's disavowal is typically expressed 'I know very well, but all the same ... '. Christian Metz invokes this phrase in his discussion of the suspension of disbelief in the cinema:

> Any spectator will tell you 'he doesn't believe it' but everything happens as if there were nevertheless someone to be deceived, someone who really would believe in it. In other words, asks Mannoni, since it is 'accepted' that the audience is incredulous, who is it who is credulous? ... This credulous person is, of course, another part of ourselves.[10]

Metz is using the psychoanalytic concept of fetishism here, with its emphasis on the human mind's ability to maintain two contradictory notions simultaneously. The cinema, particularly the industrial cinema, and most particularly the Hollywood studio system cinema which first dominated the world entertainment industry, has a close relationship with the commodity. Films are, in this mode of production, commodities and also put commodities on display. The different forms of fetishism thus find a point of convergence on the cinema screen. This point of convergence characteristically materialises in the eroticised form of the female star, producing a perfect, streamlined image of femininity which acts as a reminder of the maternal body's place in Freud's concept of fetishism.

Unlike Metz who sees the cinema's fetish object in its own technological transcendence, feminist film theory[11] has argued that the eroticisation of the cinema is a major prop for its successfully fetishised credibility. And femininity, the most obvious prop, is also dependent on an economy of fetishism. Fetishism in the cinema also leads to Marx, and a consideration of the 'aesthetics of commodity fetishism'. The popular cinema, itself a commodity, can form a bridge between the commodity as spectacle and the figure of woman as spectacle on the screen. This, in turn, leads on to the bridging function of woman as consumer, rather than producer, of commodities.[12] This series of 'bridges' suggests a topography, or spatial mapping, in which homologies, realised in image, then slide into formally similar structures. Connotations, resonances, significances can then flow, as it were, between things that do not, on the face of it, have anything in common. The formal structure typically produced by disavowal creates a conduit linking different points of social difficulty and investing in 'sight' as a defence.

It is important to emphasise that there are a variety of cinemas, with different relations of production and varying social and fantasy systems behind them. It is also important to emphasise the extent to which the fascination of Hollywood cinema itself depended on the fragility of its effect. The machine itself, always attempting to conceal the process of recording and projection, could spoil its own credibility. For instance, the star's extratextual presence produces a tension within the system even at its most glamorous, while, if the projector fails, the spectacle may suffer the humiliating demystification that the little dog Toto inflicts on the Great Wizard.[13]

During the 1970s, feminist, Marxist and modernist aesthetics united to challenge the credibility of the Hollywood illusion. Fetishism was a key concept for the political aesthetics of modernist-influenced anti-Hollywood counter-cinema and psychoanalytically influenced anti-Hollywood feminist film theory. Put together, these are the ideas behind the movement that D.N. Rodowick has called 'political modernism'.[14] The different strands within this movement came to influence each other and create the basis of a dialogue through *Screen*, the Edinburgh Film Festival events, the feminist avant-garde and structural/materialist film. Anti-fetishism, like a portmanteau, linked together different strands of the debates which aimed to exorcise: the cinema's conventional investment in willing suspension of disbelief and denial of its own materiality; the psychic process of defence against a (mis)perception of the female body as castrated; femininity fragmented and then reconstructed in image into a surface of perfect sheen; the erasure of labour processes in the society of the spectacle; the glamour of Hollywood cinema in which fascination with the erotic erases the machinery of cinema and filmic processes. All these motifs could criss-cross, especially in the politics of an aesthetic avant-garde that questioned the mechanical, mass, eroticised but censored, commercial cinema. Furthermore, an aesthetic which intends to make visible the processes hidden in cultural production could by analogy, or rather by homology, point towards labour power, also concealed by the sheen of the commodity product under capitalism. The influence of Brecht met psychoanalysis, modernist semiotics and Althusserian Marxism. In both theory and practice during this period, there was an aspiration towards the defetishisation of the film medium. This was an agenda suspended at the closing moments of the machine age.

Film theory of the 70s was political and polemical, and, in this spirit, argued that cinematic illusion worked as a total belief system at the expense of its ability to balance belief with knowledge. The concept of fetishism was invoked, therefore, without taking into account the ultimate significance of disavowal. The confusion was due, perhaps, to the fact that during the 70s, the Hollywood investment in illusion became conflated, rather confusingly, with the realism debate. The realist tradition in cinema cannot be characterised by a star system, generic forms of entertainment, eroticised spectacle (as opposed to a frankness about sex) and the fragility of illusion. Realism has tended to represent a move away from high commodification of the cinema. But the realist cinema's aspiration to close the gap between representation and the social formations it depicted fell a clear victim to contemporary concern to emphasise the constructed nature of the image and, above all, the complexities of the sign. Not only did modernist aesthetics work towards foregrounding the materiality of the signifier; the possibility of reference itself and the political implications of referring to a 'real world' came under attack both through Althusser's theories of ideology and Lacanian psychoanalytic theory.

There was, of course, an interest in common between the rejection of realism as an aesthetic strategy and the feminist critique of images of women. For feminist aesthetics, theories that conceptualised a gap between sign and referent have been a source of liberation. Semiotic and psychoanalytic theory played a central part in this conceptual liberation, not only opening up the gap in signification, but also offering a theory that could decipher the language of displacements that separated a given signifier on the screen from its apparent signified in the social world. However, for feminist psychoanalytic theory, the image refers, even though not necessarily to the referent it resembles. The image refers, through displacements of the signifier, to vulnerable or highly charged areas in the social fantasy that produced it.

Under the need to destabilise signification, the problem of reference got lost. At the same time, the influence of semiotic and psychoanalytic theory on feminism coincided with the wider ramifications of post-modern aesthetics and its pleasure in instabilities of meaning and infinite deferral of signification. In establishing the crucial point that history is a construct of discourse, post-modern theory made it difficult to relate systems of representation back to sites of social production. Fredric Jameson sums up the problem and reformulates it in the following passage:

> What Althusser's own insistence on history as an absent cause makes clear, but what is missing from the formula as it is canonically worked, is that he does not at all draw the conclusion that, because history is a text, the 'referent' does not exist. We would therefore propose the following revised formulation: that history is not a text, not a narrative, master or otherwise, but that as an absent cause it is inaccessible to us except in textual form, and that our approach to it and to the Real itself necessarily passes through prior textualisation, its narrativisation in the political unconscious.[15]

At the same time, the contemporary, post-modern rejection of reference could, perhaps, be a symptom of shifting contemporary, 'post-industrial' economic formations. From this perspective, it might be necessary to go back to Marx in order to identify a persisting link between the economic and the cultural within a post-modern, post-Marxist, era. Just as the aesthetics of realism had a specific formal relation to the economics of the machine age and industrial capitalism, so the aesthetics of post-modernism might reflect, in turn, new economic and financial structures. The problem of reference, from this angle, is not restricted to the image and aesthetics, but leads back to the economics of capitalism itself.

As industrial capitalism, in the First World, shows symptoms of crisis, finance capitalism flourishes and the advanced capitalist seems to favour economies that can create money out of money and produce surplus value outside the value produced by the labour power of the working class. In this sense, the success of finance capital over industrial capital in the advanced capitalist economies, where currency speculation can be more profitable than the exploitation of labour power, raises the issue of reference in economic terms. Money, which is first and foremost a symbolic representation of value, is now also subsumed into processes of exchange that do not necessarily represent either commodities or their production.

A Marxist approach to contemporary aesthetics might well argue that the loss of referentiality in culture is, itself, the result of shifts and changes in the economic structures which herald the advent of a capitalism based on an electronic machine age in which communication takes precedence over production. Marxism evolved within the historical context of an industrial age which was dependent both on working-class labour power to generate value and on an imbalance of political and economic power to maintain the supremacy of capitalism. The industrial and financial economics of late twentieth-century capitalism can still be analysed through Marxist theory even though the industrial and financial structures that Marx analysed have mutated over the course of the last century. Although the age of electronic media has superseded the cinematic machinery, the political and psychological importance of representation systems escalates with the growth of entertainment and communications industries. These industries not only have an ever increasing importance in contemporary capitalism, but spectacle and a diminishing reference are essential to their spread and their appeal.

While Marxist theories of ideology aimed to unveil political and economic realities, the impact of psychoanalysis and semiotics put the possibility of actually articulating the 'Real' into question. All that could be analysed would be discourses and representations. Nevertheless, it is also necessary to bear in mind that this theoretical and aesthetic shift might itself reflect changes and developments within the material reality of capitalist technology and economics. The free-floating signifier may, itself, be a signifier of changes in the economic base. Marxist principles that revealed the determining power of the economic over the social and the cultural are as relevant as ever, even as capitalism evolves and convulses in ways which Marx himself could not have foreseen. History is, undoubtedly, constructed out of representations. But these representations are themselves symptoms. They provide clues, not to ultimate or fixed meanings, but to sites of social difficulty that need to be deciphered, politically and psychoanalytically ... even though it may be too hard, ultimately, to make complete sense of the code.

It is in this context that fetishism, the carrier of such negative ideological connotations once upon a time, might be re-examined. The structure of disavowal, which Freud considered particular to fetishism, suggests a way

11

in which the difficulty of reference might be reformulated, without losing the framework of psychoanalytic and semiotic theory. Psychoanalytic theory distinguishes between fetishistic disavowal and the process of displacement in the language of the unconscious. In both cases, the link between sign and reference is lost but the concept of disavowal can contain the *question* of reference, even while displacing it. To differentiate between disavowal and repression, Freud makes the following points:

> the ego often enough finds itself in the position of fending off some demand from the external world which it feels distressing and that this is effected by a means of *disavowal* of the perceptions which bring to knowledge this demand from reality. Disavowals of this kind occur very often and not only with fetishists; and whenever we are in a position to study them they turn out to be half-measures, incomplete attempts at detachment from reality. The disavowal is always supplemented by an acknowledgement; two contrary and independent attitudes always arise and result in the situation of there being a splitting of the ego. Once more the issue depends on which of the two can seize hold of the greater [psychical] intensity.[16]

The psychic process of disavowal, though occurring 'not only with fetishists', was first elaborated by Freud in his discussion of fetishism. Disavowal includes cause and effect within its structure. The fetish acknowledges its own traumatic history like a red flag, symptomatically signalling a site of psychic pain. Psychoanalytic film theory suggests that mass culture can be interpreted similarly symptomatically. As a massive screen on which collective fantasy, anxiety, fear and their effects can be projected, it speaks the blind-spots of a culture and finds forms that make manifest socially traumatic material, through distortion, defence and disguise. Dana Polan noted:

> Mass culture becomes a kind of postmodern culture, the stability of social sense dissolved (without becoming any less ideological) into one vast spectacular show, a dissociation of cause and effect, a concentration on the allure of means and a concomitant disinterest in meaningful ends. Such spectacle creates the promise of a rich sight: not the sight of particular fetishised objects, but sight itself as richness, as the ground for extensive experience.[17]

The aesthetic of 'rich sight' erased that delicate link between cause and symptom. Processes of displacement may harness aesthetic pleasure and formal excitement disguising reference rather than acting as a defence against it. The present transcendence of the 'rich sight' aesthetic has developed out of the structures of disavowal at work in mass culture. Disavowal maintains, after all, only a tenuous link between cause and effect while its investment in visual excess and displacement of signifiers produces a very strong texture that can come to conceal *the need to conceal the relation between cause and effect*. That is, the aesthetic of disavowal can easily provide a formal basis for a displacement which moves signification considerably further away from the problem of reference. And the blind-spots, sites of social pain, that generated the processes of disavowal, get further lost on the way. Thus, the disavowal of the processes of industrial production now disguises the collapse of industrial production itself.

The visibility or invisibility of the production process has had a crucial place in film theory debates. In an extension of the Marxist model, it is logical that Hollywood, the Detroit of cinema, would evolve its characteristic style around the erasure of its own mechanics of production. The Hollywood film, as a commodity, also emerged into the market place as a self-generated object of fascination, erasing, even during the high days of genre, stars and the studio system, any easily identifiable directorial signature. And the spectacular attributes of the cinema fuse into a beautifully polished surface on the screen. It is not surprising that an interest in Brechtian foregrounding of the production process or a Vertovian formalism heralded a politically based desire to 'demystify' the magical sheen of the screen. And the aesthetics of the 1960s and 70s avant-garde was organised around the visible presence of an artisanal author and an acknowledgment of the mechanical processes that cinema depends on. But cinema is a system of production of meaning above and beyond a mechanical process of image generation, with a unique ability to play with the mind's willingness to suspend knowledge in favour of belief. The process of production gives birth to images, while the construction of the image gives birth to fascination. And feminist film theory has argued that cinema finds, not its only, but its most perfect, fetishistic object in the image of woman. As a signifier of sexuality, the image of eroticised femininity once again has a bridging function.

While Freudian analyses of fetishism in cinema have a long history in film theory, one strand of the argument is particularly relevant here. The image of woman on the screen achieves a particular spectacular intensity partly as a result, once again, of a homology of structure. Just as an elaborate and highly artificial, dressed-up, made-up appearance envelops the movie star in 'surface', so does her surface supply a glossy front for the cinema, holding the eye in fascinated distraction away from its mechanics of production. This fragile carapace shares the phantasmatic space of the fetish itself, masking the site of the wound, covering lack with beauty. In the horror genre, it can crack open to reveal its binary opposition when, for instance, a beautiful vampire disintegrates into ancient slime; or in film noir, when the seductive powers of the heroine's beauty mask her destructive and castrating powers. Psychoanalytic theory offers two interpretations of these phenomena, both to do with spatial mappings and topographies. The first, the uncanny, Freud describes as: 'In reality nothing new or alien, but something that is familiar and old established in the mind which has become alienated from it if only through the process of repression.'[18] This he associates with the subject's former home, the womb. As Barbara Creed points out, this uncanny space leads to another, the uncanny house. She says: 'The house is haunted by the ghost or trace of a memory which takes the individual back to the early, perhaps foetal, relation with the mother.'[19]

The second psychic phenomenon is Julia Kristeva's concept of the abject, that is the revulsion that the small child projects onto the mother's body in order to develop self-sufficiency and subjectivity. These are both points of psychic vulnerability, in addition to and beyond castration anxiety. When the exterior carapace of feminine beauty collapses to reveal the uncanny, abject, maternal body it is as though the fetish itself has failed. Duality of structure facilitates displacements so that images and ideas that are only residually connected can slide together, closing the gap between them like automatic doors. The topography of the phantasmatic space acts as a conduit for shifts in signification. It is this sexuality of surface, a sexuality that displaces a deep-seated anxiety about the female body, that feminist film theorists have recently analysed as a bridge between the screen and the market place where woman, consumer *par excellence*, also consumes commodities to construct *her own sexual surface into an armour of fetishistic defence against the taboos of the feminine that patriarchy depends on.*

For Freud, the body that is the source of fetishism is the mother's body, uncanny and archaic. For Marx, the source of fetishism is in the erasure of the worker's labour as value. Both become the unspeakable, and the unrepresentable, in commodity culture: repression of the mother's body, repression of labour power as a source of value. These two themes run, respectively, through the Marxist and the Freudian concepts of fetishism. They conceal (in image) structures of sexual difference and value, that, although not themselves structurally linked, reinforce each other through topographies and displacements linking the erotic spectacle of the feminine to the eroticised spectacle of the commodity. There are important differences between the two kinds of fetishism, that is, the different problems of inscription. But both are central to, and articulated within, the Hollywood cinema of the studio system. There is a logic to harnessing the overinscribed signifier to the uninscribed. The sheer force of 'rich sight', of the spectacle, creates a diversion away from inquiry or curiosity.

The 'aesthetics of fetishism', however, derives from the structure of disavowal in the Freudian model ('I know, but all the same') which creates an oscillation between what is seen and what threatens to erupt into knowledge. But danger and risk are also exciting. On a formal, as well as on a narrative level, Hollywood cinema made more use of oscillation between knowledge and belief than 'political modernism' ever acknowledged. The system built self-consciousness into its fascination, even while it apparently denied it. This *trompe-l'oeil* effect is central for post-modern aesthetics, which came to use self-referentiality, intertextual reference, direct address, ultimately in the interests of a pleasurable destabilising of perception. To look back at the aesthetics of disavowal in Hollywood cinema is, still, an attempt to rearticulate those black holes of political repression, class and woman, in the Symbolic order. But it is also an attempt to return to reconsider the relationship between cause and effect in the social Imaginary, at a time when the relation between representation and historical events becomes increasingly dislocated. Spectacle proliferates in contemporary capitalist communication systems. At the same time the reality of history in the form of war, starvation, poverty, disease and racism (as an ever escalating symptom of the persistence of the irrational in human thought) demands analysis with an urgency that contemporary theory cannot ignore.

Part One

What Price Hollywood?

Chapter 1

Americanitis: European Intellectuals and Hollywood Melodrama

In 1922 Lev Kuleshov coined the term 'Americanitis' to describe the passion for Hollywood movies that had gripped the Soviet Union. He said: 'Of all the American films the detective stories appeal the most', and 'The success of American motion pictures lies in the greatest common measure of film-ness, the presence of maximum movement and in primitive heroism, in an organic relation to contemporaneity.'[1] The detective story, the cinematic, primitive heroism, movement and modernity: Kuleshov's emphasis on the detective provides a metaphor for the criticism that emerged out of European intellectuals' fascination with Hollywood. Even the *politique des auteurs* can be compared, metaphorically, to a detective work of style, in which the director's profile is built through and across the presence of the studio contract system.

'It will be a magnificent obsession', says the strange spiritual mentor about the strange spiritual quest he proposes to Bob Merrick/Rock Hudson in Douglas Sirk's first colour A-picture melodrama, *Magnificent Obsession* (Universal, 1952). The phrase came to my mind as a figure for the persistent but shifting place the Hollywood melodrama has occupied for European film theory and criticism in general, and for its importance for feminist film theory and criticism in particular. Although the melodrama is a very different genre from the detective movie, its cinematic characteristics pushed the question of *mise en scène*, as an inscription for the unsaid, forward to a new level of articulation that was of enormous importance for the development of film theory. On the other hand, unlike the Americanitis movies, the melodrama is the genre of stasis and constraint.

I was typical of a generation of European intellectuals who, in their youth during the 60s, fell in love with Hollywood in its sunset years. Hollywood cinema was fascinating and entrancing, but also presented political and aesthetic problems that soon began to affect and trouble the first flush of transatlantic fantasy. The obsession was forced to mutate and to take political issues on board as cinephilia grew into film theory. At the same time, the aesthetics of Hollywood necessarily demanded the

19

development of new critical criteria. In this chapter, I will draw on my own changing relationship with Hollywood to think about both its intellectual impact in Europe and, more specifically, its (on the face of it) unlikely importance as a crucible for feminist film theory. I am taking a narrow perspective, focusing on the cultural and geographical instance offered by Britain, with its ambivalent attitude both to the popular entertainment that came across the Atlantic and to the intellectual ideas that came across the Channel. The conjuncture between the two affected the early development of film theory in this country and the later development of feminist theory. The melodrama genre spreads across the different moments of this history, bearing witness to its ideological twists and turns, from the first wave of pre-68 critical engagement with Hollywood through to the second more specifically feminist wave which emerged in the 70s.

Hollywood, which first perfected the mass popular appeal of the movies, stands on the side of illusion and commodity culture, escapist fantasy and the repression of its own processes of production. From this point of view, Hollywood cinema is a symptom of cultural, economic and technical fetishism. It is precisely because of these qualities that intellectuals have approached Hollywood with such ambivalence. In spite of its contribution to American cultural and economic domination, Hollywood presented, *par excellence*, questions about the relation between industrial cultural products and popular, collective fantasy patterns. And, even more crucially, it raised questions about the transparency of the cinematic image and how the spectator deciphers the signs that congeal on the screen, at the point, that is, where the social, psychoanalytic and aesthetic overlap. On the other hand, Hollywood's style of recounting and representing stories pushed critics and intellectuals to develop an appropriate film theory in order to analyse the iconographies and *mise en scènes* of genre movies.

The Hollywood cinema that first fascinated European intellectuals was energetic and cathartic, a cinema of the machine age, streamlined and commodified, able to produce and repeat successful formulas, stories or stars, as Detroit might produce motor cars. This cinema stood in direct opposition to high cultural values encrusted with the weight and authority of tradition. European intellectuals took up American cinema partly in a spirit of political polemics with the traditions and values of their own culture. A Hollywood film, brazenly generic, shamelessly star-struck, not even dignified by the presence of a single creative imagination, came to epitomise a binary opposition to the academic appropriation and fossilisation that overwhelmed the high cultures of literature, music, painting and so on. Popular cinema had fascinated the Surrealists and others on the Left, in Britain as well as France, in the 20s when Hollywood cinema established itself as world cinema. And this fascination found new life with the rediscovery of Hollywood, this time in the guise of a new film criticism, in France after the Second World War. The new criticism is associated primarily with the *Cahiers du Cinéma*, partly because of its transnational influence, which is in turn partly, of course, due to the subsequent evolution of many of its critics into the directors of the New Wave, and also due to the place of its editor André Bazin in the history of film theory.

It was European intellectuals' postwar re-evaluation of Hollywood cinema that helped to erode the value system that supported the hierarchical opposition beteen high and low art forms. So, in the strange extended romance between European intellectuals and American popular culture, the Hollywood studio system's cinema played a privileged, formative part. If the United States now, in Robin Wood's phrase, 'takes Hitchcock seriously',[2] it is partly because the European intellectual fascination with Hollywood, evoked by Thomas Elsaesser as 'Two Decades in Another Country',[3] returned American popular culture across the Atlantic, enhanced by the trappings of 'French theory'. A two-way movement: European intellectuals embraced the products of American popular culture, which were then received back into their homeland and negotiated into academia through another exchange of cultural fantasy, the arrival in the United States of European-grown ideas, particularly those associated, in the first instance, with structuralism and, in the second, with psychoanalysis. While Hollywood studio system cinema as such launched the 'first wave' of European cinephilia, the melodrama played a privileged part in a 'second wave' also enabling the negotiation of political pitfalls at stake in the first.

The legacy of the French critics was not, on the face of it, political. Their criticism of passion not only valued Hollywood precisely because it was non-literary and gestural, essentially melodramatic, as Thomas Elsaesser and others have pointed out, but it also led further. Existing critical methodologies could not be appropriately applied to commercial cinema and its particular mode of production, which subordinated individual creative autonomy to the stamp of conventions of all kinds. The *Cahiers du Cinéma* critics' investigative system that came to be known as the *politique des auteurs* was not so important as a means of restoring a traditional concept of 'the author' to non-authorial culture, but as a method of critical analysis that could be applied to and evaluate a cinema that was produced within the formulaic system of genres, and celebrate directors who managed to turn, bend or mould their material into something cinematically vivid, dramatically direct and moving.[4]

The *Cahiers* methodology was a painstaking process. Auteurist critics had to search across the whole range of a director's work to find a command of cinematic language hidden under the surface of the text. The process was a kind of decipherment; its pleasure, as well as in cinema as such, was in detection. And its method, refusing to hierarchise the good and bad, fascinated by the mythic elements of American genres, provided fertile ground for the implantation of French structuralist ideas into film theory. Perhaps strangely, this implantation also involved transplantation as the influence of French ideas took root in Britain in the mid-60s, where critics who had previously simply enjoyed the fruits of *Cahiers* criticism began moving towards theory. The characteristics of Hollywood cinema that had placed it on the 'low' side of the cultural binary opposition (generic plots, stereotypical characters, clichés and melodramatic emotion) could be magically transformed into the vocabulary of myth and into dramatic motifs of cultural meaning and significance. The anti-establishment, anti-high cultural investment in Hollywood cinema became explicitly political in Britain, as a negative gesture directed against Englishness, its elitism, its complacency and its insularity in relation to both the European theory and to US mass culture. British intellectuals in the 60s rejected our own cultural traditions and 'value' criticism, applying French theory to American popular culture, first and foremost, again following the French, to Hollywood.

The British Film Institute's Education Department under Paddy Whannel transformed these different strands and trends into an articulate policy towards film. Whannel collected together a new generation of critics, for instance Victor Perkins from the *Cahiers*-influenced *Movie* and Peter Wollen who under the pseudonym Lee Russell had been writing essays influenced by *Cahiers* and auteurism in the *New Left Review*. And the *New Left Review* had itself just recently taken a similar, but explicitly politics-directed stand, embracing European Marxist theories and consciously rejecting the traditions of the British Left. It was within the terms of this intellectual and political atmosphere that the first books of new film theory emerged: Peter Wollen's *Signs and Meaning in the Cinema* (1969), Jim Kitses's *Horizons West* (1969), David Will and Peter Wollen's *Sam Fuller* (1969), David Will and Paul Willemen's *Roger Corman* (1970) and Colin McArthur's *Underworld USA* (1972). All bear witness to the centrality of Hollywood genre cinema in formulating the new film theory, while auteurist criticism itself began to be reconfigured under the influence of structuralism.[5]

But it was, in the last resort, as Thomas Elsaesser points out, politics that brought the seeds of decay to the 'two decades in another country'. A critical engagement with Hollywood cinema could easily be seen, not only as a means of liberating British intellectuals from insularity, but also, very easily, as an unquestioning acceptance of an imperialist cinema. The recuperation of Hollywood in France had taken place in the period of the Marshall Plan, when American investment in the postwar reconstruction of Europe also opened up European markets for its products, a process in which Hollywood films played an important part, damaging the struggling national cinemas of the postwar years. In the 60s, growing political consciousness leading up to the events of 1968, the American military build-up in Vietnam and awareness of the stifling of indigenous Third World as well as European cinemas under American exports all combined to repoliticise intellectual attitudes to Hollywood. And, of course, the studio system that had been the source of the Westerns, gangster movies, musicals, films noirs, comedies and so on, and the B-pictures that had provided the stuff out of which the auteur theory developed, was itself in crisis. This 1967 statement from Godard, one of the great 'discoverers' and *aficionados* of Hollywood, reflects the changed atmosphere: 'On our own modest level, we too should try to provoke two or three Vietnams in the bosom of the vast Hollywood-Cinecittà-Mosfilm-Pinewood etc. empire, and, both economically and aesthetically, struggling on two fronts as it were, create cinemas which are national, free, brotherly, comradely and bonded in friendship.'[6] The political-historical events of the late 60s created a fissure, if not a crisis, in European Left intellectuals' relation to Hollywood.

Needless to say, my 'popular memory' account is partial in both senses of the word, both incomplete and personal, a reflection of and on my own shifting relations with Hollywood cinema. I spent the 60s under the influence of the *Cahiers du Cinéma* and absorbed in Hollywood. The crisis for me, which was also political but not that of '68, was precipitated by feminism. Although feminism irretrievably changed the terms of the debate and precipitated a highly anti-Hollywood polemic, Hollywood films, for the following reasons, had to stay on the political agenda at the very least as an object of study. First, the question of Hollywood cinema became absorbed, negatively, into the analysis of spectatorship, concentrating on images of women and woman as spectacle. Second, and partly as a result, Hollywood cinema could provide a 'pool' of narratives and iconographies symptomatic of patriarchal culture, providing the most important material for psychoanalytic criticism. Third, there was a renewed interest in the Hollywood melodrama as a mass entertainment genre specifically designed for and directed at a female audience. The melodrama emerged into film critical consciousness as a genre of interest in its own right, bit by bit: first through directors (Minnelli in *Movie* and in the *Brighton Film Review*, Nicholas Ray in *Movie*, Douglas Sirk in *Screen*), through historical period (Eisenhower's America, as in Jon Halliday's interview book *Sirk on Sirk*), through formalist aesthetics (Paul Willemen on Sirk in *Screen*), through form as expressive of content (Thomas Elsaesser's 'Tales of Sound and Fury'), through content (feminist analyses of 'women's pictures'), through origins (Griffith, the silent cinema and the legacy of theatrical melodrama, as in Christine Gledhill's introduction to *Home Is Where the Heart Is*, 1987), through psychoanalytic theory (family drama sited inside the home and the interior of the psyche). This trajectory extends from the criticism of *Cahiers du Cinéma*, through the development of film theory in Britain, to contemporary academic film theory in the United States.

The story of melodrama criticism traces a curve which marks out the debates on form versus content, and, in the last resort, psychoanalytic theory came to the rescue as a conceptual means for reconciling the two. As the 'melodrama' is constructed by feminist critics as the genre of domesticity aimed at a female audience, early critical neglect of its content has been attributed to male critics' lack of interest in 'women's pictures'. Two other considerations should be borne in mind here. First of all, the genres that initially exerted the strongest critical appeal, particularly the Western (Kitses), the gangster film (McArthur) and horror (Paul

Willemen's work on Roger Corman in 1970), allowed an understanding of Hollywood cinema as a version of myth, as a popularisation and an ideologisation of American history, belonging to the male sphere, exterior and public. The 'interior' space, gendered female in and by melodrama, demanded and had to wait for a different critical understanding. For melodrama to break out of the weepie's feminised ghetto, certain conceptual and ideological shifts in cultural methodologies had to take place.

The sphere of the feminine had to find a voice which could provide critical commentary on its genre, the domestic melodrama. At the same time, the 'interiority' of the domestic had to open up to reveal a new terrain, the terrain of the 'unspeakable'. Feminism would provide the voice and vocabulary which could transform the content aspect of the melodrama, re-evaluating the domestic interior space, while psychoanalytic theory would provide the concepts which could transform the interiority of the 'unspeakable' into the unconscious, transforming the stuffy kitschiness of the melodrama into the stuff of dreams and desire. Finally, the ahistoricity of the melodrama, as it flourished in the 50s, had to be understood as a historical phenomenon. The Hollywood melodrama is part of American 'myth' but rather than looking back and retelling and reordering the narratives of that public sphere, it symptomises the history of its own time, figuring an aspiration to retreat into the privacy of the new white suburbs out of the difficulties of contemporary political life.

Feminist engagement with Hollywood produced a theoretical second wave, giving a new political inflection to the critical interest in the studio system's cinema, which was questioned in the late 60s. In the early 70s the Women's Movement began to articulate a new politics of representation. As critics such as Claire Johnston began to use Althusser and Lacan to analyse Hollywood cinema and its representations of women, the second wave 'reinvented' and 'reconfigured' the first wave's conjuncture between French theory and Hollywood. While structuralism had provided an analytical tool for deciphering cultural products of an industrial, non-high art system of movie making, so psychoanalysis could perform a similar function. Psychoanalytic theory's concentration on gender and sexuality had, of course, a strong appeal for feminists. The pioneering work undertaken by the BFI Education Department in the 60s, shifted, in the 70s, towards *Screen* and particularly to the Edinburgh Film Festival, which, under Lynda Myles's directorship, carried on the theory/Hollywood conjuncture with its policy of organising retrospectives of auteur directors (such as Fuller, Corman, Sirk, Tashlin, Walsh and Tourneur, all between 1969 and 1975) alongside events and conferences in the mid-70s at which the new film theory, particularly its psychoanalytic component, could be publicly debated.

Psychoanalytic theory is of intrinsic interest to feminism both because of its content, its analysis of gender and sexuality, and as a formal system which identifies symptoms triggered in the human psyche by sexual difference and its social organisation, and reconfigures them as signs, to be

24

identified and decoded. Pam Cook and Claire Johnston, in their 1974 article 'The Place of Woman in the Cinema of Raoul Walsh', make the point: 'In the tradition of classic cinema, the characters are presented as autonomous individuals; but the construction of the discourse contradicts this convention by reducing these "real" women to images and tokens functioning in a circuit of signs, the values of which have been determined by and for men.'[7] The concept of displacement, which lies behind this quotation, combines Freudian theory of the language of the unconscious with semiotic theory. The melodrama, as a genre addressed to women, raised different problems of displacement and decipherment that were particular to women, so it was eagerly studied for its alternative psychic scenarios, its representations of female desire, its non-cathartic narratives and its suitability for psychoanalytic criticism.

As Elsaesser argued, the melodrama is almost characterised by the presence of a protagonist whose symptomatic behaviour emerges out of irreconcilable or inexpressible internal contradictions, and these 'unspeakable' affects overflow into the *mise en scène*. This triple displacement (the fictional character's psychic symptoms which generate the melodramatic story, the rendition of the symptoms within the constraints and limitations of the genre, the effect of these narrative limitations on the film's cinematic language) thus demands a triple critical response (psychoanalytic, narrative and cinematic/semiotic analyses). The Freudian unconscious disguises its irrepressible ideas through and into its symptoms, and cinema carries this displacement into the 'symptom-like' qualities of *mise en scène*. The spectator of the melodrama is therefore a more than usually 'deciphering' viewer, given that Hollywood cinema of the studio system by and large shares this quality. But it is further arguable that a popular cinema is symptomatic, or rather, shares certain qualities of the symptom on the wider scale of the social and historical, especially in the United States which through its cinema brought into representation the myths, repressions and aspirations of an immigrant society.

The Hollywood cinema of the studio system had as many separate but intermeshed layers as an onion. Peel away the outer skin of a conformist, censored cinema addressing an immigrant audience on the aspirations and mythologies of the American Dream; you then find an energetic form of popular entertainment, mass producing the finest-tooled spectacle of the modern age for commodity consumption. Peel away the modernist gloss and the industrial base and you find recycled versions of folk stories; heroes, heroines, villains and monsters materialise their European grandparents into contemporary American shapes and forms. Peel away the insistence on a surface sexuality, the eroticisation of the screen as spectacle and woman as sexualised spectacle and you find traces of everyday anxieties or collective fantasies that defy conscious expression. Right in the centre is emotion and its eternal, external, physical symptoms: laughter, horror, the thrill of suspense ... and tears. Although the studio system organised its genres around American mythologies, particularly the Western, the film noir, gangster, horror, adventure and science fiction movies, it also acknowledged traditional generic divisions along the lines of emotion. Tears went with women, and handkerchiefs were signs of success for the small genre of 'women's pictures' that were designed primarily for a female audience.

As a tentative working concept, the term 'collective fantasy' gathers together these strands of story telling and spectacle in popular cinema. These cultural symptoms can neither be contained within the concept of ideology nor understood as a reflective theory of historical representation. Furthermore, the 'symptomology' of collective fantasy, as a return of the repressed in a social formation, does not depend on any essential or a historical concept of the human psyche. This kind of 'collective fantasy' would be evidence of the presence of psychic symptoms within the social, traces of unassimilated historical traumas (in Freud's sense of the word). However, certain narrative structures, psychic scenarios and iconographies persist across history. Myths and narratives from traditional Western culture are recognisable, under new names and in new shapes and forms, in Hollywood cinema. One could cite work on narrative that has made use of Propp's *Morphology of the Folk-tale*[8] or Barbara Creed's and Teresa de Lauretis's different citations of the Medusa myth[9], or the reiteration of the Oedipus myth throughout Hollywood cinema, still flourishing in late Hollywood and even in the perhaps unlikely setting of Gus van Sant's *My Own Private Idaho* (1991). These narratives and figurations are not transhistorical, except in the sense that, as Propp argued, some powerful stories can outlive the moment of historical contradiction or stress that gave rise to them and survive through a story-telling tradition, in a sense almost overdetermining later mythic invention by the sheer force of familiarity and repetition. They also, obviously, may well persist if relevant psychic structures keep them alive, giving private reverie a short cut to a gallery of collective fantasy inhabited by monsters and heroes, heroines and *femmes fatales*. These short cuts can act like templates, patterning social identities while also, sometimes, simultaneously acknowledging and indicating their imperfect fit. The process of displacement itself may bear witness to the social equivalent of a geological fault, a point where intractable material (volcanic magma, as it were) is in danger of erupting. Narrative conflict, its heroes, villains supply pattern and order, but also, through the clusters of repetition, recurrence and excess, suggest the presence of a 'cultural symptomatology'.

Anyone at the movies can read significance into a *mise en scène*, and its lighting, colour, camera angles and so on. So an active process of deciphering is an essential part of cinematic spectatorship and a pleasure in spectatorship that goes beyond both the erotics of visual pleasure and the complacency of 'seeing is believing'. But the cinema has enhanced the iconography of enigma that has so often, throughout our history, been invested in images and myths of femininity. Feminist film theory, especially when addressing the cultural enigmas that materialise in images of women, analyses images in a particularly detective spirit. While all criticism involves the excitement of making sense and is, to some extent, a work of cracking a code, feminist criticism is necessarily so. A shared sense of addressing a world written in cipher may have drawn feminist film critics, like me, to psychoanalytic theory, which has then provided a, if not the, means to cracking the codes encapsulated in the 'rebus' of images of women.

Some aspects of a society's cultural production can be deciphered as symptomatic. These mythologies, images, scenarios, iconographies and so on bear witness to those aspects of social formations that are subject to censorship and repression, near to the taboos and phobias or erotic subcultures that necessarily comprise the underworld of human life. And it is these aspects of popular culture that psychoanalytic criticism focuses on, identifying and attempting to decipher and trace their symptomatic status. Feminist theory used the melodrama to push the detection metaphor beyond criticism and towards a new relation with Hollywood cinema, in which psychoanalysis contributed a further level. Ultimately, this method of decoding images on the screen searched for a means of establishing a new form of spectatorship. The pleasure of cinema could be released from subordination to the image, and move on to deciphering how and why particular images appeared and appealed. This process necessarily led back to the society that produced them and the obsessions and imitations that created its collective fantasy.

I have tried to describe a process which is like a birth of criticism, moving out of entranced fascination with the Hollywood screen, even its most semiotic of moments, to discover a distance from it that then brought its own rewards of intellectual curiosity and pleasure. The fascination also had its distance, that of foreigners looking at strange cinema, far away in terms of both myth and geography. In addition to the skill and beauty invested in the Hollywood screen, distance concealed a certain kitschiness that our formal preoccupations could first overlook and then analyse through theories of structuralism, psychoanalysis and so on. It is as though the Atlantic had widened over the decades after the collapse of the Hollywood studio system. Recent writing by black critics and theorists has also analysed the racial gap that split the United States. bell hooks has argued that the social 'distance' between black women and the images they watched on the screen necessarily created a visual 'distance' which gave rise to a deciphering mode of cinema spectatorship:

> Identifying neither with the phallocentric gaze nor the construction of white woman as lack, critical black female spectators construct a theory of looking relations where cinematic visual delight is the pleasure of interrogation.[10]

Exchanges of fantasy criss-crossed the Atlantic creating an intricate cat's cradle during the years of Hollywood's decline, reversing the movement that took exiles from fascism and the earlier generation of European 'economic migrants' to Hollywood. For instance, there is the legacy of Douglas Sirk. The films he made at Universal International Studios between 1950 and 1959 have influenced European film-makers as well as critics. *Magnificent Obsession*, released in 1954, is a founding film of the 50s genre while *Imitation of Life* marks the end of the era. In the aftermath of this success, Sirk left Hollywood and moved back to his native Europe. Looking back, from the perspective of the 90s, his move from the United States to Europe acquires a certain ironic symbolism.

Some years later, Sirk reflected back on his departure from Hollywood in his discussions with Jon Halliday:

> I felt a totally new Hollywood would soon be in the making, a Hollywood open to pictures like *Easy Rider* – at any rate pictures of a very different brand, and a different style. ... Sometimes I pondered being back there again in Hollywood, experimenting, developing a completely new style appropriate to a new time which I felt was coming. There is the undeniable lure of this rotten place, Hollywood, the joy of being again on the set, holding the reins of a picture, fighting circumstances and impossible stories, this strange lure of dreams dreamt up by cameras and men. ... But I felt I had to stick to my decision to take my illness as more than a coincidence.[11]

While Sirk's intuition about coming changes in Hollywood was undoubtedly correct, a new cinema and a new style would develop on the other side of the Atlantic that would absorb, in certain cases, his old melodramatic aesthetic translated into a new sensibility. In Europe a new generation of postwar directors, cinephiles and critics had started to emerge who had absorbed Hollywood cinema. In Hollywood, film production no longer maintained even a semblance of its former economic and cultural homogeneity. Sirk's cinema, with its focus on emotion, unbearable and inescapable human relations, performance and style, has held a special appeal for later generations of European film-makers and critics. Most particularly, his work has been a rich resource for feminist theorists' exploration of the interiorities of the domestic melodrama, the repressed emotions of the psyche and their formal, symptomatic representation on the screen.

Chapter 2

Social Hieroglyphics: Reflections on Two Films by Douglas Sirk

The melodrama, the genre of *mise en scène*, site of emotions that cannot be expressed in so many words, concentrated critical approaches to Hollywood that had tried to find a deciphering mode of reading the image on the screen. Characters could become ciphers and places could become patterns. Looking at the screen could be like looking at children's puzzle pictures, which camouflage secret objects into their overt image. To notice that lighting, colour or framing, for instance, inflected meaning would be the first stage. The next would be to work out why and whether the figure in the pattern referred to disguised social symptoms. Although the first stage is integral to any reading of the cinematic image, and open to anyone who cares to see with their mind's eye, the second stage is, obviously, more difficult. The melodrama, however, revolves so openly around sexuality and emotion that anyone who cares to do so can sense their symptomatic connection with social constraints, ideology or collective fantasy.

Made as they were for a female audience, narrative and visual conventions which organise representations of women in 'women's pictures' differed from those of most Hollywood genres. The central star characters could exert an erotic power in the stories and their diegetic worlds. However, their sexual presence within the screen world did not translate into a glossy, streamlined 'signifier of sexuality' on the screen surface that could engage and seduce the spectator's gaze. The polarisation of gender that set up this sexualised binarism collapsed in the women's picture. Films made for a female audience transformed the pleasures of spectatorship and spectacle into problems of spectatorship and spectacle. Perhaps paradoxically, the presence of a female protagonist, drained of the safe sexualisation implicit in the binary imperative, heightens the importance of performance. Rather than performing as spectacle for consumption, the female figure performs the woman who must perform, and for whom performance is invested in appearance. Performance, appearance, masquerade and their erotics shift from the surface of the screen into the story itself. For

29

Bette Davis as Charlotte Vale or Barbara Stanwyck as Stella Dallas, the artifice of successful femininity constantly cracks and out of their characters' vulnerability rise towering star performances.

The play between appearance and artifice that marks star performances in the women's picture now seems, retrospectively and possibly anachronistically, proto-post-modern. These movies were, very often, about performance and therefore necessarily draw attention to the artifice of appearance and the process of its production. And the star system itself worked overtime to blur distinctions between the constructed persona of the star and her construction of a character on the screen. The female movie star always tended to be transparently cosmetic, stylised by the skills of studio make-up artists. Stories which provided vehicles for older women stars made full use of these levels of artifice and masquerade. At the same time, neither the star persona nor the fictional character could conceal her interiority from her audience, who had a privileged insight into secrets, suffering, passion and loss.

The melodramatic performance draws attention to an identity between femininity and sexuality and to its vulnerability and instability. Joan Rivière, in contemporary criticism's most-quoted lines on this topic, puts the problem of appearance in the following terms:

> The reader may now ask how I define womanliness or where I draw the line between genuine womanliness and its 'masquerade'. My suggestion is not, however, that there is any such difference; whether radical or superficial, they are the same thing.[1]

'Womanliness as masquerade' found fertile ground in the cinema,[2] which easily exaggerated this investment in appearance; and especially so in a commercial cinema which flourished out of and celebrated the affluence and commodity orientation that marked modern America. In this sense, films which acknowledge, self-consciously, an awareness of femininity as masquerade create 'a distanciation effect' so that the different facets of performance (the social, the spectacular and the narrative) are made visible. It is often a streamlined and successful eroticism, that prevents the split between performer and performance widening in other Hollywood genres. The melodrama, with its female audience, is unable to fall back onto the erotic image of the feminine to disguise its artifices.

Sirk's cinema has often been discussed within an aesthetic of distanciation, partly because of the nature of melodramatic performance, partly because of the stylisation of his melodramas as such, partly because of the pivotal place of his cinema in film history. A German theatre director, working in the German theatre of the late 1920s and early 30s, who then turned to cinema, his career stretches back towards Brecht and forward towards Fassbinder. Fassbinder was a great admirer of Sirk and one who both wrote about his films and remade *All That Heaven Allows* (Sirk, 1955) as *Angst essen Seele/Fear Eats the Soul* (Fassbinder, 1972). Furthermore, Fassbinder's cinema with its overtly gay themes and recurring images of transvestism brought another level to the question of performance and appearance, one that focused not only on femininity as masquerade but on the instability of gender as such. The masquerade of femininity can mask other masquerades. Female impersonators have, for a long time, made use of the accoutrements of masquerade associated with Hollywood stars, emphasising and playing up tensions between surface appearance and identity, using wigs, make-up, costume all to maximum effect. In these images there is an element of *trompe-l'oeil* and a pleasure in appearance that is all the greater because of its overtly illusory nature. For instance, it is impossible to see Pedro Almodóvar's *High Heels* (1993) without thinking about aspects of *Imitation of Life*: the ageing actress trying to rediscover her daughter; the actress as star who has become the masquerade of her own performance; the star who welcomes her impersonation in a drag act, acknowledging that imitation is the best form of homage; then there is the story, reminiscent of the one in which life imitated art, of a mother and daughter in love with the same man and both suspected of his murder. And in the 'writing with the camera', the element of craziness that Sirk valued, there is a sense of imitation that is, once again, the best form of homage.

Imitation of Life is not only about performance and masquerade but goes beyond melodramatic pathos, to introduce issues of race and class, usually taboo on the Hollywood screen. The film gives a melodramatic, highly emotional and excessive materialisation to real political, social and economic issues. The oppression and intolerance of racism takes place within an everyday normality which is also an area of silence, experienced but not expressed. Throughout the fim there is a gap between what is seen and what is said. Only the spectator can decipher the relation between the two. The tension between the artifice available to the white woman, an assumed sheen of protective glamour, and the unveiling of the black woman back to essence, creates a visual discourse on race that is only possible in the cinema. *Magnificent Obsession,* on the other hand, seems to float outside the world, apparently uncontaminated by the politics of the everyday. The story seems to have stripped away the exterior accoutrements of social existence, to discover a phantasmatic scenario, solely concerned with the psyche, sexuality, *amour fou* and transgressive desire. However, the world of *Magnificent Obsession* is obsessively narrow, as though it were illuminated by a single spotlight, hinting that the exclusion is matter of repression. In retrospect, this intimation of a barely repressed subtext almost invading a love story between two characters, one played by Rock Hudson, the other by Jane Wyman, has obvious significance. When the film was made, Jane Wyman had just divorced Ronald Reagan who was building a political career out of Hollywood's McCarthy era. And Rock Hudson was one of the early celebrity AIDS victims who publicly acknowledged both his illness and his homosexuality just before his death in 1985. His biography and other writings about his life, published after his death, graphically describe the double life a gay man had to lead in Hollywood to protect his image as a heterosexual screen lover.

While *Magnificent Obsession* needs psychoanalytic theory, particularly the Freudian Oedipal drama, *Imitation of Life* grafts its obvious themes of performance, spectacle and femininity onto a scenario which needs political theory, particularly Marx's theory of labour. *Imitation of Life* tells the story of a white actress, Lora Meredith, played by Lana Turner, and her black maid, Annie, played by Juanita Moore. In a bravura performance Lana Turner acts an actress, Lora Meredith, who becomes a star, Lana/ Lora. Her appearance becomes more and more stylised with success, so that 'stardom' is depicted not so much as a social category but rather as a moulding of appearance into spectacle. Lora is hardly shown performing professionally. Her clothes, her make-up, her hair, her jewels, all combine to create an image which is constructed for the camera and the screen even though she may, in the story world, be simply moving around her house on a daily basis. Lora plays out an image just as Lana Turner plays Lora and the two star personas, the fictional and the real, condense with each other and detach from one another, so that all that is left is artifice itself. However, Lora does not achieve the status of spectacle through her own efforts. Her appearance is constructed out of Annie's labour which has the reverse visibility to Lora's fetishised image.

At the beginning of the story, Lora is struggling to establish her career as an actress, living in New York in impoverished circumstances with her daughter, Susie. She agrees to give Annie, and her daughter Sarah Jane, a home for the night after the children make friends on Coney Island beach. But Annie's arrival is the turning point which creates the foundation of Lora's future success. The first sign is Annie's deal with the milkman:

> Annie: Didn't say anything about a bill to me. He was very polite. Just gave me the order and said it looked like things were looking up for Miss Meredith.
> Lora: He thought you were my maid. Now he thinks I'm prosperous.
> Annie: No sin in lookin' prosperous. It's just a way in showing your trust in the Lord; tellin' Him you're ready whenever He is.[3]

Later, Lora manages to talk her way into the office of the theatrical agent, Alan Loomis, by 'performing' the role of Hollywood star. Her performance achieves positive if only short-lived credibility when Loomis dials her telephone number. Annie answers:

> Annie: Miss Meredith's residence.
> Loomis: Oh, this is Miss Meredith's residence?
> Lora: That'll be Annie, my maid.[4]

Annie's knowing and complicit 'performance' of the role 'maid' allows Lora the means to establish herself in the role 'actress'. As the story develops, Annie's performance congeals into reality. Her actual behind-the-scene work (cooking, washing, cleaning, child-care) produces Lora as before-the-scene spectacle in a way that is reminiscent of the worker's production of a commodity for the market. While at first her 'per-formance' invisibly supported Lora's visibility, her labour continues to support the household, materially and emotionally. However, the reality of their class relationship remains unspoken and taboo.

The visibility/invisibility of class is overdetermined by race in Sirk's *Imitation of Life*. Lora's investment in herself as spectacle renders her unable to see or decipher the world around her. The opening scenes of the film take place on a sunny *mardi gras* afternoon at Coney Island. The camera picks up Lora as she runs along the boardwalk, calling her daughter whom she has lost in the crowd. She is wearing dark glasses and the camera looks up at her as though she were on stage as she performs, in Steve Archer's words, 'the mother in distress'. He, meanwhile, is taking photographs of her. As she runs down the steps, he raises his camera and, without seeing him, she instinctively removes her glasses. The ensuing dialogue, which takes place when she literally bumps into him, underlines the point. When he points her towards the police, a few feet away, she is still unable to see. But Annie has found Susie and is looking after her and Sarah Jane, in a homely, enclosed space, *underneath* the boardwalk.

Lora's dark glasses and her inability to see other people run like a metaphor through the movie. Her life as a star, as commodity, wraps around her as though the bright lights of the stage or set leave her blinded. On one level, her work as an actress constantly removes her from her daughter, whose life becomes increasingly opaque to her. On another, and more significant, level her blindness is directed towards the problem of race and the dilemmas that face Sarah Jane, who tries, whenever possible, to 'pass' as white. Lora's response to Sarah Jane is: 'Don't you see ... it doesn't make any difference to us because we all love you.' Annie, on the other hand, certainly knows that it does make a difference. While she sees the social reality of discrimination, violence, exploitation that Sarah Jane is rebelling against, she is unable to find the words to say it. Annie's response to Sarah Jane is: 'Sush. ... Everything will be all right.' Whereas in relation to Lora she functions as worker, the invisible labour force, in her relation to Sarah Jane, Annie is excessively visible. Her mother's colour constantly returns her performance to the social reality of discrimination; without her mother she would be able to achieve a credibility of performance equal to Lora's.

For Sarah Jane the issue of race is inescapably also one of class ('Bus boys, cooks, chauffeurs! ... No thank you, I've seen your nice young folks') and she attempts to find escape and a solution to the problem of appearance through performance. Although Lora's career as a star is built up respectably on Broadway, and Sarah Jane works as a night-club singer or in a chorus line, there is a sense in which Sarah Jane is 'imitating' Lora. While artificiality and masquerade are not only acceptable but draw admiration in a white woman, Sarah Jane is not allowed to be what she appears, but is returned by society and her family to an invisible, secret, essence. She can only achieve her image by denying her relationship to her mother. Why, the film asks, does a society that is obsessed by appearance and spectacle suddenly fetishise essence when it come to race? Sarah Jane follows Lora's path into masquerade, as she, too, becomes a performer. But she understands that the masquerade only works if her black mother is wiped out and made invisible once again. To achieve certain whiteness is to achieve the performance of white femininity, to become the product that she had witnessed her mother effacing herself to produce. Lora's production as a star is not only painted, as it were, on the surface of Annie's work as her maid but the concept of whiteness as spectacle alienates her daughter into a re-performance of that spectacular femininity. In one case, Sarah Jane's, the blot of race is effaced, in the other, Lora's, it is contained within a power relation of worker and commodity.

In the last parting scene between them, Annie and Sarah Jane both have to adopt roles. Annie 'plays' the 'Mammy' to Sarah Jane's 'Miss Linda'. Earlier, Sarah Jane acts out her concept of performing 'coloured' when she waits on 'Miss Lora and her friends'. Her caricature speaks a truth, about race relations and the race relations that are concealed behind Lora's relation to Annie. In the confrontation that follows this scene Lora is depicted as white, not in a neutral sense, but as a colour. Her artificial appearance is visually concentrated into blondeness, her very pale make-up, blue eyes, white dress, jewels. This exaggeration of masquerade reflects back, through an exaggeration of racial visibility, to femininity as spectacle, and to femininity as spectacle on the cinema screen. It is as though the recurring image of the white woman, centre screen and lit up, acts as a 'blindspot', effacing any possibility of depicting the unspeakable issues that constitute race in the United States. Annie only finally achieves visibility through her death. Then, the *mise en scène* she has devised for her funeral parade erupts into a blaze of whiteness as she occupies the centre of the spectacle. However, in a final, a deeply pessimistic irony, Sarah Jane is received back into the newly constituted family: Lora, Steve and Susie embrace her in the limousine. Sarah Jane has achieved whiteness through her mother's death.

Sirk's *Imitation of Life* is a remake of John Stahl's 1934 *Imitation of Life*, the film of Fannie Hurst's best-selling novel. The Sirk version deviates from the Stahl and Hurst originals in a crucial way. While the relation between a white woman and her black servant, and the relations between the two women and their daughters, are still central, the Sirk version inflects the story by introducing the theme of performance. The original *Imitation of Life* told the story of Bea (Claudette Colbert), who becomes an extremely successful capitalist entrepreneur by marketing Delilah's (Louise Beavers) recipe for pancakes. Bea makes Delilah pose for the photograph that will become the brand image 'Aunt Delilah's Pancake Mixture' and her face, turned into a caricature of a black stereotype, haunts the movie as it flashes from a neon sign. She is stamped, as it were, into an image of alienation onto the commodity that represents her labour. Lauren Berlant has analysed the themes of the Stahl *Imitation of Life*. She points out that the white woman, a successful capitalist, is able to conceal herself behind the neutrality of her dead husband's name and the excess of Delilah's image as trade-mark:

> Bea becomes more like the classic capitalist, increasingly distant from the scene of consumption. As the brains and the name behind the business, Bea remains almost entirely behind the veil of the male moniker. In addition, Bea uses Aunt Delilah's body to stand in for her own ... in this coerced guise she she becomes the prosthetic body of 'B. Pullman', the store, and Bea Pullman, the woman.[5]

In this way, Bea can, paradoxically, maintain the fetish character of her femininity without contamination by an overt link to the process of production. She is an encapsulation of disavowal. As she becomes rich, Bea acquires glamour and fashion but displaces any labour involved, even as employer, onto Delilah's image. However, Delilah's presence is a constant reminder of the source of Bea's wealth and its origin in labour and exploitation.

The relation between the two women, the entrepreneurial skill of one and the artisanal skill of the other, also tells the story of the relation between commodity, capital and labour. Because the characters are women, economic relations acquire an extra metaphoric layer in which factors of visibility and invisibility are affected by sexuality and labour. Sirk's *Imitation of Life* eliminates the commodity object (the pancake recipe) which is replaced by Lora herself. The film can then apply issues of masquerade and spectacle to its own system of production, the cinema. But the metaphor of commodity and labour also becomes more pointed. Lora stands for the commodity rather than the entrepreneurial capitalist; Annie metaphorically stands for the labour process concealed by the spectacular nature of the commodity. While the metaphor feminises the commodity, it condenses the invisibility of labour power under capitalism with the repression of race in American society. At the same time, Annie's labour which produces Lora, Broadway and movie star, as spectacle within the story world also produces her image for audience consumption, standing in, as it were, for the invisible process of film production. As a metaphor for the relation between screen spectacle and the invisibility of the labour process, Lora's image also raises the question of the apartheid nature of Hollywood cinema. The relegation of black performers to servants' roles is well known and Sarah Jane's rebellion against her class and domestic destiny can be related back, implicitly, to this stereotyping, and thus her mother's relation to the white star. However, in the Sirk film, Sarah Jane is played by a white actress 'passing' for 'black' 'passing' for 'white'. It is the casting of the Stahl version that provides a much more vivid comment on the fate of black actresses in Hollywood. The Sarah Jane part, Peola, was played by Fredi Washington who had an established career as a stage performer, especially as a singer and dancer. Although her performance in *Imitation of Life* was outstanding, showing a real capacity for dramatic acting, the Hollywood system could not accept her. In the part of Peola, Fredi Washington truly bears witness to the racial essentialism of Hollywood, which would be carried through thematically to the story of performance, spectacle and racism in the 1958 version of the story.[6]

Lora is not an image that entrances the spectator. She is artificial to the point of self-reflexivity in performance but not self-aware as a point of empathy. Only Sarah Jane stands in the position of knowledge in the film, understanding, as it were, the full force of the accumulated metaphors. Lora's artifice is very different from Sarah Jane's. Sarah Jane is pushed into performance by the racism of the society around her. She is told that she is not what she appears to be and refused the right to perform her appearance, the social status of 'whiteness' that is the passport to not being 'different'.

While *Imitation of Life* reflects racial discrimination and persecution, but as a zone of silence and repression, marked by but outside adequate social articulation, Sirk's first successful A-picture melodrama erases the external world altogether. Although *Magnificent Obsession* mainly takes place in the well-to-do milieu of an ideal, semi-rural, semi-small-town America, the setting is atopian rather than social. Always despised by critics, ignored even by Sirk critics and melodrama theorists, the film's interest primarily lies in its unusual reversed Oedipal fantasy. Father/son rivalry, conflict and different forms of reconciliation make up far the most frequent form of Oedipal narrative, a negotiation into the patriarchal Symbolic, which is supposed to involve the subordination of desire. In *Magnificent Obsession* desire outwits, as it were, the patriarchal principle. And the narrative topography of the home, its constraints and interiority which almost always characterise the melodrama, gives way to a narrative topography of movement and journey. While the male hero's journey is one of search or pursuit, the heroine's journey is one of flight and escape. The heroine's flight from her desire, once into blindness, then into a literal journey of escape, leaves her nomadic, unable to settle until the object of her desire has completed his emotional and psychic journey into maturity.

Bob Merrick's Oedipal trajectory is internal and more precisely portrayed than in film narratives whose Oedipality is exteriorised and carried forward by action. Here the plot is fuelled simply by movements generated by desire. In a sense, therefore, it loses the social implications that are of central importance in the domestic melodrama and the woman's picture. *All That Heaven Allows*, the direct follow-up to the success of *Magnificent Obsession*, makes thorough use of the social as a delaying mechanism to the movement of desire. The love story between Ron and Cary is disrupted by differences of age and class, but there is no implied metaphor of mother/son incestuous desire. *Magnificent Obsession*, while obviously unable to depict a literal blood relationship, creates a romance which constantly places the two lovers within an incestuous frame of reference.

The film's opening premise is that Bob Merrick, a very rich and self-indulgent playboy obsessed with the thrill of speed, has an accident through his own irresponsibility, as a result of which Dr Phillips, head of the local hospital and much-loved and respected philanthropist, dies. Dr Phillips succumbs to a heart attack because the medical equipment he depended on, in an emergency, is tied up saving Bob Merrick. The film story emphasises this sequence of cause and effect. The immature and irresponsible younger man causes the death of a man who occupies the place of the law, culture and moral worth invested in the Symbolic order. Merrick's subsequent behaviour is depicted less as immature than as infantile, in Freud's term, His Majesty the Baby. His life is changed when he meets Helen, Dr Phillips's widow, with whom he falls instantly and passionately in love. The film's next move is precipitated by Helen's attempt to ward off Merrick's pursuit. She is knocked down by a passing car and loses her sight. Her blindness allows him to meet her on the beach under an assumed name, where they read the funnies with Helen's minder, a tomboy little girl who represents the de-gendered latency period. She marks Merrick's progression from self-centred infancy into an asexual childhood idyll.

In the meantime, Merrick is initiated into a pseudo-Symbolic order by Phillips's old friend who teaches him the doctor's own recipe for self-fulfilment: a secret philanthropy which sustains the donor purely through giving without demanding social recognition in exchange. The ego's wish for recognition is subsumed into a higher ideal. Sublimation is accompanied by a new sexual maturity and restraint. Merrick takes up his abandoned medical career and, during the rest of the film, his trajectory is directed towards acquiring the place of the 'father', whose death he has caused, in order to marry his widow. And she now passionately reciprocates his love, even acknowledging that she knows that the man she loves caused her husband's death. The resolution of the love story is delayed, not through the intervention of any exterior force, but through her flight from the danger of her reciprocated desire. It is not until she is at the point of death that Merrick finds her, operates on her himself and restores both her life and her sight. By then all the outraged witnesses of their romance, in particular Dr Phillips's daughter, have also acknowledged that true love has won over past wrongs and the couple are united. The 'son' has found not only a way to take his 'father's' place in the world, but to marry his 'father's' wife.

This story, if my argument for its Oedipal implications holds good, fails to subordinate an illicit desire to the law. Merrick successfully assumes the position of the dead doctor, the father figure in my terms, without having to give up his love for the mother figure, the doctor's widow. Without making any great claims for *Magnificent Obsession,* I would use it as an example of how, with only a little help from psychoanalytic theory, a story of forbidden love can be shown to conceal an incestuous day-dream ... The film strips away any extraneous elements exterior to the love story; the relationship between Bob and Helen is all there is to it. The middle-class, well-to-do social milieu serves two functions. First, as I said earlier, it is atopian, neutral, safe from any possible interference from social or economic pressures. Bob Merrick's money funds the utopian romance just as money funds a movie. Second, the well-to-do milieu does have social connotations. It puts an idealised American lifestyle and landscape, interior and exterior, on show to a very different America and to the world at a time when American movies were a show case for this lifestyle. The realisation of an impossible desire condenses with the aspiration to an impossible way of life. Sexuality effaces all contradiction, and the screen is simply surface. Significantly, when Helen travels to Europe for medical consultations, her destination is Switzerland, unravaged by the Second World War and available for folksy, kitschy representations of a village lifestyle that has remained unchanged, like a movie fantasy of an ahistorical Middle Ages. But during the scene in which Bob acts as Helen's eyes, and describes the ritual burning of an effigy of a witch, the spectre of the United States in 1952 and its witch hunts haunt the screen.

While *Imitation of Life* deals specifically with race, *Magnificent Obsession* is a film of total whiteness. Both films revolve around 'blind-spots'. Helen, the heroine of *Magnificent Obsession*, literally blind for most of the film, can fall, illicitly, in love under the mask of blindness. Lora, in *Imitation of Life,* although literally sighted, is blinded by her ambition to be seen as spectacle and while the bright lights of stardom shine on her, she is unable to discern, to make out, the emotional events that are taking place around her. Her inability to understand the tragic reality of racial oppression and exploitation is realised under the guise of spectacle which prioritises appearance.

Obsession and imitation: these two ideas evoke psychic processes. First, the irrational, obsessive, psychic energy that activates the unconscious; second, the imitations, substitutions and masquerades that characterise the language of the unconscious. While contemporary intellectuals, especially film theorists, may be accused of an obsession with Hollywood cinema, from the days of auteurism and *mise-en-scène* analysis onwards the kind of criticism they produced has been concerned with clues and their decipherment rather than with intentional and innate meanings. The melodrama could condense this critical tendency with the methodologies of psychoanalysis and feminist interest in challenging the transcendent power of the visual. While in Hollywood generally the spectacle of woman is a symptom that relates back to the male psyche and blocks the understanding of the social, the melodramatic symptom tends to de-eroticise its female spectacle. The 'symptom' can, residually, reflect on its own imitation and acknowledge its own 'blind-spot'.

Chapter 3

Close-ups and Commodities

The close-up, specifically the close-up of the female star, played its part in the development of the cinema as an industry and as a set of conventions. Jean-Luc Godard, in the following quotation, associates female beauty almost ontologically with the cinema:

> A beautiful face, as La Bruyère wrote, is the most beautiful of sights. There is a famous legend which has it that Griffith, moved by the beauty of his leading lady, invented the close-up in order to capture it in greater detail. Paradoxically, therefore, the simplest close-up is also the most moving. Here our art reveals its transcendence most strongly, making the beauty of the object signified burst forth in the sign.[1]

The D.W. Griffith story is undoubtedly a legend. However, Godard's observation, which links the close-up, fascination with feminine beauty and the specifics of the cinema, illuminates another of the film industry's legendary beginnings. The star system developed in the early days of film production in the United States, predating the industry's move, *en masse*, to Hollywood in the years before the First World War. In 1910, Florence Lawrence, until then only known by the brand-name of her company as The Vitagraph Girl, demanded to be named in response to the fan-mail she had been receiving. Vitagraph refused her request and she moved to an independent company which allowed her to build up her own publicity machine around her own name. Trade magazines commented on the way that newer companies gained publicity by sending out pictures of beautiful women to the press.[2] The rival attractions of female performers became a factor in the competition between companies in the infant industry. As companies struggled for dominance or even survival, consumer seduction and the seductive powers of the female image on the screen grew side by side. Just as the other new industries developed advertising, promoting desirability, gloss and glamour, so the film industry invested in the visibility of the star. Perhaps the chrome on a motor car, shining, modern and streamlined, had an equivalent in the image of sexualised femininity in the cinema. Male stars, of course, also appealed to the public. But the female stars came to be idolised by both sexes, and their popularity far outran that of male stars (with the exception of the great comedians). As female star glamour and the development of the cinema as industry fell into step, control over the most popular stars aided vertical integration. Crowds were drawn to the theatres by stars' names and posters (exhibition), the exhibitors were forced to show films made by companies that contracted popular stars (distribution), and popular stars were launched and promoted in appropriate films (production).[3]

Although it may not have been D.W. Griffith who invented the close-up, he pioneered the use of special diffused lighting and specially adapted lenses to film his favourite star, Lillian Gish.[4] On the one hand, the cinema was developing the conventions of continuity editing that gave the Hollywood product its movement and excitement, on the other hand, the star close-up would hold the story in stasis, cutting her image out from the general flow of the narrative, emphasising her function as spectacle in its own right. Thus, a disjuncture appeared between the image of woman on the screen enhanced as spectacle and the general flow of narrative continuity organising the action. Film theorists have drawn attention to the way in which the cinema echoes the excitement of other kinds of modern movement, the movement of train travel or the movement of visualised suspense, for instance, enhanced by the movement of the camera and of editing. But the discourse of sexuality develops its own rhetoric of stasis, holding back the excitement of movement into a moment of eroticised visual pleasure.[5]

But D.W. Griffith's work and his typical Gish close-up were out of synch with the rise of modernity after the First World War. The 1920s saw the emergence of the 'new woman', who cut her hair, shortened her skirt, went to work, earned money, began to take control over her own sexuality, and finally had to be taken into account at the movie box-office. Lary May summarises Hollywood's response to this phenomenon:

> Films that featured a new woman were usually written by female sce-
> narists and played by one of the large number of actresses under twenty
> five who worked in the Hollywood industry. The female heroine was
> generally found in contemporary urban society and whether she was an
> emancipated wife or a flapper played by Clara Bow, Mae Murray, Joan
> Crawford, Gloria Swanson or Norma or Constance Talmadge, she por-
> trayed a restless young woman eager to escape from an ascetic home.
> Seeking a new role, she could take a job in search of freedom or money
> but these heroines find their true emancipation in short skirts, glamour
> and innocent sexuality.[6]

Hollywood managed to acknowledge and address the 'new woman', while simultaneously acknowledging and addressing her through the discourse of consumerism. Lauren Rabinovitz notes that as the female labour force increased twice as fast as the adult female population between 1880 and 1930, certain genres of early cinema played to the new discourse of female sexuality while constructing the female body as object of an eroticised gaze: 'This double-edged process of subjectivity and objectivity was fundamental to recuperating female desire so that it functioned in the service of patriarchy. The temptations of pleasure defined by early cinema were, indeed, as dangerous as early social reformers said they were.'[7] And Gaylyn Studlar, pointing out that in the 20s 'the American film industry operated on the assumption that women formed their most mportant audience', analyses contemporary fan magazines to show that:

> By actively seeking sexual pleasure, American women of the 1920s were widely believed to be usurping a male privilege more powerful and precious than the vote. In response countless social commentators accused American women of destroying the norms of heterosexual relations, eroding the boundaries between the sexes and sending American masculinity into rapid decline. Universal suffrage and female employment were not cited as the chief culprits in these distressing trends: women's assertion of their right to sexual gratification was.[8]

As a result, discourses addressed to women had to be couched in terms of both liberation and repression, negotiating between 'the old standard of sexual restraint and the "new" possibility of sexual desire'.

It is during this period that Hollywood established its characteristic modernity. Hollywood quickly came to dominate the European market, suffering as it was from the aftermath of the First World War which reversed the previous flow of film imports from Europe to the United States. It is obviously true that trade factors were crucial here; Hollywood's power was asserted through its economic power and its industrially organised, vertically integrated system of production, distribution and exhibition. At the same time, the image of America as a modern, affluent, free-thinking and progressive society drew audiences into the cinema outside the United States. And Hollywood's domination of the entertainment industry attracted the great European directors whose work came to be among the best of the late silent period, producing movies that could triumph due to their own talent realised through technology and production values unparalleled in the world. And, to complicate the issue further, directors such as Lubitsch and Stroheim brought a sophisticated sexuality to the audiences of the New World. This concept of modernity included a troubling new discourse of sexuality, projected onto the iconography of the 'new woman'.

On the other hand, the 20s was not simply the decade of modernity. The discourse of sexual freedom signified by the 'new woman' produced a backlash. The casual amorality of the times was vigorously challenged by the supporters of what would, today, be known as 'family values'. Their fury was focused on the cinema as the perpetrator of the decline in morals and their instrument was organisation for censorship. This crisis was not new to the cinema. It had taken a different form earlier in the century when the industry and moral reformers had combined to move the cinema out of the ghettos to find a 'respectable' audience. As film historians have argued, such a move generalised the appeal of the cinema to a mass audience but one which had no class specificity, and its emblem was 'the respectable American mother and her children'. During the 20s, Hollywood began to lose its veneer of respectability. It became, rather, synonymous with an eroticised glamour and a sophisticated amorality. The scandal-ridden lives of the stars were exaggerated to create a moral panic in the United States, which threatened by the end of the silent period to affect box-office attendance. The moral panic was answered by the financial panic of the movie moguls, who began to search for ways of regulating their industry without abandoning control to outside censorship forces.

The Hollywood cinema in the late silent period confronts today's critics with certain dilemmas. It has to be approached from different angles, allowing its multiple facets to be understood in context, rather than assessed according to preconceived values. To put this point another way, from a feminist perspective the image of sexuality in the great days of silent cinema is contradictory. It traces a zigzag path, simultaneously liberating in address and constraining and objectifying as liberation is couched in terms of commodity culture. However, the very contradictions inherent in mythologies of sexuality in the period are central to the contradictions inherent in American modernism and its favourite emblem, the cinema.[9] Thus, on the one hand, Hollywood movies gave a respectable veneer to the sexualised image of woman as signifier of the erotic and as a 'trade-mark' for the seductive potential of the cinema itself. From this point of view the image of woman was conflated with the commodity spectacle. On the other hand, the modernity of the 'flapper', her first steps towards sexual autonomy, were reflected on the cinema screen. Woman might still signify sexuality and erotic objectification, but female desire had to be acknowledged and accommodated. Thus a discourse of sexuality could emerge from the depths of nineteenth-century Manichaean division between the repression of respectable society and the licentiousness of the underworld, the city at night.

At the same time, this cinema with its liberating ability to capture the discourse of feminine desire used its glamour in the interests of commodity capitalism. In Will Hays's own words: 'More and more is the motion picture being recognised as a stimulant to trade. No longer does the girl in Sullivan, Indiana guess what the styles are going to be in three months. She knows because she sees them on the screen.'[10]

Furthermore, Hollywood projected across the movie-going world a shimmering mirage of desirability that held up the United States to view as the democracy of glamour and the democracy of commodity acquisition. Already in 1926, William Fox had said (to Upton Sinclair) the famous words: 'I have tried to bring government officials to realise that American trade follows the American motion picture, not the American flag.'[11] No other production system has been able to challenge the American entertainment industry to this day. And, even, today, in the GATT negotiations of 1994, the Americans continue to defend the supremacy established in the 20s.

Into this already contradictory configuration came the challenge of moral panic. By the end of the silent period, the moral majority was fighting back and Hollywood capitulated to pressure by appointing Will Hays as their own internal censor. Hays confided his understanding of his responsibilities to Carl Laemmle in the following terms, explaining that he had no wish to ignore the public's interest in sex: 'Films had to be made passionate but pure ... giving the public all the sex it wants with compensating values for all those church and women's groups.'[12] By this means, and by the submission of all movies to censorship scrutiny before their release into the public domain, Hollywood held at bay demands for formal, legislated censorship either at federal or state level. But this compromise was thrown off balance by the arrival of the talkies. As early as 1915, the cinema had been denied the automatic, constitutional right of free speech by the Supreme Court. Its ruling proclaimed that 'freedom of speech must be denied to moving pictures because they may be used for evil.' The talkies took the the guardians' national morality to new heights of frenzy. The movies' depiction of 'sex and crime' could now not only be shown but spoken, and even casually discussed outside traditional moral boundaries. It was said that 'the talkies opened up new dramatic possibilities. Now sexy starlets could rationalise their criminal behaviour.'

It is impossible to trace the details of the Machiavellian negotiations that led up to the formation of the Production Code Administration in 1934. The main protagonists of the campaign were dedicated Catholics, particularly Martin Quigley and Father Lord, who were convinced of the enormous immoral influence exerted by the cinema. They were equally convinced of its potential for good. Father Lord had grasped this potential when he saw *Birth of a Nation* as a young priest. He had been deeply impressed by its moral stance and the portrayal of good and evil on the screen. And it was this question of the relation between good and evil that became central to the new struggle for censorship. As the new Production Code demanded that scripts be submitted for censorship before production, the narrative line of movie scripts could be moulded in advance, emphasising an opposition between moral and immoral behaviour. The Code deeply affected certain genres, the gangster film, for instance, as it was no longer possible to identify with characters on the wrong side of the law; and it deeply affected the depiction of sexuality. The free and easy approach to sex epitomised by the 'new woman' reached its zenith in the pre-Code raciness and sexual self-sufficiency of screen heroines. Although

Mae West has now become emblematic of this period, there are many other examples of her sophisticated disregard for traditional sexual morality. The movies dramatised sex, allowing a negotiation between men and women in which women were able to assert not only desire, but also autonomy. And although many movies ended with marriage, the negotiations, the wit and the light-hearted rapid exchanges took up most of the story time.

The imposition of censorship did not take sexuality out of the movies. The effect was to displace sexuality from the realm of a tentative modernity into a new apotheosis of the visual concentrated on woman as signifier of sexuality. As a Manichaean sense of good versus evil came to dominate the structure of stories, in any negotiation around or about female sexuality the image of woman became primarily a matter of visual coding. And, at the same time, although a tendency to code female sexuality as spectacle had always existed in the cinema (as expressed, for instance, in the ontology that Godard drew attention to in my earlier quotation) the imposition of the 1934 Code literally codified this tendency. Thus the impact of the Code was to produce a cinema in which sexuality became the 'unspoken'; as a site of repression, the image of woman embodies its symptomatic return. It became difficult, if not impossible, to represent autonomous female desire on the screen, while femininity took on an acutely polarised function in opposition to masculine action and authority.

The cultural phenomenon of polarisation of values, the construction of antinomies around good versus evil, obviously has a long and complex history. Not only does religious ideology build up antinomies, but folktales also often depend on a hero/villain structure for their narratives to function. This cultural phenomenon has persisted into the popular culture of the century of cinema and Hollywood has played an important part in perpetuating it. The moral crusades of the early 30s demanded the imposition of a value system built on polarisations of good and evil. Although Hollywood attempted to modify and wriggle out of the strait-jacket imposed even by self-censorship, formulaic stories in which a moral stance can be provided by demonising and erasing a villain had their uses both ideologically and in terms of the constant demand for product. Out of this opposition, the hero/villain polarisation tends to focus the action aspect of a story, its violence and its catharsis. Within the narrative structure, femininity and sexual spectacle tend to condense, exaggerating the cinema's (in Godard's terms) specific condensation between the beauty of woman, the close-up, and the stasis of spectacle as opposed to the movement of action.

These points are still significant today for understanding popular culture, particularly that of the United States. As the cinema's first century draws to a close, and Hollywood's investment in entertainment has diversified, it still produces show-case movies. In its decline, Hollywood has become more and more dependent on demonisations, on hero/villain violence and a good/evil polarisation. This decline was, of course, presided over by Ronald Reagan, a politician formed by Hollywood in its cold war period, in which the social erasure of liberalism was echoed on the screen by the fictional erasure of villains. At the same time, violence takes over the screen as spectacle, almost, one might argue, usurping the other antinomy: the erotic role played by the image of woman.

Now I would like to return to the quotation from Godard and complete it by adding another sentence:

> A beautiful face, as La Bruyère wrote, is the most beautiful of sights. There is a famous legend which has it that Griffith, moved by the beauty of his leading lady, invented the close-up in order to capture it in greater detail. Paradoxically, therefore, the simplest close-up is also the most moving. Here our art reveals its transcendence most strongly, making the beauty of the object signified burst forth in the sign. With these huge eyes half-closing in discretion and desire, with these blenching lips, all we see in their anguish is the dark design they imply, and in their avowal only the illusions they conceal.[13]

Here Godard not only links the close-up and femininity to cinema, but associates both the image and femininity with secrets, with something that lies 'darkly' behind the mask. And the spectacle of female sexuality becomes one of 'topography', one of surface and secret. The celluloid image thus acquires an 'unconscious' that has its source in male anxiety and desire projected onto an uncertainty about femininity.

Mary Ann Doane has associated this iconography most particularly with the image of the *femme fatale*:

> The femme fatale is the figure of a certain discursive unease, a potential epistemological trauma. For her most striking characteristic is the fact that she never really is what she seems to be. In thus transforming the threat of the woman into a secret, something which must be aggressively revealed, unmasked, discovered, the figure is fully compatible with the epistemological drive of narrative. Sexuality becomes the site of questions about what can and cannot be known. This imbrication of knowledge and sexuality of epistemophilia and scopophilia has crucial implications for the cinema. Cinematic claims to truth about women rely to a striking extent on judgements about vision and its stability or instability.[14]

I want to take these ideas out of the context of an analysis of the *femme fatale* and relocate them in the context of the 'enigma' of Marilyn Monroe. Quite clearly, Marilyn is outside the film-noir genre and her exaggerated sexuality is not that of the *femme fatale*. However, some of the same issues of 'topography', the surface/secret opposition, are relevant to her image, returning the argument back to interconnections between the mask of femininity and commodity consumption.

After Marilyn made *Gentlemen Prefer Blondes* (Howard Hawks, 1952), her image rapidly became an emblem of perfectly eroticised features that could be recognised immediately in a reduced form, a silhouette of her body or a few lines conveying her face in diagram. Her face provided the perfect base for the cosmetic appearance of the time, with the features painted onto a surface that then, almost magically, acquired an iridescent glamour that had a special relation with the camera. There are three phases of imprint here: the cosmetic, the photographic and the diagrammatic. Eve Arnold, who did several photo stories on her, noted: 'Her make-up was a total mystery. According to Whitey Snyder, her veteran make-up man, she knew more secrets about shadowing her eyes and using special lipstick to keep her mouth glossy than anyone else in the business. These "secrets" were kept even from him.' And after her last photo session with Marilyn, when a waiting reporter waylaid her and asked: 'What was it like to photograph Marilyn?' she commented:

I waved him off and went on my way. But the question would not be denied. What was it like to photograph her? It was like watching a print come up in the developer. The latent image was there – it needed just her time and temperature controls to bring it into being. It was a stroboscopic display, and all the photographer had to do was to stop time at any given instant and Marilyn would bring forth a new image.[15]

Marilyn thus became emblematic, through cosmetics and on celluloid and in the popular imagination, of 50s America and its representation of self in Hollywood cinema.

In the 50s, America became the world's image of a democracy of glamour, completing a process, through the movies and through mass-produced clothes and cosmetics, that had been launched in the 30s and interrupted by the Second World War. It was a paradigmatic moment for commodity fetishism. Jean Baudrillard pointed out that originally the word 'fetish' derived from the Portuguese *feitico,* which in its turn stemmed from the Latin *factitius*, the root of the Spanish *afeitar,* meaning 'to paint, to adorn, to embellish', and *afeite,* meaning 'preparation, ornamentation, cosmetics'.[16] He suggests that this etymology implies a homology between the fetishised figure of bodily beauty and the fetishism of the commodity. Both are constructed, made out of raw material or the body, to acquire value. In both cases, the embellished surface conceals and enables a sliding of connotation from the eroticised feminine to the eroticisation of consumption.

There are obvious ways in which the female star sets up a possible point of conjuncture between the figure on the screen as fetishised commodity and her function as signifier in a complex social discourse of sexuality.

America in the 50s, Marilyn's particular moment in history, poses these issues with unusual precision. One privileged image, such as Marilyn Monroe, who still today represents an apex of the star system, may represent a construction of female glamour as a fantasy space: its investment in surface is so intense that it seems to suggest that the surface conceals 'something else'. What might this 'something else' be? To what extent does it guard against nameless anxieties associated with the female body outside its glamour mode? What is repressed, and then reinvested even more intensely in the fascination of surface? Marilyn's own form of cosmetic appearance is particularly fascinating, because it is so artificial, so mask-like, that she manages to use her performance to 'comment on' or 'draw attention to' or 'foreground' both its constructedness and its vulnerability and instability. But there is a further point. Marilyn's image is an ethnic image; her extreme whiteness, her make-up, her peroxide blonde hair bear witness to a fetishisation of race. But its cosmetic, artificial character also bears witness to an element of masquerade. Her image triumphantly creates a spectacle that holds the eye and distracts it from what should not be seen.

In her last interview in *Life*, Marilyn said: 'That's the trouble, a sex symbol becomes a thing and I just hate to be a thing. But if I'm going to be a symbol of something, I would rather have it sex.' Marilyn Monroe came to superstardom just as, or indeed as part of, a new, more explicit discourse of sexuality was coming into being in the United States. *Gentlemen Prefer Blondes* was released in 1953. The same year saw the publication of the Kinsey Report on female sexuality and the first issue of *Playboy* with Marilyn on the front cover and her notorious nude calendar pin-up photograph 'Golden Dreams' reissued as the centre-spread. While the Kinsey Report focused attention on the 'problem' of female sexuality and women's widespread difficulties in achieving sexual pleasure, *Playboy* marketed a representation of female sexuality that was tailored exclusively to the tastes of men. It produced an airbrushed cosmeticised image that found a consumer acceptability that had evaded previous sex publications, and that was perfectly in keeping with the ethos of the time. The commodity boom in the aftermath of the Korean War and the Marshall Plan gave American culture a streamlined gloss of mass consumption. This was a time when, in the context of the cold war particularly, advertising, movies and the actual packaging and se-ductiveness of commodities all marketed glamour. Glamour proclaimed the desirability of American capitalism to the outside world and, inside, secured a particular style of Americanness as an image for the newly suburbanised white population. In this sense the new discourse of marketed sexuality and the new discourse of commodity consumption were articulated together, reinforcing each other as though in acknowledgment of a mutual interest.

These themes mesh together in *Gentlemen Prefer Blondes,* in which Jane Russell and Marilyn Monroe play two American showgirls, Dorothy and Lorelei, who sail across the Atlantic, implicitly carrying American star quality and glamour to war-torn Europe. The 'characters' hardly mask the stars. The film is a comedy and exaggerates the uncertainty associated with femininity as masquerade, not through the film-noir motif of the *femme fatale*, but through its comic extension, the 'dumb blonde'. Jane Russell plays the 'straight man' to Marilyn's wild divergence from common sense. Lorelei's attitude to life zigzags between calculation and naiveté, so that, combined with her intensely spectacular sexuality, the instability of her persona becomes inscribed into the comedy. But this kind of comic performance involves another level of instability, in which the audience has difficulty separating the performance from the performer. Surely, it takes the most consummate actor to construct a foolish persona? But, on the other hand, Marilyn's public image was of the dumb blonde personified. In this way, the spectator's oscillation between belief in the image and knowledge of its construction is doubly layered through the genre of comedy and through the iconography of female sexuality.

However, the comedy also systematically undermines masculine power. The male look is turned upside down to become a site of weakness rather than control. As a result, the main point of exploration for the plot to unfold focuses on Lorelei's meaning and her value in a system of commodity exchange. She replaces an exchange of sex/love with money/diamonds. And, the film implies, she understands her erotic value simply as exchange value, and her position as woman as that of ultimate consumer. To paraphrase Madonna's tribute to the Marilyn of *Gentlemen Prefer Blondes,* she may be a 'Material Girl', but she is also a materialist, in that she encapsulates, both in iconography and understanding, the commodification of sexuality and the sexualisation of the commodity in 50s American capitalist society.

Although the discourse of sexuality epitomised by Marilyn Monroe is that of *Playboy*, and its address is thus male-directed, *Gentlemen Prefer Blondes* has its roots in the contradictory image of femininity that addressed a predominantly female audience in the 20s. The film is based on Anita Loos's novel, published in 1926. In this context, the polarisation between the two characters, Dorothy and Lorelei, has a contemporary significance. The two women personify the double, contradictory address of the time. While Lorelei is placed on the side of commodification, aiming only to consume, Dorothy represents the other side. Cynical and wisecracking, she is only interested in erotic adventure, with no concern for a pay-off, apart from romantic pleasure and sexual autonomy. In the book, Dorothy's modernity is aggressive, intended to amaze or even shock. Lorelei's modernity takes her from her beginnings as a chorus girl on the stage in New York to a power on and behind the screen in Hollywood. Anita Loos transforms Lorelei into her destiny: the eroticised, commodified, celluloid image.

In Anita Loos's novel, Lorelei consults Freud in Vienna, at a moment when her machinations are finally taking their toll. In a witty account of the encounter, Loos has Lorelei write in her diary:

So Dr Froyd asked me, what I seem to dream about. So I told him I never really dream about anything. I mean I use my brains so much during the day time that at night they do not seem to do anything but rest. So Dr Froyd was very very surprized at a girl who did not dream about anything. So then he asked me all about my life. I mean he is very very sympathetic, and he seems to know how to draw a girl out a lot. I mean I told things I really would not put in my diary. So then he seemed very very intreeged at a girl who always seemed to do everything she wanted to.[17]

Freud recommends that Lorelei should cultivate a few inhibitions and get some sleep, implying, perhaps, that she has no unconscious. Perhaps, the interest that feminist film theory has had in psychoanalysis has been to discover the unconscious behind Lorelei's image. Although this unconscious has been understood first and foremost as that of patriarchal fantasy, the contradictions of the 20s tell a more complex story. At the same time, throughout the story runs the particular imbrication between sexuality, commodity, cinema and enigma that has haunted images of women on the Hollywood screen.

To return to Mary Ann Doane: 'Sexuality becomes the site of questions about what can and cannot be known. This imbrication of knowledge and sexuality, of epistemophilia and scopophilia, has crucial implications for the cinema.'

Part Two

Dialectics of Division

Chapter 4

Pandora's Box: Topographies of Curiosity

Chests, especially small caskets, over which we have more complete mastery, are objects that may be opened. When a casket is closed, it is returned to the general community of objects; it takes its place in exterior space. But it opens! For this reason a philosopher-mathematician would say it is the first differential of discovery. ... From the moment the casket is opened dialectics [of inside and outside] no longer exist. The outside is effaced with one stroke, an atmosphere of novelty and surprise reigns. The outside has no more meaning. And quite paradoxically, even cubic dimensions have no more meaning, for the reason that a new dimension – the dimension of intimacy – has just opened up. ...

Outside and inside form a dialectic of division, the obvious geometry of which blinds us as soon as we bring it into play in metaphorical domains. It has the sharpness of the dialectics of yes *and* no, *which decides everything. Unless one is careful, it is made into the basis of images that govern all thoughts of positive and negative.*

Gaston Bachelard[1]

Pandora, in the Greek myth, was a beautiful woman, manufactured by the gods to seduce and bring harm to man. She was sent to earth with a box that secretly contained all the evils of the world. The box and the forbidden nature of its contents excited her curiosity and she opened it. So evil ecaped into the world and woman brought misery to man. Only hope remained.

I

A secret thing may be hidden away, in a concealed place, but a secret meaning must be transformed into a code. One can be simply discovered by the eye, the other has to be deciphered. The topographies of the Pandora myth move between the two. While the box has the space of a dangerous secret that can literally be opened and revealed, its significance for myths and iconographies of the feminine is coded and has to be deciphered through theory. I found it impossible to begin to untangle the significance of the 'dialectics of inside and outside' that permeates Pandora's iconography without having recourse to psychoanalytic theory, so that the process became almost like a test case for the use of Freudian ideas for feminist aesthetics. I began to see parallels between Pandora's story, feminist theory and the influence that psychoanalysis has had on feminist theory, and these parallels indicated that the alliance between feminism and psychoanalysis is neither accidental nor arbitrary. Furthermore, the process involved a certain pleasure and excitement in discovery that seemed similar to riddle or puzzle solving. So this essay became an experiment with an intellectual analysis which could merge with the pleasure of curiosity and seeing with the mind's eye. The myth of Pandora is about feminine curiosity but it can only be decoded by *feminist* curiosity, transforming and translating her iconography and attributes into the segments of a puzzle, riddle or enigma.

The image of woman has become conventionally accepted as very often meaning something other than herself:[2] for instance, the sign of justice as a woman carrying scales. In semiotic terms, the signifier supports a symbolic as well as a literal signified and the two come to inflect and inform each other. Feminist theory has always drawn attention to the way in which images of women have assumed another special visibility in iconographies of sexuality. These images, however, cannot be decoded simply through a knowlege of emblems and symbols. They often bear witness to a difficulty of sexuality and sexual difference and mark sites of repression where 'something' that cannot find conscious articulation is displaced onto 'something else'. It is here that feminists have turned to psychoanalytic and semiotic theory first and foremost as implements for this task of deciphering and decoding images of women that disguise other meanings, most particularly the censored discourse of sexuality. I am using the myth of Pandora to illustrate the effect of such displacements on a particular iconography of the feminine.

Pandora's Creation: Beauty, Artifice and Danger

The myth of Pandora first appears in Greek mythology in Hesiod's *Works and Days* (c.700 BC), returning in his *Theogony* as an account of the first woman. Prometheus tricked Zeus and stole fire and gave it to man. Zeus, determined to have his revenge, answered one deception with another. He said 'I will give men as the price of fire an evil thing in which they may all be glad of heart while they embrace their own destruction.' He told Hephaestus to mix earth with water and put in it the voice and strength of the humankind and 'fashion a sweet and lovely maiden shape, like to the immortal goddesses in face'. Aphrodite, the goddess of love, gave her the power to seduce, putting 'grace upon her head' and the 'cruel longing and cares that weary the limbs'. Hermes gave her 'a shameless mind and deceitful nature, lies and crafty words', while the Divine Graces gave her gold necklaces and crowned her head with spring flowers. Pallas Athena girded and clothed her with a silver raiment, an embroidered veil and a crown of gold with much curious work. Zeus then told Hermes to take Pandora to earth, as a snare and a plague to men, to seduce Prometheus's brother, Epimetheus, as Prometheus himself was too cunning and would see through the trick. When Epimetheus saw her, he forgot Prometheus's warning to reject any gift from Zeus and send it back for fear it would bring harm to man. 'He took the gift and afterwards, when the evil thing was already his, he understood. Previously men lived on earth free from ills and hard toil and sickness. But the woman took off the great lid of the jar and scattered all these and caused sorrow and mischief to man.' Pandora was an artefact, crafted by Hephaestus as a living trick, and all the gods had contributed to creating her extraordinary beauty. Hesiod describes her as 'a steel trap from which there is no escape'.[3]

In *Monuments and Maidens*, Marina Warner describes Pandora in the following manner:

> A most subtle complex and revealing symbol of the feminine, of its contradictory compulsion, peril and lovableness. ... Female forms are associated from the very start with beauty and artistic adornment and its contradictory and often dangerous consequences. ... These mythological principles ... have assisted the projection of immaterial concepts onto the female form, in both rhetoric and iconography.[4]

The story of Pandora's creation, and the story of the purpose behind her creation, also install her as a mythic origin of the surface/secret and interior/exterior topography. She is artificial, made up, cosmetic. As a manufactured object, Pandora evokes the double meaning of the word fabrication. She is made, not born, and she is also a lie, a deception. There is a dislocation between her appearance and her meaning. She is a Trojan horse, a lure and a trap, a *trompe-l'oeil*. Her appearance dissembles.

Pandora is the prototype for the exquisite female android and, as a dangerous enchantress, she is also the prototype for the *femme fatale*. Both these iconographies depend on an inside/outside topography. A beautiful surface that is appealing and charming to man masks either an 'interior' that is mechanical or an 'outside' that is deceitful. Both these iconographies connote uncertainty, mystery, and are only readable in death. Pandora prefigures mechanical, erotic female androids, such as Olympia in E.T.A. Hoffmann's story 'The Sandman' (1816–17), the False Maria in Fritz Lang's *Metropolis* (1925), Hadaly in Villiers de l'Isle-Adam's *The Eve of the Future* (1886), all of whom personify the combination of female beauty with a mechanical artifice. As the mission for which she had been fabricated was to entrance, seduce and bring about the downfall of man, Pandora highlights the ease with which the seductive android merges into the figure of the *femme fatale* who reappears as the film-noir heroine, such as Rita Hayworth in *Gilda* (1946) or *The Lady From Shanghai* (1948), or Jane Greer/Kathy in *Out of the Past* (1947).

In her essay 'On the Eve of the Future', Annette Michelson identifies the invention of the cinema machine with the perfect android, Hadaly, made by Edison, inventor of cinema, to replace the imperfections of female flesh and blood: 'The female body then comes into focus as the very site of the cinema's invention, and we may, in an effect of stereoscopic vision, see the philosophical toy we know as the cinema marked in the very moment of its invention by the inscription of desire.'[5] And she ends by evoking the familiar murmur, equally applicable to the fascinating android and the fascination of cinema, 'I know, but all the same ...' that characterises fetishism.

The cinema has enhanced the image of feminine seductiveness as a surface that conceals. That is to say: the codes and conventions of Hollywood cinema refined the representation of femininity, heightened by the star system, to the point where the spectator's entrancement with the effects of the cinema itself became almost indistinguishable from the draw exerted by an eroticised image of woman. It is as though the scopophilic draw of the cinema, the flickering shadows, the contrasts between light and dark became concentrated in and around the female form. Framing, make-up and lighting stylised the female star, inflecting the way representations of female sexuality slip into 'to-be-looked-at-ness', creating the ultimate screen spectacle. The luminous surface of the screen reinforces the sense of surface radiated by the mask of femininity, flattening the image, so that its usual transparency, its simulation of a window on the world, becomes opaque.

The figure 'Pandora' condenses different topographies of femininity. These themes unravel into strands but link together like the rings in a chain. While she collapses different ideas into a single image in a concertina effect, the different motifs in her story set in motion a series of displacements. An 'inside' space may generate connotations of a maternal femininity (the womb, the home), but may also link to the enclosed, concealed space of secrecy (a box, a room). These associations, one feminine, the other secret, link further to the topography which splits femininity into an inside/outside polarisation. A mask-like surface enhances the concept of feminine beauty as an 'outside', as artifice and masquerade, which conceals danger and deception. And lingering alongside is the structure of the fetish, which, with its investment in eye-catching surface, distracts the gaze from the hidden wound on the female, or rather the mother's, body. It is as though the repeated spatial structure creates a homology across these different ideas which then enables them to flow across each other, as though by conduit. The imaginary space, that is, supports the process of displacement.

The Box: Sexual Metaphor and its Poetics of Space

Such displacements are borne out, but also complicated, by the juxtaposition of Pandora and her box. The spatial configuration that characterises Pandora is also extended to the box. So two topographies make up the mystery and danger in the myth, that of the woman and that of the box. And both are patterned around an inside and an outside, a 'dialectic of division', as Bachelard put it.

In classical mythology, Pandora had with her a different iconographical attribute. It was a large jar that contained all the evils of the world. In their book *Pandora's Box*,[6] Dora and Erwin Panofksy have shown how during the Renaissance the jar shrank into another version of the attribute, a small box that Pandora generally carried in her hand. Jars and boxes both belong to the same set of objects, that is both are containers for storage, and thus have the potential to set up an inflection or shift of meaning through a metonymic linkage. Both containers carried a forbidden secret locked away, and both are subject to 'the dialectics of inside and outside'. But the container's shrinking from jar size, that is from the approximate size of Pandora herself, to the small box allows an extension of meaning to take place. The box easily allows a metaphoric relationship to come into existence between the box and the female genitals, providing a substitute, suggested by shape and imaginative similarity rather than by contiguity, while both are associated with secrecy, and therefore once again linked by a metonymy. The motif of secrecy that is associated with the female body is discussed by Ludmilla Jordanova in *Sexual Visions* in the following terms:

> Veiling implies secrecy. Women's bodies, and, by extension, female attributes, cannot be treated as fully public, something dangerous might happen, secrets be let out, if they were open to view. Yet in presenting something as inaccessible and dangerous an invitation to know and to possess is extended. The secrecy associated with female bodies is sexual and linked to the multiple associations between women and privacy. ... In the Pandora story secrecy is reified as a box.[7]

These links between the space of a box and the female body, with their attendant connotations of secrecy and sexuality, reminded me of the following exchange between Freud and Dora, whose case history he discussed in 'Fragment of an Analysis'. They are analysing Dora's 'first dream':

> 'Does nothing occur to you in connection with the jewel-case? So far you have only talked about jewellery and said nothing about the case.'
> 'Yes, Herr K. had made me a present of an expensive jewel-case a little time before.'
> 'Then a return present would have been very appropriate. Perhaps you do not know that "jewel-case" [*Schmuckkästchen*] is a favourite

expression for the same thing that you alluded to not so long ago by means of the reticule you were wearing – for the female genitals, I mean.'

'I knew you would say that.'[8]

Freud's point is confirmed by general usage, by polite speech that uses metaphor in order to avoid calling a spade a spade, and vulgar speech that uses metaphor for 'poetic' reasons, in order to proliferate and vary the ways in which the taboos of sexuality can be named and described, either erotically or derogatorily. He, himself, is referring to the language of the unconscious and its use of displacement as a form of censorship. However, the metaphor of the female body as 'container' also refers to the womb, the enclosing space inside the mother's body, that provides an instant source of connotation and a 'poetics of space' quite usual in culture and the first link in the chain of displacements that I mentioned earlier. Here metonymy invades metaphor. In Freud's example, the jewel-case, though strictly speaking a metaphor for the genitals, also belongs to the 'container' class of objects, with a 'dialectics of inside and outside', so that it, too, is tinged with metonymy.

Iconographically, the figure of a woman can be identified as Pandora by the presence of her box, and a box attracts and repels by association with Pandora. Iconographical associations are usually formed by juxtaposing a character with the most significant object associated with their figure or their story. We can only identify Hercules by his club or St Catherine by her wheel through awareness of cultural convention and familiarity with the relevant details of the story. This is also true, on one level, of Pandora and her box. However, her attribute has an added significance, taking it beyond the realm of iconography. In addition to representing her story, the box has a spatial structure that relates back to the topography of Pandora herself: her exterior mask of beauty concealing an interior of combined mystery and danger. Pandora's box becomes, through another rhetorical figure, a synecdoche for those aspects of the feminine that should be 'hidden away' and concealed in a secret place.

The seductive mask and the box: each conceal a secret that is dangerous to man. The Panofskys record two examples of Pandora iconography in which the sexual significance of the box is made explicit. One, an engraving by Abraham van Diepenbeek dating from the mid-17th century, shows Pandora 'holding the fateful pyxis as a fig-leaf' and a contemporary commentary by Michel de Marolles points out that Pandora is

holding her box in her right hand, lowered to that part, which she covers, from which has flowed so many of the miseries and anxieties that afflict man, as though the artist wished to show that there is always something bitter in the midst of a fountain of pleasure and that the thorn pricks among the flowers.[9]

The second is a drawing by Paul Klee dating from 1920, *Die Büchse der Pandora als Stilleben*. The Panofskys comment that he 'represent[ed] the ominous receptacle as a kind of goblet rather than a box and converted it into a psychoanalytical symbol: it is rendered as a kantharos-shaped vase containing some flowers but emitting evil vapours from an opening clearly suggestive of the female genitals.'[10] Thus the sexual connotation is tinged with anxiety and disgust.

There is a long history to the mythologisation of female sexuality as something to be afraid of and repelled by, which deepens the phantasmatic topography of the female body itself. In her book *Decadent Genealogies*,[11] Barbara Spackman analyses the implication of these 'evil vapours'. She uses the figure of Pandora in her discussion of d'Annunzio's aesthetics to analyse the Symbolist obsession with the unveiling of the woman's body as a gesture of fascinated repulsion. It is a gesture that reveals the woman's body as the site of her wound and the sight of Medusa. Within this aesthetic, masculine desire is caught in an oscillation between erotic obsession with the female body and fear of the castration that it signifies. It is, of course, the fear of castration, and subsequent disavowal of the woman's body as castrated, that Freud saw as the cause of male fetishism. The association between the female body and either castration, the wound, or a more profound horror is displaced onto the box. These reverberations between Pandora and her box are set in motion in the first place by contiguity (in the juxtaposition of the figure to its iconographic attribute) but also by the structural similarity between two containing, enclosed spaces, their 'dialectics of inside and outside'. While Pandora's surface image, fabricated and fascinating, is highly fetishistic, the inside of the box contains everything that fetishism disavows. It is a defetishised body, deprived of the fetish's semiotic, reduced to being the 'unspeakable' other of the mask and devoid of significance. Whatever is concealed by Pandora's surface is secretly stored in the box.

Curiosity: Where the Woman Looks
Pandora's gesture of looking into the forbidden space, the literal figuration of curiosity as looking in, becomes a figure for the desire to know rather than the desire to see, an epistemophilia. If the box represents the 'unspeakable' of femininity, her curiosity appears as a desire to uncover the secret of the very figuration she represents.

Pandora is now better known for her curiosity than for her origin as artefact and lure. Although she was forbidden to open the box and warned of the danger it contained, she gave way to her curiosity and released all the evils into the world. Only hope remained. In Nathaniel Hawthorne's version of the myth, told for children in *Tanglewood Tales* (1853), Pandora's story is a warning of the dangers of curiosity. He describes the allure of the box:

It was a very handsome article of furniture, and would positively have been quite an ornament to any room in which it should be placed. It was made of a very beautiful kind of wood with dark and rich veins spreading over its surface which was so highly polished that little Pandora could see her face in it.[12]

The motif of curiosity also links Pandora's story to Eve, the first woman of Judaeo-Christian mythology, who persuaded Adam to eat the apple of knowledge. The Panofskys point out that this parallel was noted by late medieval mythographers wanting to use classical precedent to corroborate the Christian story of the fall of man. Although Eve's story highlights the knowledge theme, the epistemophilia inherent in the drive of curiosity, the myth associates female curiosity with forbidden fruit rather than with forbidden space. The motif of space and curiosity can be found again symptomatically in the fairy story *Bluebeard*. The story is about his last wife, a young girl who is given the free run of his vast palace with the exception of one room which her husband forbids her to enter. Its little key begins to excite her curiosity until she ignores the luxury all around her and thinks of nothing else. Then, one day, when she thinks her husband is away, she opens the door and finds the bodies of all his former wives still bleeding magically from terrible wounds and tortures. Her husband sees the bloodstain that cannot be removed from the key and tells her that the punishment for breaking his prohibition, for curiosity, is death alongside his former wives, who he explains had also been irresistibly drawn to the little room. Angela Carter retells this story in *The Bloody Chamber*[13] and compares the room with Pandora's box and the heroine with Eve.

Curiosity projects itself onto, and into, space through its drive to investigate and uncover secrets, carrying with it connotations of transgression and danger. In 'The Woman's Film: Possession and Address', Mary Ann Doane discusses the woman's look of paranoia in films with a female investigative protagonist set in a home suddenly invested with the uncanny:

> One could formulate a veritable topography of spaces within the home along the axis of this perverted specularisation. ... Many of these films are marked by the existence of a room to which the woman is barred access. *Gaslight* – the attic; *Dragonwyck* – a tower room. In *Rebecca* it is both the boathouse and Rebecca's bedroom, ultimately approached by the female protagonist with a characteristically Hitchcockian moving point of view shot towards the closed door. ... Dramas of seeing that become invested with horror within the context of the home [whose] narrative structures produce an insistence upon situating the woman as agent of the gaze, an investigator in charge of the epistemological trajectory of the text, as the one for whom the 'secret behind the door' is really at stake.[14]

In other words, the woman's look of curiosity is associated with enclosed, secret and forbidden spaces. There are three themes associated with curiosity implicit in my argument so far: it involves an active look and one that has been associated primarily, although not of course exclusively, with women; it relates to the enclosed space of secrets that echoes the interior/exterior topography associated with a particular mythology of the feminine; it is experienced almost like a drive with an aim and object to discover something felt so strongly that it overwhelms prohibition or danger. Pandora's myth juxtaposes an iconography of enigma with a narrative of curiosity. If, as I suggested earlier, the box is a displaced materialisation, a synecdoche, of those aspects of the female body that are the site of anxiety and revulsion, and Pandora herself personifies both their threat and their disguise, then her gesture (opening the box) may be read as curiosity about the enigma of femininity itself. The female figure not only is driven by transgressive curiosity, to open the box, but is able to look at the supposed horror of those aspects of the female body that are repressed under patriarchal culture. It is here that the myth, otherwise from its very beginnings truly a symptom of misogyny, can find a point of transformation.

Pandora's gesture, however, can only be read as 'self-reflexive' if the process of displacement that has taken place, the distortions of the psyche around the representation of femininity and its significance for sexual difference, are seen to be encoded in the signifiers 'Pandora'/'box'. The opening of the box as a gesture taken on its own can only release the evil-smelling vapours into the world, all the evils of the world, and expose the horrid wound and so on that no one wants to see. But she does want to see ... To refer back to Bachelard, it is at this point that a new dimension is opened up: 'The outside is effaced with one stroke, an atmosphere of novelty and surprise reigns. ... And quite paradoxically even cubic dimensions have no more meaning, for the reason that a new dimension ... has just opened up.' Curiosity shifts, with this new dimension, from a literal desire to see with one's own eyes to the thrill of deciphering an enigma. The point, then, is to recast the figure of Pandora, her action and its fearful consequences in such a way that the literal topography of her structure can shift from the register of the visual into the register of the theoretical. Pandora, caught in the myth, cannot make this step, but feminist theorists, seeking to translate the iconographies of the feminine to reveal their origins, can take her curiosity and transform it into a seeing with the mind.

To sum up, there are three 'cliché' motifs, elements of myth, that are central to Pandora's iconography: (a) femininity as enigma; (b) female curiosity as transgressive and dangerous; (c) the spatial or topographical figuration of the female body as an inside and outside. And I would like to try to reformulate them, to illuminate the tautology, as follows: (a) Pandora's curiosity acts out a transgressive desire to see inside her own surface or exterior, into the inside of the female body metaphorically represented by the box and its attendant horrors; (b) *feminist* curiosity transforms the topography of Pandora and her box into a new pattern or configuration, which can then be deciphered to reveal symptoms of the erotic economy of patriarchy; (c) feminist curiosity can constitute a political, critical and creative drive.

II

My interest in the Pandora myth stemmed originally from a wish to consider the aesthetics of curiosity, in order to give greater complexity to the argument in my article 'Visual Pleasure and Narrative Cinema'.[15] An active, investigative look, but one that was also associated with the feminine, suggested a way out of the rather too neat binary opposition between the spectator's gaze, constructed as active and voyeuristic, implicitly coded as masculine, and the female image on the screen, passive and exhibitionist.

As in the myth of Pandora, the woman's look is often directed towards enclosed, secret and forbidden space. I was first struck by the female gaze of curiosity and investigation in Hitchcock's film *Notorious* (1947). Ingrid Bergman is sent as an undercover agent to investigate a house that is redolent of uncanniness. She, only temporarily, becomes the investigative force, empowered with an active look, that carries the narrative forward in its desire to penetrate the secrets hidden in the house. When she arrives at the house for the first time, the scene is orchestrated around closed doors, simultaneously creating an enclosed space (the interior of the house) and mysterious spaces (behind the closed doors). Her look is emphasised by the tracking of the camera, as well as the 'characteristically Hitchcockian moving point of view shot towards the closed door'. She, who has been established at the opening of the film as object of the gaze, as enigma, and probably dangerous, then conceals the investigative power of the cinematic look behind her 'cosmetic' mask. And her mask of seductiveness and beauty is echoed in the topography of the house, its closed doors and locked cupboards potentially containing a secret, dangerous to man, order and the Law. Her own structure of concealment replicates these topographies. There is a displacement here, reminiscent of the displacement in the Pandora myth, between the dialectics of division figured through the woman's secret, and the secret spaces of the house. As she investigates these spaces, she mobilises the spectator's curiosity which is invested in her, an emblem of female curiosity.

Feminists, trying to understand how femininity is socially constituted, subject to historical and cultural constraints, and transformed into a signifier, found common ground with Freud's emphasis on the contingent nature of sexual difference. But feminist theory also used Freudian theory as a formal methodology, as an analytical tool that could start to make sense of representations of the female body in culture. In this sense, psychoanalytic theory that had been evolved for the analysis of the individual psyche was appropriated and applied to the workings of collective fantasy. Popular cultures, myths, iconographies, narratives could be understood as having a symptomatic relationship to the repressions and obsessions of the society that generated them. In the myth of Pandora, the Freudian primary processes, displacement and condensation, are clearly at work. Nowadays accoutrements of feminine fascination are associated with artifice (make-up, cosmetics, constructed allure), and Pandora's ancient, pre-consumer-society origins as an artificial construction highlights the deep-rooted linkage between images of feminine seduction, artifice and deception.

Processes of displacement and condensation are evidence that the anguage of the unconscious is at work on a formal level. But there is the further question of content. What is it, in the collective psyche, that has transformed the image of woman into a vehicle for the inscription of sexual fantasy and anxiety? And what are these anxieties that need to be 'warded off' by an exquisite defensive construct? It is at this point that the vexed issue of castration has to be faced and that Freud's ideas are both useful and problematic for feminist theory. To ward off castration anxiety, the female body's topography presents a façade of fascination and surface that distracts the male psyche from the wound concealed beneath, creating an inside and outside of binary opposition. While the mask attracts and holds the gaze, anxiety produces a dread of what might be secretly hidden. This structure, of belief in the female phantasmagoria, followed by deception and disgust, is close to the structure of fetishism.

The space of secrets is, as Bachelard pointed out, organised around the logic of binary opposition, the antinomy of inside and outside. Pandora's iconography shares this pattern. Her secret danger is veiled by a surface that is proportionately eye-catching, shining, invested with extra attributes of visibility. The surface is like a beautiful carapace, an exquisite mask. But it is vulnerable. It threatens to crack, hinting that through the cracks might seep whatever the 'stuff' might be that it is supposed to conceal and hold in check. This phantasmagoric topography has haunted representations of femininity across the ages, not consistently manifest, but persisting as an intermittent strand of patriarchal mythology and misogyny.

In the Pandora story, castration, as a source of horror and disgust, needs to be supplemented by the Kristevan concept of the abject.[16] For Kristeva, abjection is an effect of a child's first desire for separation from the mother's body. The small child, of both sexes, in the process of establishing its autonomous subjectivity, has to establish an autonomous 'clean and proper body'. The child who has found pleasure in its bodily wastes and lack of differentiation between its body and that of its mother, comes to need its own boundaries and separations. Suddenly feelings of disgust come into play. Barbara Creed traces the 'monstrous feminine' in horror movies to this archaic mother:

> Within patriarchal signifying practices, particularly the horror film, she is reconstructed and represented as a negative figure, one associated with the dread of the generative mother seen only in the abyss, the monstrous vagina, the origin of all life threatening to reabsorb what it

once birthed. ... In horror films such as *Alien,* we are given a representation of the female genitals as uncanny, horrific objects of dread and fascination.

She goes on to point out that there is also a series of displacements between different aspects of the maternal figure:

Clearly it is difficult to separate out completely the figure of the archaic mother ... from other aspects of the maternal figure: the maternal authority of Kristeva's semiotic, the mother of Lacan's imaginary, the phallic woman, the castrated woman. ... At times the horrific nature of the monstrous-feminine is dependent on the merging together of all the aspects of the maternal figure into one – the horrifying image of woman as archaic mother, phallic woman and castrated body represented in a single figure.[17]

The Pandora myth and the examples of Hitchcock's heroines who investigate the uncanny house suggest that, although both sexes are subject to abjection, it is the heroine rather than the hero who can explore and analyse the phenomenon with greater equanimity. It is the female body that has come, not exclusively but predominantly, to represent the shudder aroused by liquidity and decay. When, in *Notorious,* Ingrid Bergman investigates the house of spies, its uncanniness is confirmed, and personified, by the Hitchcockian figure of 'Mother'. The *Notorious* house and Mother prefigure the cinema's most uncanny house ever, the Bates' house in *Psycho* (1960). Once again, Hitchcock uses the characteristic 'Hitchcockian moving point of view shot' to represent the way that the Bates' house and its internal spaces draw the heroine into its interior with the physical force of her curiosity. Hitchcock's *mise en scène* suggests that the gradual movement of the heroine towards and into the house is a movement leading to a confrontation between the body of the young woman, alluring and cosmetic, and the mother's body, redolent (especially, of course, in *Psycho)* of disintegration, decay and death. The mask of feminine beauty then takes on another level of disavowal, that is the specific, psychoanalytic, problem of the mother's body.

While curiosity is a compulsive desire to see and to know, to investigate something secret, fetishism is born out of a refusal to see, a refusal to accept the difference the female body represents for the male. These complex series of turnings away, of covering over, not of the eyes but of understanding, of fixating on a substitute object to hold the gaze, leave the female body as an enigma and threat, condemned to return as a symbol of anxiety while simultaneously being transformed into its own screen in representation.

Chapter 5

Cosmetics and Abjection: Cindy Sherman 1977–87

When I was in school I was getting disgusted with the attitude of art being so religious or sacred, so I wanted to make something which people could relate to without having read a book about it first. So that anybody off the street could appreciate it, even if they couldn't fully understand it; they could still get something out of it. That's the reason by I wanted to imitate something out of the culture, and also make fun of the culture as I was doing it.

Cindy Sherman[1]

Cindy Sherman's works are photographs. She is not a photographer but an artist who uses photography. Each image is built around a photographic depiction of a woman. And each of the women is Sherman herself, simultaneously artist and model, transformed, chameleon-like, into a glossary of pose, gesture and facial expression. As her work developed, between 1977 and 1987, a strange process of metamorphosis took place. Apparently easy and accessible post-modern pastiche underwent a gradual transformation into difficult, but still accessible, images that raise serious and challenging questions for contemporary feminist aesthetics. And the metamorphosis provides a new perspective that then alters, with hindsight, the significance of her early work. In order to work through the critical implications of this altered perspective, it is necessary to fly in the face of her own expressly non-theoretical, even anti-theoretical stance. Paradoxically, it is because there is no explicit citation of theory in the work, no explanatory words, no linguistic signposts, that theory can then come into its own. Sherman's work stays on the side of enigma, but as a critical challenge, not an insoluble mystery. Figuring out the enigma, deciphering its pictographic clues, applying the theoretical tools associated with feminist aesthetics, is, to use one of her favourite words, fun, and draws attention to the way that, through feminist aesthetics, theory, decipherment and the entertainment of riddle or puzzle solving may be connected.

During the 70s, feminist aesthetics and women artists contributed greatly to questioning two great cultural boundary divisions. Throughout the 20th century, inexorably but discontinuously, pressure had been building up against the separation between art theory and art practice on the one hand, and between high culture and low culture on the other. The collapse of these divisions was crucial to the many and varied components of post-modernism, and also to feminist art. Women artists made use of both theory and popular culture through reference and quotation. Cindy Sherman, first showing work in the late 70s, used popular culture as her source material without using theory as commentary and distanciation device. When her photographs were first shown, their insistent reiteration of representations of the feminine, and her use of herself, as model, in infinite varieties of masquerade, won immediate attention from critics who welcomed her as a counterpoint to feminist theoretical and conceptual art. The success of her early work, its acceptance by the centre (art market and institutions) at a time when many artists were arguing for a politics of the margins, helped to obscure both that the work has intrinsic interest for feminist aesthetics and that the ideas raised by the work could not have been formulated without a prehistory of feminism and feminist theorisation of the body and representation. Her arrival on the art scene certainly marks the beginning of the end of that era in which the female body had become, if not quite unrepresentable, only representable if refracted through theory. But rather than sidestepping, Sherman reacts and shifts the agenda. She brings a different perspective to the 'images of women question' and brings back a politics of the body that had, perhaps, been lost or neglected in the twists and turns of 70s feminism.

In the early 70s, the Women's Movement claimed the female body as a site for political struggle, mobilising around abortion rights above all, but with other ancillary issues spiralling out into agitation over medical marginalisation and sexuality itself as a source of women's oppression. A politics of the body led logically to a politics of representation of the body. It was only a small step to include the question of images of women in the debates and campaigns around the body, but it was a step that also moved feminism out of familiar terrains of political action into a terrain of political aesthetics. And this small step, from one terrain to another, called for a new conceptual vocabulary, and opened the way for the influence that semiotics and psychoanalysis have had on feminist theory. The initial idea that images contributed to women's alienation from their bodies and from their sexuality, with an attendant hope of liberation and recuperation, gave way to theories of representation as symptom and signifier of the way that problems posed by sexual difference under patriarchy could be displaced onto the feminine.

Not surprisingly, this kind of theoretical/political aesthetics also affected artists working in the climate of 70s feminism, and the representability of the female body underwent a crisis. At an extreme, the film-maker Peter Gidal said in 1978: 'I have had a vehement refusal over the last decade, with one or two minor aberrations, to allow images of women into my films at all, since I do not see how those images can be separated from the dominant meanings.'[2]

Women artists and film-makers, while rejecting this wholesale banishment, were extremely wary about the investment of 'dominant meanings' in images of women and while feminist theorists turned to popular culture to analyse these meanings, artists turned to theory, juxtaposing images and ideas, to negate dominant meanings and, slowly and polemically, to invent different ones. Although in this climate, Cindy Sherman's concentration on the female body seemed almost shocking, her representations of femininity were not a sign of regression, but a re-representation, a making strange.

A visitor to a Cindy Sherman retrospective, who moves through the work in its chronological order, must be almost as struck by the dramatic nature of its development, as by the individual, very striking, works themselves. It is not only a question of observing an increasing maturity, a changed style, or new directions, but of following a certain narrative of the feminine from an initial premise to the very end of its road. And this development takes place over ten years, between 1977 and 1987. The journey through time, through the work's chronological development, is also a journey into space. Sherman dissects the phantasmagoric space conjured up by the female body, from its exteriority to its interiority. The visitor who reaches the final images and then returns, reversing the order, finds that with the hindsight of what was to come, the early images are transformed. The first process of discovery, amusement and amazement is complemented by the discovery of curiosity, reverie and decipherment. And then, once the process of bodily disintegration is established in the later work, the early, innocent, images acquire a retrospective uncanniness.

The first series of photographs, which also established Sherman's reputation, are called *Untitled Film Stills*. In each photograph Sherman poses for the camera, as though in a scene from a movie. Each photograph has its own *mise en scène*, evoking a style of film-making that is highly connotative but elusive. The black and white photographs seem to refer to the 50s, to the New Wave, to neo-realism, to Hitchcock, or Hollywood B-pictures. This use of an amorphous connotation places them in a nostalgia genre, comparable to the American movies of the 80s that Fredric Jameson describes as having the post-modern characterisic of evoking the past while denying the reference of history.[3] They have the Barthesian quality of 'fifties-ness', that American collective fantasy of the 50s as the time of everyone's youth in a white and mainly middle America setting, in the last moment of calm before the storms of civil rights, Vietnam and finally feminism. Nostalgia is selective memory and its effect is often to draw attention to its repressions, to the fact that it always conceals more than it records. And the 50s saw a last flowering of a particular culture of appearances and, particularly, the feminine appearance. The accoutrements of the feminine struggle to conform to a façade of desirability haunt Sherman's iconography. Make-up, high heels, back-combed hair, respectable but eroticised clothes are all carefully 'put on' and 'done'. Sherman, the model, dresses up into character while Sherman, the artist, reveals her character's masquerade. The juxtaposition begins to refer to a 'surfaceness', so that nostalgia begins to dissolve into unease. Sherman accentuates the uneasiness by inscribing vulnerability into both the *mise en scène* of the photographs and the women's poses and expressions.

These *Film Still* scenes are set mainly in exteriors. Their fascination is derived from their quality as *trompe-l'oeil*. The viewer is subjected to a series of doubletakes, estrangements and recognitions. The camera looks; it 'captures' the female character in a parody of different voyeurisms. It intrudes into moments in which she is unguarded, sometimes undressed, absorbed into her own world in the privacy of her own environment. Or it witnesses a moment in which her guard drops as she is suddenly startled by a presence, unseen and off screen, watching her. Or it observes her composed, simultaneously demure and alluring, for the outside world and its intrusive gaze. The viewer is immediately caught by the voyeurisms on offer. But the obvious fact that each character is Sherman herself, disguised, introduces a sense of wonder at the illusion and its credibility. And, as is well known in the cinema, any moment of marvelling at an illusion immediately destroys its credibility. The lure of voyeurism turns around like a trap, and the viewer ends up aware that Sherman, the artist, has set up a machine for making the gaze materialise uncomfortably in alliance with Sherman, the model. Then the viewer's curiosity may be attracted to the surrounding narrative. But any speculation about a story, about actual events and the character depicted, quickly reaches a dead end. The visitor at a Cindy Sherman show must be well aware that the *Film Still* is constructed for this one image only, and that nothing exists either before or after the moment shown. Each pregnant moment is a cut-out, a tableau suggesting and denying the presence of a story. As they pretend to be something more, the *Film Stills* parody the stillness of the photograph and they ironically enact the poignancy of a 'frozen moment'. The women in the photographs are almost always in stasis, halted by something more than photography, like surprise, reverie, decorum, anxiety or just waiting.

The viewer's voyeurism is uncomfortable. There is no complementary exhibitionism on the part of the female figures and the sense of looking on, unobserved, provokes a mixture of curiosity and anxiety. The images are, however, erotic. Sexuality pervades the figures and their implied narratives. Sherman performs femininity as an appearance, in which the insistent sexualisation of woman hovers in oscillation with respectability. Because Sherman uses cosmetics literally as a mask she makes visible the feminine as masquerade. And it is this culture of appearance, a homogeneity of look that characterises 'fifties-ness', that Sherman makes use of to adopt such a variety of similar, but different, figurations. Identity, she seems to say, lies in looks for white femininity at the time. But just as she is artist and model, voyeur and looked at, active and passive, subject and object, the photographs set up a comparable variety of positions and responses for the viewer. There is no stable subject position in her work, no resting point that does not quickly shift into something else. So the *Film Stills'* initial sense of homogeneity and credibility breaks up into the kind of heterogeneity of subject position that feminist aesthetics espoused in advance of post-modernism proper.

In 1980 Sherman made her first series of colour photographs, using back projections of exteriors rather than actual locations, moving into a closer concentration on the face, and flattening the space of the photograph. Then, in 1981, she made a series of colour photographs that start to suggest an interiority to the figure's exterior appearance. These photographs initiate her exploration inside the masquerade of femininity's interior/exterior binary opposition. The photographs all have the same format, horizontal like a cinemascope screen, so most of the figures lie on sofas or beds or on the floor. As the series originated as a 'centrefold' for *Artforum,* they parody soft-core pastiche. These photographs concentrate on the sphere of feminine emotion, longing and reverie, and are set in private spaces that reduplicate the privacy of emotion. But, once again, an exact sensation is impossible to pin down. The young women that Sherman impersonates may be day-dreaming about a future romance or they may be mourning a lost one. They may be waiting, in enforced passivity, for a letter or telephone call. Their eyes gaze into the distance. They are not aware of their clothes which are sometimes carelessly rumpled, so that, safe alone with their thoughts, their bodies are, slightly, revealed to the viewer. They exude vulnerability and sexual availability like love-sick heroines/victims in a romantic melodrama. There are some precedents in the *Untitled Film Stills* for this series, but the use of colour, the horizontal format and the repeated pose create a double theme of inside space and of reverie. The intimate space of a bedroom provides an appropriate setting for day-dream or reverie, and combines with Sherman's erotic, suggestive, poses to accumulate connotations of sexuality. These photographs reiterate the 'to-be-looked-at-ness' of femininity. The *Untitled Film Stills* fake a surrounding narrative, so the camera should not draw undue attention to its presence and the 'to-be-looked-at-ness' is a matter of social and cultural conformity. The 1981 *Untitleds,* on the other hand, announce themselves as photographs and, as in a pin-up, the model's eroticism, and her pose, are directed towards the camera, and ultimately towards the spectator.

In most of the *Untitled Film Stills*, the female figure stands out in sharp contrast to her surroundings, exaggerating her vulnerability in an exterior world. In some, however, a visible grain merges the figure with the texture and material of the photograph. In the 1981 series, Sherman's use of colour and light and shade merges the female figure and her surroundings into a continuum, without hard edges. Pools of light illuminate patches of skin or bathe the picture in a soft glow. Above all, the photographs have a glossy, high-quality finish in keeping with the codes and conventions of commercial photography. While the poses are soft and limp, polar opposites of a popular idea of fetishised femininity (high-heeled and corseted, erect, flamboyant and exhibitionist), fetishism returns in the formal qualities of the photography. The sense of surface now resides, not in the female figure's attempt to save her face in a masquerade of femininity, but in the model's subordination to, and imbrication with, the texture of the photographic medium itself.

Sherman's next important phase, the *Untitleds* of 1983, first manifests the darkness of mood that will, from then on, increasingly overwhelm her work. This turn was, in the first place, a reaction against the fashion industry that had invited her to design photographs for them and then tried to modify and tone down the results:

> From the beginning there was something that didn't work with me, like there was friction. I picked out some clothes I wanted to use. I was sent completely different clothes that I found boring to use. I really started to make fun, not of the clothes, but much more of the fashion. I was starting to put scar tissue on my face to become really ugly.[4]

These photographs use bright, harsh light and high-contrast colour. The characters are theatrical and ham up their roles. A new Sherman body is beginning to emerge. She grotesquely parodies the kind of feminine image that is geared to erotic consumption and she turns upside down conventional codes of female allure and elegance. Whereas the language of fashion photography gives great emphasis to lightness, so that its models seem to defy gravity, Sherman's figures are heavy in body and groundedness. Their lack of self-consciousness verges on the exhibitionist, and they strike professional poses to display costumes which exaggerate their awkward physiques, which are then exaggerated again by camera angle and lighting. There is absolutely nothing to do with nature or the natural in this response to the cosmetic svelteness of fashion. Rather, they suggest that the binary opposition to the perfect body of the fashion model is the grotesque, and that the smooth glossy body, polished by photography, is a defence against an anxiety-provoking, uneasy and uncanny body. From this perspective the surface of the body, so carefully conveyed in the early photographs, seems to be dissolving to reveal a monstrous otherness behind the cosmetic façade. The 'something' that had seemed to be lurking somewhere in the phantasmatic topography of femininity begins, as it were, to congeal.

After the *Untitleds* of 1983, the anti-fashion series, the metamorphoses become more acute and disturbing. The series *Untitled 1984* is like a reversal of Dorian Gray, as though the pain, anger and stupidity of human nature left their traces clearly on human features, as though the surface was failing in its task of masking. In the next series, inspired by the monsters of fairy stories, the figures become supernatural, and, rather like animistic personifications, they tower above or return to the elements. By this time the figures seem to be the emanations of irrational fears, verging on terror, relics of childhood nightmares. If the 'centrefold' series conveyed, through pose and facial expression, the interiority of secret thoughts, now Sherman seems to personify the stuff of the unconscious itself. While the earlier interiority suggested soft, erotic reverie, these are materialisations of anxiety and dread. Sherman seems to have moved from suggesting the presence of a hidden otherness to representing its inhabitants. Increasingly grotesque and deforming make-up blurs gender identity, and some figures are horned or snouted, like horrific mythological hybrids. If the earlier iconography suggested a passive aspiration to please, deformation and distortion seem to erupt in some kind of ratio to repression. These figures are active and threatening.

Finally, in the last phase, the figure disappears completely. Sometimes body bits are replaced by prostheses, such as false breasts or buttocks, but, in the last resort, nothing is left but disgust; the disgust of sexual detritus, decaying food, vomit, slime, menstrual blood, hair. These traces represent the end of the road, the secret stuff of bodily fluids that the cosmetic is designed to conceal. The topography of exterior/interior is exhausted. Previously, all Sherman's work had been centred and structured around a portrait, so that a single figure had provided a focus for the viewer's gaze. Surrounding *mise en scènes* had gradually vanished as though Sherman was denying the viewer any distraction or mitigation from the figures themselves as they gradually became more and more grotesque. Around 1985, settings make a come-back in the photographs, but diffused into textures. Natural elements, pebbles, sand or soil, for instance, develop expressive and threatening connotations. Colour, lighting and the texture of the figures make them merge visually into their settings. The camera angle now looks down onto the ground where the figures lie lifeless or, perhaps, trapped in their own materiality.

The shift in perspective, to downward camera angle, heralds Sherman's last phase. When the body, in any homogeneous or cohesive form, disappears from the scene, its traces and detritus are spread out on the ground, on pebbles or sand or submerged in water. With the disintegration of the body, the photographs also lose any homogeneous and cohesive formal organisation, and the sense of physical fragmentation is echoed in the fragmentation of the images. Now the edge of the image may be as significant as any other section of its space. At the same time the photographs have become enormously enlarged. The early series, *Untitled Film Stills*, were all 8 by 10 inches, while the late series have grown to dimensions such as 72 by 49 inches. The viewer could take in the early work with a glance and sense of command over the image; the late photographs overwhelm the viewer and force the eye to scan the surface, searching for a specific shape or pattern that might offer some formal reassurance against the disturbing content.

This narrative of disintegration, horror and finally disgust raises, first and foremost, the question of the source, or origin, of this phantasmagoria of the female body, and, second, how it might be analysed. Woman becomes 'the favoured vehicle of the metaphor' once she is inscribed into the regime of castration anxiety, so the question of origin returns, once again, to the question of the male unconscious. A cosmetic, artificial surface covers, like a carapace, the wound or void left in the male psyche when it perceives the mark of sexual difference on the female body as an absence, a void, a castration. In this sense, the topography of the feminine masquerade echoes the topography of the fetish itself. But whereas, for instance, the Pandora phenomenon remains, in the last resort, a symptom of these anxieties and disavowals, Sherman has slowly stripped the symptom away from its disavowal mechanisms, at the same time revealing the mechanisms for what they are. Sherman's ironic 'unveiling' also 'unveils' the use of the female body as a metaphor for division between surface allure and concealed decay, as though the stuff that has been projected for so long into a mythic space 'behind' the mask of femininity had suddenly broken through the delicately painted veil. The female body's metamorphoses, in Sherman's 'narrative trajectory', trace a gradual collapse of surface. In parodying the metaphor, she returns to the 'literal', to the bodily fluids and wastes that become inseparable from the castrated body in the iconography of misogyny. But she also dramatically draws attention to the regime of representational and mythological contradiction lived by women under patriarchy. Although the origin of the image may be in the unconscious and although the image may be a phantasm, these collective fantasies also have an impact in reality, and produce symptoms that mediate between the two. The late photographs are a reminder that the female psyche may well identify with misogynist revulsion against the female body and attempt to erase signs that mark her physically as feminine. The images of decaying food and vomit raise the spectre of the anorexic girl, who tragically acts out the fashion fetish of the female as an eviscerated, cosmetic and artificial construction designed to ward off the 'otherness' hidden in the 'interior'.

It is hard to trace the female body's collapse as successful fetish without re-representing the anxieties and dreads that give rise to the fetish in the first place, and Sherman might be open to the accusation that she re-produces the narrative without a sufficiently critical context. It is here that the *Untitled Film Stills* may be reread with the hindsight of the future development of Sherman's work in mind. To return to the early photographs, with hindsight, is to see how the female body can become a conduit for different ideas condensed into a single image. For instance, the uncanniness of the women characters, behind their cosmetic façades, starts to merge with the instability of the photograph as object of belief. The structure of fetishism indicates a homology between these different ideas and the theory of fetishism helps to unravel the process of condensation.

For Freud, fetishism (apart, that is, from his view that it 'confirmed the castration complex') demonstrates that the psyche can sustain incompatible ideas at one and the same time through a process of disavowal. Fetishistic disavowal acknowledges the woman's castration and simultaneously constructs a substitute to deny it and replace the missing object. Freud saw the coexistence of these two contradictory ideas, maintained in a single psyche, as a model for the ego's relation to reality, the 'splitting of the ego', which allowed two parallel, but opposed, attitudes to be maintained with uneasy balance. Switching back and forth between visual duping, followed by perception of the duping mechanism, a willing suspension of disbelief followed by a wave of disillusion, 'I know ... but all the same', the viewer of Sherman's *Film Stills* can feel almost physically, and almost relish, the splitting open of the gap between knowledge and belief.

An 'oscillation effect' contributes to post-modern aesthetics. The viewer looks, recognises a style or trope, doubts, does a doubletake, recognises the citation; and meanings shift and change their reference like shifting perceptions of perspective from an optical illusion. This effect is, perhaps, particularly exciting because it dices with the credibility of the fetish. In this sense, Cindy Sherman pushes post-modern play to its limits in the contested terrain of the female body. When the viewer reaches the final photographs of disintegration and only reluctantly recognises the content for what it is, the art aspect of Sherman's work returns. It is not so much that the colours of the detritus images are more 'painterly' and their reference is more to the shape of the frame than the figure, but that their place on the gallery wall affirms their status, just as the viewer is about to turn away in revolted disbelief. In this sense, they, too, create an 'oscillation effect', this time between reverence and revulsion. This kind of theme is present in Sherman's latest works, which are outside the 1977–87 'narrative' and return to the figuration of the human body, now refracted through art itself. She reproduces Old Masters, putting herself in the role of the central figure, or impersonating a portrait. Again, she distorts the body with false additions, such as the breast in a Virgin and Child. Although these images lack the inexorability and complexity of her previous phase, she still plays on the structures of disavowal and draws attention to the art-historical fetishisation of great works and their value.

For Freud, the structure of fetishism was not the same as the structure of repression. While providing a substitute and a replacement and literally a screen against a traumatic memory, the fetish is also a memento of loss and substitution. And in these circumstances, how the female body, the original provoker of castration anxiety, is represented may be symptomatic and revealing. When Sherman depicts femininity as a masquerade in her succession of 'dressings-up', the female body asserts itself as a site of anxiety that it must, at all costs, conceal. And it acquires a self-conscious vulnerability that seems to exude tension between an exterior appearance and its interiority. In this way, Sherman plays with a 'topography' of the female body. But the early photographs illustrate the extent to which this

73

'topography' has been integrated into a culture of the feminine. In order to create a 'cosmetic' body a cosmetics industry has come into being, so that the psychic investment the patriarchy makes in feminine appearance is echoed by an investment on the part of capitalism. And cosmetics are also, of course, the tools of Sherman's trade.

Fetishism depends on a phantasmatic topography, setting up a screen and shield, closely linked to the ego's defence mechanism, as Freud pointed out. At the same time, fetishism is the most semiotic of perversions, screening and shielding by means of an object that is, unavoidably, also a sign of loss and substitution. But its semiotic enterprise is invested in an acknowledgment of artifice. The fetish is, as Nietzsche said of woman, 'so artistic'. And, for instance, in Godard's representations of women, the female body reduplicates the surface that covers over a mysterious void, but it can incarnate the fetish object itself. This syndrome came into its own with the Hollywood star system, the mass production of pin-ups, and the equation, in contemporary consumer culture, between the feminine and glamour.

Cindy Sherman traces the abyss or morass that overwhelms the defetishised body, deprived of the fetish's semiotic, reduced to being 'unspeakable' and devoid of significance. Her late work, as I suggested in the Pandora myth, raises the question of Julia Kristeva's concept of the abject.[5] Barbara Creed's argument that abjection is central to the recurring image of the 'monstrous feminine' in horror movies[6] is also applicable to the monstrous in Sherman. Although her figures materialise the stuff of irrational terror, they also have pathos and could easily be understood in terms of 'the monster as victim'. Her photographs of atrophied figures, for instance the corpse that lies like a soiled wax work, eyes staring and blending with colour tones into the grass, could be collected into a lexicon of horror and the uncanny, just as the Untitled Film Stills are like a lexicon of poses and gestures typical of respectable, but still uncanny, femininity. Just as the development of individual subjectivity depends on marking out a boundary between the self, the mother and subsequently anything reminiscent of the boundarilessness of infancy, so Sherman's photographs work in reverse. Starting off with Untitled Film Stills, mounted within a white border and enclosed in a black frame, the images gradually lose their definite outlines, both in relation to the frame and the depiction of the figures themselves.

By referring to the 50s in her early work, Sherman joins many others in identifying Eisenhower's America as the mythic birthplace of post-modern culture. Reference to the 50s invokes the aftermath of the Korean War and the success of the Marshall Plan, American mass consumption, the 'society of the spectacle' and, indeed, the Hollywood melodrama. It was a time when, in the context of the cold war, advertising, movies and the actual packaging and seductiveness of commodities all marketed glamour. Glamour proclaimed the desirability of American capitalism to the outside world and, inside, secured Americanness as an aspiration for the newly suburbanised white population as it buried incompatible memories of immigrant origins. In Sherman's early photographs, connotations of vulnerability and instability flow over onto the construction and credibility of the wider social masquerade. The image of 'fifties-ness' as a particular emblem of Americanness also masks the fact that it was a decade of social and political repression while profound change gathered on the horizon, the transition, that is, from Joe McCarthy to James Dean, from Governor Maddox to Martin Luther King. Rather than simply referring to 'fifties-ness' in nostalgia mode, Sherman hints at a world ingesting the seeds of its own decay.

In 1982 Cindy Sherman appeared on the cover of the Ango-American avant-garde magazine *ZG*. She is immediately recognisable as Marilyn Monroe in a cover-girl pose. She is not the Marilyn of bright lights and diamonds, but the other equally familiar Marilyn in slacks and a shirt, still epitomising the glamour of the period, hand held to thrown-back head, eyes half-closed, lips open. But refracted through Sherman's masquerade, Marilyn's masquerade fails to mask her interior anxiety and unhappiness seems to seep through the cracks. America's favourite fetish never fully succeeded in papering over her interiority and the veil of sexual allure now seems, in retrospect, to be haunted by death. While American postmodernism cites the 50s, Marilyn Monroe is its emblem, as an icon in her own right, and as source of all the subsequent Marilyn iconography, kept alive by gay subculture, surfacing with Debbie Harry in the late 70s and recycled by Madonna in the 80s.

Cindy Sherman's impersonations predate, and in some ways prefigure, those of Madonna. Madonna's performances make full use of the potential of cosmetics. As well as fast changing her own chameleon-like appearance on a day-to-day basis, she performs homages to the cosmetic perfection of the movie stars and also integrates the 'oscillation effect' into the rhythm of her videos, synchronising editing, personality change and sexual role reversals. Although Madonna, obviously, does not follow the Cindy Sherman narrative of disintegration, her awareness of this, other, side of the topography of feminine masquerade is evidenced in her well-known admiration for Frida Kahlo. Frida depicted her face as a mask in a large number of self-portraits, and veiled her body in elaborate Tehuana dresses. Sometimes the veil falls, and her wounded body comes to the surface, condensing her real, physical, wounds with both the imaginary wound of castration and the literal interior space of the female body, the womb, bleeding, in her autobiographical paintings, from miscarriage. Frida Kahlo's mask was always her own. Marilyn's was like a trade-mark. While Cindy Sherman and Madonna shift appearance into a fascinating debunking of stable identity, Marilyn's masquerade had to be always absolutely identical. Her features were able to accept cosmetic modelling into an instantly recognisable sign of 'Marilyn-ness'. But here, too, the mask is taut, threatened by the gap between public stardom and private pressures (as was the case for everyone caught in the Hollywood Babylon of the studio system's double standards) and also by the logic of the topography itself.

In refusing the word/image juxtaposition, so prevalent in the art of the 70s and 80s, Sherman may draw the accusation that she is, herself, stuck in the topographic doublebind of the fetish and its collapse. She would thus be unable to inscribe the means of decipherment into the work itself. Her use of 'Untitled' to describe her works turns inability into refusal. Her work vividly illustrates the way that images are able to address their spectator, and are completely available to the process of deciphering, through *mise en scène*, connotations, juxtapositions and so on. In this sense, the iconicity of a photograph, its meaning through resemblance to what it represents, may be an illusion. Like children's puzzle pictures which have objects concealed in other objects, like the *double entendre* of a *trompe-l'oeil*, like the adjustment of vision needed to see a holographic image, Sherman's work bears witness to the photograph's ability to mean more than what it seems to represent.

Futhermore, the human psyche thrives on the division between surface and secret, which, as a metaphor for repression of all kinds, cannot be swept away. Topographies of the female body are formed out of the uncertainty inscribed into femininity by misogynist culture and this kind of imbrication between a psychic (social) order and the culture that reflects it will necessarily exist. But the wordlessness and despair in Sherman's work represents the wordlessness and despair that ensue when a fetishistic structure, the means of erasing history and memory, collapses, either as a result of individual trauma or social repression. The fetish necessarily wants history to be overlooked. That is its function. The fetish is also a symptom and, as such, has a history which may be deciphered, but only by refusing its phantasmatic topography. Freud described his first concept of the unconscious as a topography to convey the burying action of repression, but he analysed the language of the unconscious, its formal expression in condensation and displacement, in terms of signification and decipherment. In the last resort, decipherment is dependent on language and the analysand's exegesis, which transforms the symptom into language and traces its displaced history. The complete lack of verbal clues and signifiers in Cindy Sherman's work draws attention to the semiotic that precedes a successful translation of the symptom into language, the semiotic of displacements and fetishism, desperately attempting to disguise unconscious ideas from the conscious mind. She uses iconography, connotation or the sliding of the signifier in a trajectory that ends by stripping away all accrued meaning to the limit of bodily matter. However, even this bedrock, the vomit and the blood for instance, return to cultural significance, that is to the difficulty of the body, and above all the female body, while it is subjected to the icons and narratives of fetishism.

Chapter 6

The Hole and the Zero: Godard's Visions of Femininity

In an early article, written in 1952 in *Cahiers du Cinéma*, 'Defence and Illustration of the Cinema's Classical Construction', Godard associates female beauty, almost ontologically, with the cinema:

> A beautiful face, as La Bruyère wrote, is the most beautiful of sights. There is a famous legend which has it that Griffith, moved by the beauty of his leading lady, invented the close-up in order to capture it in greater detail. Paradoxically, therefore, the simplest close-up is also the most moving. Here our art reveals its transcendence most strongly, making the beauty of the object signified burst forth in the sign. With these huge eyes half closing in discretion and desire, with these blenching lips, all we see in their anguish is the dark design they imply, and in their avowal only the illusions they conceal. The cinema does not query the beauty of a woman, it only doubts her heart, records her perfidy (it is an art, La Bruyère says, of the entire person to place a word or an action so that it puts one off the scent), sees only her movements.[1]

Reading these words it is impossible not to think of the profoundly cinematic beauty of Godard's actresses, of Jean Seberg's insouciant treachery in *A bout de souffle* (1960) and, most of all, of Anna Karina and her lying glance into camera in *Pierrot le fou* (1965). The dichotomy between surface and secret, artifice and truth, is paradoxical. The artificial surface of feminine beauty may disguise an inside that that can only be unveiled to reveal the danger of the *femme fatale*. But the artificial surface of cinematic illusion may disguise an inside that can be unveiled to reveal the true beauty of its materiality and its potential to analyse political reality.

Godard's move towards an aesthetics of materialism in the militant late 60s was accompanied by a move towards Marxism. During his Marxist period, he reformulated the surface/secret, beauty/deception oppositions that had characterised his representations of women in keeping with the struggle against capitalist, commodity society. Out of this struggle he developed his politically radical and aesthetically avant-garde counter-cinema. In the place of a femininity of mystery, a femininity of enigma emerged. The artifice and illusion of femininity could be stripped away, alongside the artifice and illusion of the cinema and the artifice and illusion of consumer society. Then, Godard's late, post-Marxist, cinema of the 80s moved away from enigma and back towards mystery and away from curiosity and investigation and towards a new sense of awe. These political changes affected both his cinema and his representations of women. The changes can be mapped through the painful but obstinate engagement with sex, sexual difference and femininity that has zigzagged across his cinema and his politics.

Why, Godard has taught us to ask, these sounds and these images? In *Je vous salue Marie* (1982), Marie visits her family doctor. Before the doctor examines her and verifies her virgin pregnancy, he goes behind a screen to wash his hands, meanwhile making a remark that she cannot hear. The camera is in long shot, composed around Marie sitting in her underwear on the examining table. She asks him to repeat his remark, and the camera is repositioned in medium shot on the doctor, as he says, seemingly for the benefit of the audience rather than Marie: 'I've always wondered what we can know about a woman and then I discovered that all you can know is what men knew already: there is a mystery there.' Faced with the Virgin Mary, of course mystery becomes Mystery. It is as though Godard had struggled for so long to get behind the surface that, in this film, he has taken a step back to examine it with awe, if also with a certain irony. However, in doing so, he installs a fetishised concept of beauty, smooth and complete, in cinema, in the woman's body and in a concept of nature that includes the unknowable.

The cinema, the woman's body, 'nature'. The aesthetic that emerges from this triad is very different from the aesthetic of Godard's political phases. In the mid-60s, in what could be called his Debord phase[2] (especially *Une femme mariée* (1964) and *Deux ou trois choses que je sais d'elle* (1966)), the triad was, rather: cinema, the woman's body, consumer society. In his Marxist phase (for instance *British Sounds* (1969) and *Tout va bien* (1972)), he tried to look beyond consumerism at the process of the commodity's production itself. The cinema, the body, the factory. Although these triads are necessarily reductive conceptually, they draw attention to an important aspect of Godard's aesthetic in which the woman continues to play a nodal role despite shifts and changes in his political agendas. By the 80s the significant relation between the first two terms has altered so that the elements that contributed to Godard's enormous theoretical influence in the 60s and 70s emerge in a different 'mix' with *Passion* (1981), *Prénom: Carmen* (1982) and *Je vous salue Marie*. *Passion* is a watershed film, a point at which Godard's changing aesthetic and political priorities take shape. *Carmen* is a transitional film, a film of crisis marking the distance that lies between *Passion* and *Je vous salue Marie*.

Two different topographies underlie the network of links between ideas, slippages of meaning, displacements and condensations that are exchanged across the triads. For instance, the cinema, the eroticised female body, and the consumer commodity all share the attribute of spectacle. They can reinforce and overlay each other in a series of analogies. On the other hand they can create a network of interconnections, more along the lines of metonymy, so that the connection between woman and commodity consumption is a social alignment rather than one of analogy or metaphor. On the other hand again, in the form of the prostitute, the woman's relationship with the commodity is analogous. Both offer themselves for sale in the market place. Both have to produce a desirable surface. Both have to circulate without reference to any history outside the moment of exchange.

In *Deux ou trois choses que je sais d'elle*, Juliette/Marina Vlady is a working-class housewife who becomes a prostitute in order to buy consumer goods for herself and her family. She thus condenses into a single figure a metaphorical analogy of commodity and a metonymy, shopping. She also, of course, shops to produce the desirable surface, the 'look' that comes with make-up and clothes, which then, in turn, implies the seductiveness of an eroticised surface that implies something hidden, a secret or mystery. While Godard draws attention to the commodification of woman, in the advertisements of consumer capitalism as well as literally in prostitution, he also draws attention to an eroticisation of the commodity. Again, a seductive surface implies something hidden. The two share a similarity of structure, which can also be extended to the cinema and its investment in a surface fascination that conceals its mechanisms. And the cinema is also itself a commodity that circulates successfully through its seductive power, and its seductiveness is very often encapsulated in the presence of the eroticised female body on the screen. The similarity of structure thus creates a channel through which processes of displacement may flow, and in this sense metaphoric or metonymic connections are structured by a phantasmatic homology. The homology reinforces movements of ideas and sets up deep subliminal linkages across figurations that would not seem on the surface to be so intricately imbricated. The figuration of femininity is central and the feminine enigma allows Godard to suggest other enigmas, aesthetic, cinematic and socio-economic (that of the commodity). The homology of surface and its suggestion of a phantasmic 'depth' projected behind it channels ideas and images into a network of criss-crossed displacements and condensations.

The question of visibility emerges here. Juliette's opaque, placid, passive exterior as sexual object is juxtaposed to her inner thoughts conveyed, on the soundtrack, to the audience but not to the characters on the screen, while Godard's own whispering voice also mediates, commenting on the action on the screen and questioning its spontaneity and its autonomy. In Marina Vlady's introduction to *Deux ou trois choses* she, or rather (probably) Godard, cites Brecht. The citation also created a bridge between a

Brechtian dismantling of the 'plenitude' of the spectacle, the cinema's function as commodity to be consumed, and the structure and function of commodity fetishism in late capitalist society. Although the mediation is enabled through the figure of the prostitute (also movie star, spectacle and commodity in herself), Godard's first concern is with the fetishistic aspects of cinema. If the shiny, glossy surface fascination of the screen could be unmasked to reveal the process of production concealed behind it, cinema would be stripped of its fetishistic aspects. In Godard, this desire to free the cinema into the complex space and time of intertextual reference, direct address, self-reflexivity, material specificity and so on parallels the Marxist desire to defetishise the commodity, by making visible, through political analysis, the specificity of its process of production. The materialism of a modernist aesthetics meets the materialism of Marxism in Brecht and through to Godard.

During his radical phase, Godard's cinema was aimed at remoulding spectatorship, attempting to create and to address an audience that would be excited by an image and excited by its cinematic specificity and excited by deciphering its meaning. I have argued that the drive of curiosity can be a critical response to the lure of voyeurism. The critic attempts to transform fascinating images into enigmatic images and decipher their meaning. A counter-cinema attempts to create images that fascinate because they arouse curiosity and challenge the audience to decipher their meaning. In this sense, the curiosity generated by a secret, something hidden and forbidden, is extended into the curiosity generated by a puzzle, something that has to be figured out. Images of woman, long associated with fascination and enigma, stand centre screen. They act as signs that, like a puzzle, can be deciphered to reveal something that was previously incomprehensible, a source of mystery. In the image of the prostitute, Godard subjected mystery to the materiality of sexuality, of capitalist production and, implicitly, of cinema.

In two complementary scenes, Godard uses the figure of the prostitute to forge further chains of reference between two contrasting aspects of capitalism and sexuality. In *Deux ou trois choses,* the two prostitutes are called to an American business man's hotel suite. Their client asks them to walk in front of him, one wearing a Pan Am flight bag, the other a TWA, over their heads, while he photographs them. The American's erotic investment in his powerful and expensive camera, the girls masked by the two great logos, turn the prostitute/client relationship into a ritual which grotesquely celebrates the dependence of American consumer capitalism on the representation of its phallic power as fetish for sexual pleasure and condenses the commodity with sexuality. In the second scene, in *Sauve qui peut (la vie)* (1979), the prostitute and other subordinate employees create a Heath Robinson sex machine of cold, impersonal, Taylorised, erotic gestures under the management of their boss for his profit and satisfaction. While the first scene revolves around images of consumption, the second mimics the production line. While the first explores the fetishism of the commodity, the second caricatures capitalism's relations of production, which fetishism conceals.

However, the sex machine is, itself, obviously, at one and the same time, deeply fetishistic. It uses the mechanical, synchronised movements of the robot through which the process of production, otherwise dangerously close to exposing the labour theory of value, can conceal its secrets. Robert Stam describes it in the following manner: 'Like a filmmaker [the boss] assigns precise movements to his actors. ... The orgy participants, like assembly line workers, are reduced to well-defined jerks, twists, moans and quivers'.[3] Raymond Bellour and Pascal Bonitzer have similarly drawn attention to the analogy. Bellour has pointed out that the stop-motion frames privilege particular moments in *Sauve qui peut* and 'make impossible the the imaginary pause that the image needs in order to satisfy its false plenitude', and that they allow 'the rebirth of the image, this move toward a writing-painting freed from the deceptive imaginary plenitude prescribed by the forward movement of the machine'.[4] There is also a sense of terminal loss, suggesting that Godard, this time, is not engaged so much in the deconstruction of the cinema machine, or its liberation, but rather in recording the blockage of these processes. The imbrication of the cinema, the factory and the body is there, visibly in motion, but it no longer signifies more than just that.

Factory–body–cinema. The last traces of analytical, politically radical Godard, mainly personified in Isabelle Huppert's character in both films, drained away somewhere between *Sauve qui peut* and *Passion*. In *Passion*, these three grand themes that preoccupied Godard for so long come to occupy three distinct spaces, that overflow into each other through the intertwined strands of the narrative. Work–sex–sound/image. The factory sphere is represented by Isabelle Huppert as worker and Michel Piccoli as boss. Piccoli's character is reminiscent of the boss/client in the *Sauve qui peut* sex machine scene. Isabelle's character is only connected to that scene through the presence of the actress and the fact that her character is, at the opening of the film, within the 'sphere' of the factory/ machine and subject to the power of the boss. The 'sphere' of the cinema is represented by the director, his cast, crew and the studio ('the most expensive in Europe') where they are making a movie, itself called *Passion*. The factory/cinema analogy continues and there are numerous overlaps between these two spheres. Piccoli's presence, although here on the side of the factory, provides a ghostly trace of his role as the scriptwriter in *Le Mépris* (1963), rewriting *The Odyssey* rather as, in this film, the director tries to recreate Old Master paintings. In their behaviour and social gestures, the dramatis personae of the film crew echo the factory hierarchy and division of labour. Jerzy, the director, is authoritarian and peremptory on set. Sophie, the production assistant, behaves very much like a factory manageress; she insists on the rules, the importance of productivity and the place of narrative in cinema. Patrick, the assistant director, behaves very much like a foreman; he bullies and exhorts the extras to 'work', rounding them up and overseeing the management of the set, literally chasing the girls. The 'sphere' of sex/the body is represented by Hanna Schygulla, Piccoli's wife, who owns the hotel where the cast and crew stay, and the film world overlaps with that of the factory next door. Jerzy spends time with Hanna when he should be directing the film, making her watch a video of her face, in close-up, recorded under the sway of strong emotion, as he tries to persuade her to move into the world of the cinema and play a part in the 'Rubens'.

Isabelle, the factory worker, is sacked at the beginning of *Passion*. Her narrative is concentrated primarily on her struggle for reinstatement or compensation, and is thus apparently in keeping with Godard's earlier commitment to working-class struggle. Her character is physically and emotionally vulnerable. Her slight stutter conveys a lack of mastery over language and the discourses of culture which isolates her from the world of the film and art. Towards the end of the movie, Piccoli capitulates and pays her off, too exhausted by his racking cough to continue the fight. She is suddenly transformed from worker into a free agent, a potential entrepreneur, able to choose her future, as though the narrative had decided to move away from the signifier of the working class and its struggle, in a gesture towards another kind of production, artistic rather than economic and political. The cinema, however, remains a central point for investigation and inquiry, but the 'how' is now decidedly directed more towards questions of creativity, although the economic and technical are still present.

The relationship between Jerzy and Isabelle points to parallels between her struggle with the factory boss and his struggle to reconcile the industrial demands of production and distribution with creative autonomy. On another level, there is a parallel between Isabelle's stammer, her struggle for articulate speech, and the director's loss of direction in his film project. Both are trying to find a flowing form of expression and find themselves blocked. The director has to find a way through his film without having recourse to a story, as required by the investors, Sophie and general expectation. He is obsessed by his inability to master the lighting on the set. He wants to recreate in tableaux, and then film in their three dimensions, some of the great and famous paintings of Western art. Created on a flat surface by the painter, with the illusion of depth and movement frozen for one split second, these images have to move from the *trompe-l'oeil* of the canvas surface into the *trompe-l'oeil* of the screen surface. In the process, the director, like Michelange in *Les Carabiniers* (1963), is attempting to penetrate *inside* the space implied by these familiar paintings, transforming them into the round for the camera's participation and exploration. The stunningly beautiful tableaux are recreated on huge sets like labyrinths, channelling and then blocking the flowing movement of the camera. A technician with video camera and cables, or other external interloping elements, may break up the magical *trompe-l'oeil* by presenting, in the image on screen, the processes of its production. While the meta-phor 'unveiling' evoked a surface/secret dichotomy suggested by the fetish, the appropriate metaphor here is 'penetration', not behind but into the surface. The surface now possesses a channel to its own behind, not to a mode of production or something that it overlays, but into a celebration of the fetishisation of surface as such. The escape from the dilemma of fetishism, from the radical need to defetishise cultural production, is a sign of the passing of the machine age, of the end of the problematics of modernism and the politics that characterised both.

Isabelle and Jerzy's mutual recognition is like a last remaining trace of a theoretical condensation between the process of production, in capitalism and in art, that characterised Godard's earlier, deconstructive, Brechtian aesthetics. In *Passion* Godard's priorities seem to change direction. It is as though he were describing the shift of emphasis in his work, away from materialist modernism, into an exploration of art and the problems of creativity itself. Isabelle, from this perspective, would (until her victory) represent the past to Godard's own shifting political trajectory and the changing climate of the 80s which said, in André Gorz's words, 'Farewell to the working class'. Jerzy describes himself as searching for a solution to his problems with cinema in between the two women, 'as different as day from night'. The problem of cinema is imbricated with the female body, in a strange reversal of the 60s preoccupation with the demystification of the society of the spectacle and its investment in sexuality.

In *Passion*, Godard begins to reconstitute the female body as the prop of the cinema. At the end of the film, in a gesture which acknowledges his move away from the everyday of political struggle, Godard moves away from the everyday into a more 'real' world of fiction and fantasy. A young girl, dancer and acrobat, who works as a maid at the hotel provides the film with an ending. Jerzy is her 'prince' and she accepts a lift in his car when he tells her, his 'princess', that it is not a car but a magic carpet which will transport them back to Poland. The film ends with an escape from the space of the film and the space of the factory, but the space of the body, signified by the feminine, has been incorporated into the fantasy escape of a fairy story.

After *Passion*, Godard made two films in succession both of which deal directly with myths of feminine mystery and the enigma of the female body. They also form a diptych through which he can return to his old, pre-Marxist obsession with the duality of cinema, its magic versus its real-ity. The two mythologies of the feminine are, on the face of it, diametri-cally opposed to each other. One, *Prénom: Carmen*, reworks, in its main narrative strand, Prosper Mérimée's 1845 story whose heroine, due to the success of Bizet's 1875 opera, quickly became an icon of feminine seduc-tiveness and infidelity, and a rampant, independent sexuality. The other, *Je vous salue Marie*, daringly retells the myth of the Annunciation and the Virgin Birth and the story of Mary, Christian culture's icon of feminine chastity, submission to the will of God, and spirituality. The problem of cinema once again finds an analogue or a metaphorical representation in the mystery of woman. The two kinds of cinema, the cinema of magic/ desire (Carmen) and the cinema of spirituality/truth (Marie), are reworked through metonymies which both link back to the place of the female body in Godard's earlier work and represent a point of crisis. There is a sudden, numbing, realisation that creativity depends on desire but that desire deflects creativity.

In *Je vous salue Marie* Godard finds an apparently paradoxical means of restoring the spiritual (the unnatural nature of the Virgin Birth) to cinema. This is not so much a new departure but a return to the spiritual tradition of cinematic realism and some of Godard's earliest mentors: Dreyer, Rossellini, Bresson. Godard subordinates magic, implied by a belief in the Virgin Birth, to mystery and returns his cinema to nature through the hand of God. The cinematic representation of nature is now mysterious, cynically stripped of its former realist aspiration. Only Godard's instinctive understanding of cinema's inherent contradictions, his deep involvement with debates about the nature of cinema, could realise its paradox so precisely. And only a despairing obsession with the enigma of femininity could invoke the Virgin Mary as the paradox itself. So, as the two films polarise femininity into a binary opposition, the carnal and the spiritual, ghosts of earlier polarisations also return.

Godard's dualistic, almost Manichaean, attitudes are there at the very beginning of his work as a director, or even from before the beginning, when, as a critic, he first started to articulate his concept of cinema. As a critic, Godard encapsulated his ideas through names ('criticism taught us to love both Rouch and Eisenstein') constantly reiterating an opposition between research or documentary (Lumière) and spectacle or fiction (Méliès), on the one hand Rossellini, on the other Nicholas Ray. Through these oppositions Godard tried to negotiate the problem of truth and the aesthetic in the cinema. From the beginning, that is from Patricia's betrayal of Michel Poiccard in *A bout de souffle*, the split between feminine seductive appearance and either deceitful or mysteriously unknowable essence was a recurring theme in Godard's work. It is not only a dramatic trope but also a metaphor for the more profound philosophical problem of the split between appearance and essence. It is a problem of inscription. *Je vous salue Marie* returns to this problem but by a strange route, one that is mapped through/across the question of truth as the presence of the invisible and spiritual made manifest through/across the body of woman. Godard's homology between female sexuality, artifice and deception has, of course, a rich history in Western culture and there are many *femmes fatales* who could represent the myth that he realised with the Carmen story, while only one woman, the Virgin Mary herself, could represent the other side of the antinomy. In the myth of the Mother of God, the enigmatic and dangerous mystery of female sexuality is exorcised, but only through the further mystery of God's power. And paradoxically, this mystery can only be grasped by a blind subservience to irrational belief. Belief in God depends on belief in the woman's impossible virginity which represents her 'wholeness', an evisceration of the psychologically threatening and physically disgusting 'inside'. It is only as 'whole' that woman can drop the mask of artifice with which she both deceives man and conceals the truth of her body.

But the simple fact of polarisation will always link, as well as oppose, and the attributes that separate Carmen and Marie only superficially conceal the underlying 'fit' between them. Both myths revolve around mysteries of the female body and its ultimate unknowableness. Both myths symbolise a zero point for Godard, at which the mystery of the feminine, profoundly destructive on one level, becomes a threshold to and signifier of, other *more profound* mysteries. There is a complex conflation between the enigmatic properties of femininity and the mystery of origins, particularly the origins of creativity, whether the creation of life or the creative processes of art. In both films the forces of nature have a presence unprecedented in Godard's cinema. Although landscape has often played its part, alongside quotations and works of art, in his cinema (the journey through France in *Pierrot le fou*, the Mediterranean in *Le Mépris*, Denise's bicycle ride in *Sauve qui peut,* the sky in *Passion*) in these two films, landscape has evolved into nature, and, in both films, is associated with the feminine.

On the other hand, femininity cannot be separated from performance. Nietzsche ends 'On the problem of the actor' in *The Gay Science* thus:

> Finally women. Reflect on the whole history of women: do they not have to be first of all and above all else actresses? Listen to the physicians who have hypnotised women; finally, love them – let yourself be hypnotised by them! What is always the end result? That they 'put on something' even when they take off everything. Women are so artistic.[5]

It is easy to see the phrase 'women are so artistic' in Godard's mind's eye. At what point does art turn into artifice and artifice into art? The aesthetic problem posed by the dissembling nature of the actor preoccupied Godard in the spirit of Nietzsche's comment: 'Falseness with a good conscience; the delight in simulation exploding as a power that pushes aside one's so called "character", flooding it and at times extinguishing it; the inner craving for a role and a mask, for *appearance*.'[6]

In *Une femme mariée*, Charlotte interrogates her actor/lover, showing the same doubts about how to read his inner being in his appearance that are more usually projected by the man onto the woman. It was this mistrust of performance that pushed Godard towards the distanciated, visible separation between actor and role that characterised his late-60s cinema.[7] And this mistrust then extends to the simulation and fiction of cinema itself. The woman's simulation, like the cinema's, is spectacle and what can only be seen as a surface still conceals its secrets.

Many critics were struck, seeing *Prénom: Carmen,* by Myriem Roussel's likeness to Anna Karina. As the Virgin Mary in *Je vous salue Marie*, Roussel transforms perfidy into purity, transforming Marianne (*Pierrot le fou*) into a Nana (*Vivre sa vie*) whose sexuality has been erased. The beauty of her body can still transfix the camera, but it acts as a conduit towards a new kind of cinema which can transcend materiality. Man and the cinema can fantasise liberation from an enslavement to sexuality. While Carmen encapsulates the theme of beauty and faithlessness in the *femme fatale* and, by extension, the cinema of Hollywood, the theme of the spiritual in nature, represented by Marie, resurrects the ghost of another cinema and Rossellini's one-time significance for Godard. In a 1962 interview with *Cahiers du Cinéma* he said:

> Rossellini is something else again. With him a shot is beautiful because it is right: with most others, a shot becomes right because it is beautiful. They try to construct something wonderful, and if in fact it becomes so, one can see that there were reasons for doing it. Rossellini does something he had a reason for doing in the first place. It is beautiful because it is.[8]

The cinema is the only art which, as Cocteau says (in *Orphée*, I believe), shows 'death at work', a phrase glossed by Godard as 'death twenty-four times a second'. This citation resurrects another less obvious influence on Godard: André Bazin, the devout Catholic who co-founded *Cahiers du Cinéma* and edited it from 1951 until his death in 1958. Bazin argues in 'The Ontology of the Photographic Image' that the origins of art lie in the human desire to overcome death, to mummify the body and conquer time: 'the preservation of life by a representation of life'. In the history of art, this 'creation of an ideal world in the likeness of the real' was vitiated by the need for illusion, the 'proclivity of the mind towards magic', and it was only Niépce and Lumière who redeemed art from this sin. Bazin wrote: 'For the first time, between the originating object and its reproduction there intervenes only the instrumentality of a nonliving agent. ... Photography affects us like a phenomenon in nature, like a flower or a snowflake whose vegetable or earthly origins are an inseparable part of their beauty.'[9] And he compares the shared nature of the object and its photograph to the fingerprint.

In the semiotic categories of Charles Peirce, the fingerprint is an index, the sign in which the object leaves its own unmediated trace just as light, in photography, carries the image onto celluloid. Peter Wollen associates Bazin's aesthetic of the index with his concern for the spiritual:

> It was the existential bond between fact and image, world and film, which counted for most in Bazin's aesthetic, rather than any quality of similarity or resemblance. Hence the possibility – even the necessity – of an art which could reveal spiritual states. There was, for Bazin, a

double movement of impression, of moulding and imprinting: the first, the interior spiritual suffering, was stamped on the exterior physiognomy; then the exterior physiognomy was stamped and printed upon sensitive film.[10]

Here the problem of the relationship between interior and exterior, between an appearance and what it might conceal, is effaced as the presence of the deity is inscribed into the world, into nature and into the soul, inscribed onto the face of man. The cinema, thus, in turn, finds an integration between its mechanical nature and its ability to record. The split between the cinema as a surface illusion, and the disillusioning mechanics that produce it, is effaced. But, for Godard, there is a difficult tension between the cinema's imbrication with the beauty of woman, and therefore her perfidy, and its potential realisation of Bazin's aesthetic. When, in *Vivre sa vie* (1962), Anna Karina as Nana weeps as she watches Falconetti's face in Dreyer's *La Passion de Jeanne d'Arc* (1927), Godard is paying a tribute to Dreyer's image, in which the spirituality of the soul is indistinguishable from the spirituality of the cinema. Myriem Roussel's Marie could be born out of the gap between Karina/Nana, innocent but a prostitute, irrevocably subordinated to the body and the sexual, and Falconetti's Joan, uncontaminated by the sexual and inscribed with the spiritual power of God. Peter Wollen noted that in Bresson's films Bazin saw

> 'the outward revelation of an interior destiny', and that in those of Rossellini, 'the presence of the spiritual' is expressed with 'breathtaking obviousness'. The exterior, through the transparence of images stripped of all inessentials, reveals the interior. Bazin emphasised the importance of the physiognomy, upon which – as in the films of Dreyer – the interior spiritual life was etched and printed.[11]

Raymond Bellour has pointed out that the index is both the most material and the most spiritual of signs. In his Marxist period, Godard sought reality through materialism, rather than through a cinema that lay on the cusp of illusion and spirituality. From a materialist point of view, truth lies in revealing the relations of production, whether those of capitalist society or those of cinema itself. In this sense the beauty of the filmic image comes not from recording something mystically inherent in the pro-filmic, but in the inscription of the usually obscured presence of the processes of cinematic production. The presence of the camera, its inscription onto the scene, lights up the nowness of the film moment into its indexicality and, when Godard's characters spoke directly to camera, not only did documentary break into fiction, but that moment was then carried into the actual screening of the finished film and the screen would speak, whenever it was projected, at that moment in time, to the spectator of the future. It is as though with the acknowledgment of the apparatus of the cinema, everything that is usually concealed and glossed over in the process of making a film could open out the secret space of cinema's truth. Direct address, therefore, opens out the darkened space of the auditorium. The realist aesthetics of Brecht are not the same as those of Bazin. Furthermore, while Godard was capable of defetishising the cinema and illuminating the fetishistic imbrication between woman as appearance and the dissembling nature of the late capitalist commodity, his iconography of the feminine on the screen was never freed from a fetishistic gloss.

I described *Passion*, earlier, as a watershed in Godard's work. The spheres of narrative space, separated out into thematic strands, replaced the chapter structure that Godard had used in *Sauve qui peut* and also often in his earlier films. In *Passion*, Godard's new search for purity, earlier transmuted into materialism, now takes the form of splitting the different component narrative parts of the film into distinct, almost autonomous spheres. These divisions are even more significant in *Prénom: Carmen*. Carmen and eroticism are a function of image, while Claire and purity materialise through the music. It is as though the elements of film, that are usually wound together in a hierarchical organisation, have been unravelled, so that sound acquires image track and image is used to generate soundtrack. In *Prénom: Carmen* the film is divided into different spaces according to formal strands rather than narrative or theme. The music is taken from Beethoven's late string quartets. A string quartet is intended for informal performance, and a 'chamber', space in which the members of the quartet practise, materialises, alongside the space of the story, to give an image to the music on the soundtrack.[12] In an interview, Godard described the sound in this film as 'sculpted'.

In *Prénom: Carmen,* the only character from the sphere of the music to have contact with the narrative is Claire (Myriem Roussel, who will play Marie in the next film), although the quartet are present, as, indeed are the whole of the rest of the cast, in the final scene in the hotel. While the sky and the countryside will have an important place in *Je vous salue Marie*, in *Prénom: Carmen* the sea creates both a sound and image track, creating a counterpoint to the Beethoven (and Claire), and acting as a metaphoric extension of Carmen. Equally, the strand of narration, or the desire for cinema, is personified by the director's presence on the screen. He exists in a kind of limbo, occasionally overlapping with the space of the story itself, dominated by 'Carmen'. The narrator's participation in the narrative is true to Mérimée's original story, but Godard's presence is also like a materialisation of his whispered voice, so familiar from previous soundtracks, and also, again, a reversal of his earlier, deconstructive, appearances as part of the process of production.

In *Prénom: Carmen* Godard plays the film director who has taken refuge in a nursing home (for the physically and mentally ill) because he cannot make films. He is not literally ill. On the contrary, the fever that he needs in order to stay in hospital seems to be also the fever that he lacks in order to make films. For the director, Godard implies, the cinema is a necessary object without which the world is unbearable. Although his special camera is there with him, like a fetish object, in his hospital room, it cannot, alone, conjure up the cinema. When the nurse comes to take his temperature, gently encouraging his hopes for a fever, he says: 'If I put my finger up your ass and counted to thirty-three, do you think I would get a fever?' In the next scene, on cue, as it were, Carmen appears. Unlike the nurse, who seems to function more as a channel to desire, Carmen represents the feminine as 'to be looked at'. And this investment in her seductiveness creates the sense of surface, of sheen and gloss, that the theoreticians of the 60s and 70s associated with the fetishism of both the commodity and the cinema, and that feminist theorists associated with the specularisation of the female body. Carmen is the director's niece, whom he has desired since she was a little girl. She asks her Uncle Jean's help for a film she is making with some friends and she marks both the onset of desire and the onset of the fiction, the adventure, the fantasy. Like the tower that starts to crash at the beginning of *Le Sang d'un poète* (1930) and then crumbles on the ground at the end, bracketing all the action in between as subjective, outside space and time, so the nurse appears to bracket the narrative action in *Prénom: Carmen*. When Uncle Jean's coat needs mending during a production meeting, the nurse reappears as the wardrobe mistress, and then remains his constant, inseparable companion, performing (in the sense of acting a part, with appropriate gestures and phrases) the role of production assistant, a trace of the Sophie part in *Passion*. At the end of the film Uncle Jean says to her: 'That was a long thirty-three seconds.'

Godard's performance is ironic, sad and harshly self-parodic, as though to pre-empt the accusations that his late cinema is likely to draw from, say, feminist or political quarters. He depicts the film director's dilemma as hopelessly fetishistic, his obsession with cinema and the female body as helplessly dependent, masochistic, exploitative. Cinema and sexuality merge into a condensation that is unashamedly masculine, while also being apologetically impotent. The director's fever is roused by and through the female body, as though, at the zero moment of creativity, Godard confronts bedrock and finds nothing left except the desire for desire. The cinema that slowly materialises, like a genie masturbated out of its bottle, is therefore a distillation, almost an abstraction or a reverie on the very limits of the film-maker's fantasy. And the genie appears in the form of a *femme fatale*, Carmen, also summoning up, generically, Godard's first great passion: film noir.

When I first saw *Prénom: Carmen,* I was very moved. It was not the film, its story or the plight of the director that moved me. It was, probably, the film's situation in Godard's own history, its lapse out of self-referentiality into nostalgia. The final title 'In Memoriam small movies' brought back the memory of the *A bout de souffle* dedication to Monogram Pictures. There is, thus, a double palimpsest, one layer tracing his own early work and, deeper still, the traces of the Hollywood cinema that had originally been his point of departure. The bridge that links the past to the present also inscribes the presence of what is crossed. Just as Godard represents the greatest of 60s radical cinema, so also his work is bound to raise the question of what happens after innovation. The political film-maker, working within the ethos of a particular historical conjuncture, has to deal directly with time, its passing and its propensity to wash over a radical movement, an avant-garde, leaving its members stranded above the tideline. The theme and imagery of 'stranded-ness' is central to *Prénom: Carmen*. It is there in the repeated shots of the sea. And the director's sense of being abandoned by the cinema is dramatically replayed when Joseph is ultimately abandoned by Carmen. The cinema itself, or rather the video camera, is only made use of, by the young people, reductively, as a masquerade to cover their attempted kidnapping.

If *Prénom: Carmen* marks a moment of crisis in Godard's history, it also reveals the bare constitutive elements of his late cinema, all that remains when everything else is stripped away. In the early 80s, with *Prénom: Carmen* Godard's return to the cinema 'as such' takes the form of a despairing return to zero, ironically inverting the thrill of the return to zero in 1968. The return to zero is a return to the origins of the director's own primal desire for cinema, rather than to the point zero that investigates the social circulation and significance of images as, for instance, in *Le Gai Savoir* (1968). His struggle is now to represent what makes the making of cinema possible: its obsessive, romantic, delusory hold over the director, rather than a modernist, Brechtian struggle to represent the process of production of cinema and the process of production of meaning. Although there is an obstinate courage in Godard's 'self-portrait' as the director who sees the cinema slipping through his fingers and a poetic heroism in his ability to turn even such an intimation of loss into new 'sounds and images', the question persists: why, at the moment of crisis, should he return to these particular sounds and these particular images? And, above all, what is the significance of the juxtaposition between Carmen and Claire/Marie as two polarised icons of the feminine?

My sudden rush of nostalgia after seeing *Prénom: Carmen* was focused above all on *Pierrot le fou. Pierrot le fou* was already a version of the Carmen story. That is, it was a story of *amour fou*, in which an essentially respectable and law-abiding hero is seduced by an irresistible, unfaithful woman into a descent into an underworld and a life of crime, on the run from the police. The end is death. Ferdinand kills Marianne and then kills himself; Don Jose kills Carmen, who prefers death to losing her freedom, and, in Mérimée's original, as well as *Prénom: Carmen,* Don Jose/Joseph gives himself up to the police willingly. The Carmen story is pivoted on a separation between the hero's settled, everyday life, and the other netherworld of passion, violence and adventure. The gap that separates the two is bridged by the spell cast over Ferdinand by Marianne, over Joseph/Don Jose by Carmen, over Michael O'Hara by Elsa Bannister in

The Lady from Shanghai (1948). In all these cases the hero's passion for the heroine is ambivalent.

'Carmen' returns to 'Pierrot' not only with almost subliminal references such as a whistled phrase of 'Au clair de la lune' and Joseph's repeated refusal to be called Joe ('Je m'appelle Ferdinand/Joseph'), but with a return to the kind of cinema defined towards the beginning of *Pierrot le fou* by Sam Fuller, appearing as himself: 'A film is a battleground. Love. Hate. Action. Violence. Death. In one word: Emotion.' The bank robbery that Carmen stages shifts Joe from the side of the law to that of the criminal, just as Marianne's confrontation with the gun-runners shifts Ferdinand from a respectable member of the bourgeoisie to the underworld. The shift is an effect of the Hollywood cinema that had so affected the *Cahiers* critics. Ferdinand had forgotten that he was expected to go to a party with his wife and had sent the maid to see *Johnny Guitar* (1954). In the maid's absence, Marianne appears as the baby sitter. Just as Sterling Hayden and Joan Crawford meet again after five years' separation, Marianne and Ferdinand meet again and move back five years in time. In both *Pierrot* and *Carmen*, *amour fou* leads to violence and a journey of crime, pursuit and death ('*Une saison en enfer*'). The 'emotion' is also motion, the moving pictures, the movement of the narrative, the adventure that takes over the hero, and the fascination exerted by the heroine that binds together all the other levels of movement. Both Joe and Ferdinand are abandoned by the story when they are no longer desired by the heroine. Ferdinand is exploited in the final heist and then left behind on the dock. Joe has no 'role' in the final heist, and his sexual impotence is compounded by his narrative impotence.

For both Josephs (the Don and the Saint) sexual desire is an emasculating enslavement to the feminine, leading to abasement, whether with reconciled exaltation, in Marie, or with antagonised aggression in Carmen. Both men are subjected to the irrational and unknowable in woman, and both women are described as 'taboo'. The reference in *Prénom: Carmen* is derived from the lines in Preminger's *Carmen Jones* (1954): 'You go for me, and I'm taboo – But if you're hard to get – I'll go for you, and if I do – Then you are through – 'Cos, if I love you, that's the end of you!' In *Je vous salue Marie,* the angel explains to Joseph that 'the taboo outweighs the sacrifice'.) Both the men have to endure extremes of jealousy. Carmen wants to find out 'what a woman can do with a man', Marie has to teach a man to relate to her body without sexuality. In each film the iconography of the central female character contrasts with the iconography of a secondary female character. While Claire, in *Prénom: Carmen,* prefigures Marie, and is detached from the carnal world of Carmen by the spiritual abstraction of music, Eve, in *Je vous salue Marie,* is a presence of sexuality. She is a student taking classes on the origins of the universe from an exiled Czech professor with whom she falls in love. Eve is first shown sitting in the sunlight trying to solve the puzzle of the Rubik cube. She represents the curiosity of her namesake, but, at the same time, the puzzle reflects the overall theme of mystery and enigma that runs through the film. In juxtaposition to the ultimate enigma, Marie's virgin pregnancy and birth, the mystery of the origins of life is discussed by the students. The professor holds the view that the beginnings of life were 'organised and desired by a resolute intelligence' which interacted with chance at a certain moment to overdetermine the course of nature. To prove his point, Eve stands behind Pascal, covering his eyes, and guides him step by step through the Rubik cube puzzle. Her directions – 'yes ... no ... no ... yes ... yes ... yes' – are repeated by Marie as she guides Joseph's hand to her stomach, teaching him to approach her body without touching it and accept the mystery that had befallen her.

While Carmen is linked to the restless movement of the sea, waves on the shore and the tide, Marie is linked to the moon and the still surfaces of water, sometimes broken by ripples. The moon and water are ancient symbols of the feminine (as opposed to the sun and the earth) and the moon and the tide coexist in a cyclical time of repetition and return, which breaks radically with the linear time of, for instance, history and its utopian aspiration towards progress. Godard associates the cyclical with the sacred and the feminine. The roundness of the moon is reduplicated by Marie's other iconographical attribute, the netball she takes with her to team practice and that Joseph hits from her hand whenever he challenges her chastity. The ball is round and complete, the circle of the feminine once again, but impenetrable, with no *hole*. In this sense the ball functions like an object of disavowal, not in the classic scenario of fetishism that denies and finds a substitute for the absence of the mother's penis, but, rather, a denial of the wound, the open vagina, the hole.

In one of the most complex and beautifully orchestrated shots in *Passion*, the camera moves between the film crew's space and the space of the set, contrasting the work involved in producing the image with the 'finish' of the image itself. In this case, the image consists of a beautiful young and naked girl, who, at the director's request, floats, spread in the shape of a star, in an Oriental pool. As the camera moves slowly across the surface of the water, it seems opaque with the reflection of tiny points of light, like the reflected stars rippling at the opening of *Je vous salue Marie*. As the camera moves closer to the director, his friend asks him what he is looking at. He answers: 'The wound of the world', and then turns away to try to perfect the lighting on the set. The theme returns in *Prénom: Carmen,* when, after making love to Carmen for the first time, Joseph says, 'Now I understand why prison is called "the Hole".' Marie's virginal body, on the other hand, is perfect. At one point in their stormy, aggressive relationship the angel interrogates Joseph: 'What is the common denominator between the zero and Marie?' and he answers himself 'Marie's body, idiot.' The zero, the magical point of return for a new departure, the perfect circle, the space of the womb, that inside of the female body that is not the hole/ vulva/wound. When the *habilleuse* sews up the hole in Godard's jacket in *Prénom: Carmen*, he seems to suggest an affinity between the function of suture in cinema (the element considered most responsible, during the deconstructive 70s, for the false cohesion of conventional cinema and the subject it produced) and fear of the gaping hole, the wound. The fetishism of the smooth cinematic surface, and the perfect surface of the female body, reassures, but only so far as 'I know but all the same...'.

Marie separates female sexuality, the female genitalia that represent the wound, from reproduction, the space of the womb. The most frequently reproduced still from the film has, in itself, acquired something like fetish status. Joseph's hand reaches towards Marie's stomach, which is stretched into the shape of a curve, and framed, cut off precisely at groin and shoulder height. Joseph accepts the mystery, in relation to and through Marie's body, so that the enigmas of femininity and female sexuality are solved and sanitised in polar opposition to Carmen's sexualised body, which has to remain ultimately uncertain and unknowable.

In *Sauve qui peut* the prostitute, Isabelle, acts sex with her client, Paul, while her interior monologue can be heard on the soundtrack. Constance Penley commented: 'Isabelle, at the moment when she is presented exactly as the inevitable icon of the pornographic love-making scene, the close-up of the moaning woman's face serving as the guarantee of pleasure, is heard thinking about the errands she has to run.'[13] Godard is illustrating a gap between the visible and the invisible, an external artifice that engages belief and an interiority that demands knowledge. This gap in men's knowledge of women's sexual pleasure reinforces the castration anxiety provoked by the female genitals, separated, as they are, from female reproductive organs, lacking any visible 'sign' of pleasure. Gayatri Spivak discusses the problem, for men, presented by female sexuality as unknowable. She quotes Nietzsche about women being 'so artistic' and comments: 'Women impersonate themselves as having an orgasm even at the time of orgasm. Within the historical understanding of women as incapable of orgasm, Nietzsche is arguing that impersonation is woman's only sexual pleasure. At the time of greatest self-possession-cum-ecstasy, the woman is self-possessed enough to organise a self-(re)presentation without an actual presence of sexual pleasure to (re)present.'[14] It is easy to see, as I said before, the phrase 'women are so artistic' in Godard's mind's eye. At what point does art turn into artifice and vice versa? The woman's simulation, like the cinema's, is spectacle and what can only be seen as a surface still conceals its secrets; whatever the spectator wants to see, he may still suspect ...

At the very end of *Je vous salue Marie*, Marie sits alone in a car, her face in close-up. She takes some lipstick from her bag, and applies it to her lips. The camera moves in to fill the frame with the shape of her mouth, which becomes dark and cavernous, surrounded by her bright, newly painted lips. She lights a cigarette. The cycle is complete: the Virgin turns into a whore, the hole returns to break the perfection of the zero. The representation of woman puts on, simultaneously with sexuality, her cosmetic appearance and, simultaneously, is restored to her place among that set of objects defined by an inside/outside, surface/secret topography.

I have tried to show how a common topographical structure facilitates the construction of analogies which, although changing in content, are central to the structure of Godard's ideas. It is, perhaps, as though analogy were enabled by homology. The image of an exterior casing protecting an interior space or contents from view usually carries with it the implication that if the exterior cracks, the interior contents may disgust and possibly harm. From a psychoanalytic point of view, the protective surface is a defence constructed by the ego along the lines of a fetish. It denies the interior but because it knows the exterior *is* an exterior it thus acknowledges the interior. Female beauty, in a sense, fulfils this function by fixing the eye on something that pleases it and prevents the psyche from bringing to mind those aspects of the feminine that are displeasing. So even if Carmen brings death and destruction, the female figure who personifies her brings an image of youthful perfection to the screen. On the screen this image is a projected photograph, a shadow, eviscerated of bodily fluids associated with the maternal body. But the cinema, too, has insides less sightly and fascinating than its screen. It is a machine that can only work with money, and that produces a commodity for circulation in the market, one which must also disguise the labour that created it and its own creaky, unwieldy mechanics while it waits to be ultimately overwhelmed by electronics.

Although Godard's cinema becomes more and more absorbed into the surface, he does not return to a cinema of plenitude and cohesion. He rigorously splits open the components of sound, image and narrative. His films still foreground their process, especially through the soundtrack's relation to the image. But the struggle to articulate social contradiction and the struggle for change are no longer there. And Godard's longstanding political concern with work and the relationship of production to contemporary capitalist society is replaced in *Je vous salue Marie* by concern with creativity, and the relationship of the spiritual to the origins of being. And these mysteries, particularly nature and woman, cannot be penetrated except by God. The myths, clichés and fantasies surrounding both Carmen and Marie constitute, not a mystery, but a rebus for a feminist criticism of Godard. But, as Godard retells these stories he shows not only that they are Janus-faced, but how particularly *telling* they are for our culture. While trying to decode a deep-seated, but interesting, misogyny, I came to think that Godard's cinema knows its own entrapment, and that it is still probing, struggling to give sounds and images to mythologies that haunt our culture although no longer able to challenge them. For feminist curiosity, it is still a goldmine.

Part Three

Dollar-Book Freud

Chapter 7

From Log Cabin to Xanadu: Psychoanalysis and History in *Citizen Kane*

My generation of psychoanalytically orientated film critics has never paid much attention to *Citizen Kane*. Perhaps Pauline Kael's triumphant citation of Orson Welles's own comment on the film's psychoanalytic themes as 'dollar-book Freud' warned everyone off. Even so, a single glance at the film from a Freudian point of view reveals a wealth of psychoanalytic reference and a narrative structure informed by psychoanalytic theory. The question of whether or not the Freud is 'dollar-book' is irrelevant. The relevant questions are to do with how and why Welles used psychoanalytic themes, clichéd or not, to inflect his pseudo-biographical portrait of a major newspaper tycoon. My interest in the portrait is, in the first instance, in its politics, but most particularly in the way that the film includes the psychoanalytic within its politics. There is a fascinating shamelessness in the film's ability to shift between a fictional Oedipal narrative, cannibalised elements taken from the real life of a recognisable public figure, and, by implication, a Freudian reading of American politics at a time of crisis and polarisation. My interest is not whether such an obviously Freudian film is Freudian, but how the psychoanalytic strands mesh with the political strands. And then, how these meshed strands turn into an intellectual polemic that is as original and startling as the film's visual style. The question that then arises, of course, is whether the film's visual style is, in turn, yet another essential element in its political and intellectual perspective.

However, Welles's famous 'dollar-book' remark, taken in context, is more complicated than it seems and can illuminate the way that *Citizen Kane,* from the very first, has had a skewed critical reception. The film's release was completely overshadowed by press interest in its portrait of newspaper tycoon William Randolph Hearst. In order to protect the film from the damage the Hearst papers could easily inflict on it, and to protect the film from such completely one-sided attention, Welles issued a careful press statement. He said that the characteristics that linked Kane to Hearst were simply necessitated by the film's psychological themes and he insisted on moving the discussion away from the biographical (Hearst) into the more general (capitalism and psychoanalysis). He discussed Kane's separation from his mother, his subsequent 'parenting by a bank' and the significance of the sled 'Rosebud' which

> in his subconscious ... stood for his mother's love which Kane never lost. In his waking hours, Kane certainly forgot the sled and the name which was painted on it. Case books of psychiatrists are full of these stories. It was important for me in the picture to tell the audience as effectively as possible what this really meant. ... The best solution was the sled itself. ... It was necessary for my character to be a collector, the kind of man who never throws anything away ... etc.

The assembled press were reluctant to accept this blatantly diversionary tactic. In response to their irritation, Welles said 'I admit that it's "dollar-book" Freud *but that's how I understand the film.*'[1]

I want to take Welles's own analysis, whatever spirit it might have been delivered in, and examine its implications. This involves trying to unravel the intricate interweaving of the quite obviously factual references to Hearst with their, by and large fictional, psychoanalytic underpinnings and, finally, speculate about the wider ideological significance of both. Above all, I am attempting to analyse the film as a conscious, considered experiment in psychoanalysis and politics, and furthermore, as an experiment which could only have been realised in film form.

I want to place the film historically before embarking on the theoretical sections of my analysis and I will then come back to its politics at the end of the chapter. Some dates: work started on the *Citizen Kane* script in February 1940, during the 'phoney war period' that followed the German invasion of Poland in 1939. While scripting continued in the spring and early summer, the German offensive moved across Europe, and *Citizen Kane* went into production on 29 June during the bleakest moments of the war, between the fall of France in May and the Battle of Britain which stretched out, in an apparently last stand against Hitler, from July to September 1940. As Europe appeared to be falling inexorably to fascism, the battle between intervention and isolationism was bitterly engaged in America. And when *Citizen Kane* opened in New York, in May 1941, Pearl Harbor was still six months away. Not only was the question of the war in Europe the burning public issue of the time, but it was of passionate personal importance to Orson Welles. He was deeply committed to Roosevelt, the New Deal and the struggle against fascism, but he was also deeply influenced by European culture. Hearst, on the other hand, had always been a major exponent of isolationism, particularly where Europe was concerned. He had broken with the Democrats over Wilson's involvement of the United States in the First World War and with the Republicans over, among other things, Hoover's support for the League of Nations. These historical and political factors are hardly visible explicitly in *Citizen*

Kane. However, their traces can be discerned in the film's imagery and in its metaphoric allusions.

Psychoanalysis and History: the Inscription of a Mode of Spectatorship

My analysis of the mode of spectatorship in *Citizen Kane* emerges out of my work with psychoanalytically influenced feminist film theory, which has developed a criticism of decipherment directed first and foremost at the meanings invested in images of women. *Citizen Kane* conspicuously lacks a female figure encapsulating spectacle and enigma. Whereas in *The Lady from Shanghai,* for instance, spectacle and enigma are concentrated on the *femme fatale* played by Rita Hayworth, in *Citizen Kane* Welles's own towering presence and performance leave little space for sexualised voyeurism. Instead, the film weaves together an enigma constructed across its use of cinema and its ability to carry displacements and condensations of meaning from image to image, from one frame to another, and link themes that are widely separated in the narration. Liberated from its erotic obsession with the female form, cinematic 'voyeurism' is itself displaced and replaced by a different currency of exchange between screen and spectator.

Citizen Kane makes a particular call on the spectator's powers of 'reading' the image, which has a political significance that goes beyond avoiding conventional voyeurism and beyond Bazin's deep-focus theories. The psychoanalytic content of the film overflows onto its use of cinematic language. Miriam Hansen has compared the language of film with the hieroglyph and, then, the language of the unconscious: 'The model of hieroglyphic writing seems useful [for film] because of its emphasis on the irreducibly composite character of the sign (consisting of pictographic, ideogrammatic and phonetic elements) and its constitutive plurality of meanings.' She draws attention to the connection made by Freud between hieroglyphic writing and the figurative script of dreams: 'Both these textual phenomena in their way resist immediate perception and understanding, requiring instead an activity of reading and interpretation.'[2]

While 'Rosebud' signifies 'the Kane mystery' within the story, Welles presents the spectator with a series of visual clues which transform the literal mystery into images on the screen. The enigmatic text that then gradually materialises appeals to an active, curious, spectator who takes pleasure in identifying, deciphering and interpreting signs. The music also plays its part. Bernard Herrmann wrote about the necessity for musical leitmotifs in *Citizen Kane*:

> There are two main motifs. One – a simple four note figure in brass – is that of Kane's power. It is given out in the first two bars of the film. The second motif is that of Rosebud. Heard as a solo on the vibraphone, it first appears during the death scene at the very beginning of the picture. It is heard again and again throughout the film under various guises,

and, if followed closely, is a clue to the ultimate identity of Rosebud itself.[3]

The Kane mystery is neatly displaced onto 'Rosebud', which then becomes the focus of the journalist/investigator's quest. But the enigma is never resolved within the fictional world on the screen, through either the protagonist's investigation or the witnesses' testimony. Welles detaches the spectator's understanding from that of the characters and upsets our normal assumption that they, or a hero, or an investigator, will control a story's resolution. The film avoids the conventions of the hermetically sealed narrative usually associated with the Hollywood cinema. It experiments with another kind of narrational strategy, which breaks down the gap between the screen and the spectator, moving out of the diegetically contained third-person and into the second-person mode of address.

By its very use of inconsistency and contradiction, the film warns the audience against any reliance on the protagonists as credible sources of truth, and, in the last resort, it deflects understanding away from character and away from a dramatic interplay between people and their destinies. In *Citizen Kane* the audience can come to their own conclusions, but only if they break through the barrier of character as the source of meaning, and start to interpret clues and symptoms on the screen as might a detective or a psychoanalyst. Once the characters fall into place as just one element in an intricately patterned web, the film's own internal consistency and logic, independent of character, come clearly into focus. The clues then spread through the story on the screen, hidden in all the varied elements that make up a film: camera movements, objects, gestures, events, repetitions, *mise en scène*. And, among these elements, the characters are only one more link in the chain, another piece in the jigsaw puzzle. So *Citizen Kane* transforms the usual human-dominated hierarchy in story telling. The spectator is left to 'figure out' what is going on (beyond, in Lucy's famous words to Linus, 'Rosebud's his sled') and pick up hints at messages that are quite clearly not delivered by Western Union.

The film's opening sequence sets up the relationship between camera and spectator, and invokes the spectator's investigative gaze through a collaboration with the investigation of the seeing camera rather than the unseeing character. When the title *Citizen Kane* fades from the screen and the film's initial image takes its place, the audience is swept into the story with an interdiction and a camera movement. A sign saying 'No Trespassing' can be easily seen through the murky lighting, and a wire fence fills the screen barring the way forward. This sign, though rationalised through its place on the gate of the Xanadu estate, directly addresses the audience. Everyone knows that prohibited space becomes immediately fascinating and that nothing arouses curiosity more than to be excluded from a secret. In immediate response, hardly even pausing on the first image, the camera cranes up and over the top of the fence moving forward through a series of lap dissolves and grounds of neglected grandeur, towards a fairy-tale castle on the top of a hill. There is no grounding of the camera here. It is freed from an establishing character's presence, literally approaching the gate, on the ground. The space is simply that of the screen and the frame, and the gravity-defying movement of the camera.

The camera's movement functions both literally and figuratively. First of all, it establishes a place and a mystery but it also gives a literal rendering of the opening of a narrative space. The space of the story is depicted as an enclosed place from which the audience is excluded and the camera's effortless passage from outside to inside acts as a magic eye, and it opens a way into the storyteller's world and imagination. The end of the film reverses the camera movement, so the space that opened up the story is symmetrically closed, returning the audience back to the original position, outside the wire fence, ultimately back into the auditorium, back to square one, the same as they were, but different for having undergone the experience of the previous ninety minutes.

There is an echo, in this narrating camera, of the grand experiment that Welles had planned for his first Hollywood project, the adaptation of *Heart of Darkness*. This project grew out of the Mercury Theater's radio series *First Person Singular* in which novels built around a narrating 'I' were adapted for dramatic performance combined with the storyteller's 'voice over'. *Heart of Darkness* had been one of these. To transform the first-person narration into the new medium, cinema, Welles wanted to shoot the film with the camera as the eye of the 'I', using a subjective camera throughout, of the kind later used by Robert Montgomery in *The Lady in the Lake*. The difficulties involved in shooting the film in this way greatly inflated the *Heart of Darkness* budget and the project was shelved. The film would have been introduced by a prologue in which Welles himself would give an illustrated lecture on subjective camera and explain directly to the audience that the camera's point of view was also theirs. Robert Carringer, in his book *The Making of Citizen Kane,* says:

> To Welles's explanatory narration, the camera would adopt the points of view, successively, of a bird in a cage, a condemned man about to be electrocuted, and a golfer driving a ball. Then it would take up Welles's point of view from the screen, looking into a movie audience made up entirely of motion picture cameras. In the final shot, an eye would appear on the left side of a blank screen, then the equals sign, then the pronoun I. The eye would wink, and a dissolve would lead to the opening shot of the film.[4]

The opening of *Citizen Kane* offers an infinitely more sophisticated version of subjective camera. As the camera's look is not associated with a character, a literal first-person participant in the story, it takes on, rather, the function of narrator outside the world of the story. While it still assimilates and represents the audience's eye as they look at the screen, it also sets up an invocation to decipher. Later in the film, the shadowy presence of Thompson, the investigating journalist, acts as a surrogate for the audience's curiosity, carrying the narrative forward and precipitating the film's flashbacks to the past. But he never has the transcendent look that is the sign of a character's assimilation to a subjective camera.

As the overt solution to the 'Rosebud' enigma only appears in the film's closing seconds, many important signs and clues set up earlier in the film will, more likely than not, have gone by unnoticed on a first viewing. *Citizen Kane* has, built into its structure, the need to think back and reflect on what has taken place in the main body of the film as soon as it finishes. And when the camera tracks into the furnace and supplies the 'missing piece of the jigsaw puzzle', it throws everything that has led up to that moment into a new relief. Anyone whose curiosity has been truly engaged by the film must want to see it again. The next and subsequent viewings are bound to be experienced quite differently from the first. There is, in a sense, a didactic metaphor at play here. The film's 'active spectator' is forced to look back at and re-examine events as though the film were suggesting that history itself should be constantly subjected to re-examination and re-reading. Not only should history never be accepted at face, or story, value, but also, from a political perspective, it should be detached from personality and point of view and rediscovered, as it were, in its materiality and through the decoding of its symptoms. And this inscribed return to the past to decode the film as history overlaps with the question of the unconscious and its enigmas.

The sled, for instance, functions as lost object and as screen memory. Buried in the snow, it is both hidden and preserved, perfectly in keeping with Freud's picture of memory within the unconscious. It is displaced, within Kane's psyche and the spectator's interpretation, onto the little glass paperweight which contains a log cabin and snow scene, and which activates the memory of his first loss at the moment of his last. The paperweight makes three appearances, one at the very beginning of the film, Kane's death scene; one at the end, when Susan leaves him; and one in the middle when Kane and Susan meet for the first time. As the 'snowstorm' belongs to Susan, Kane is able to use it as a signifier of the two losses, condensed together. It first appears in the chronology of Kane's story when she does, that is in the middle of the film, during Leland's turning-point narration. Kane meets Susan in the street, at a crossroad, and she stops, in its tracks, Kane's journey back into his past. He explains to her: 'You see, my mother died, a long time ago. Well, her things were put in storage out West. There wasn't any other place to put them. I thought I'd send for them now. Tonight I was going to take a look at them. A sort of sentimental journey.'[5]

This scene includes the second of the only two times in the film that Kane mentions his mother. And this moment of nostalgia for his past also reintroduces the theme of motherly love and ambition:

> *Susan*: I wanted to be a singer. That is, I didn't. My mother did. ...
> It's just – well you know what mothers are like.
> *Kane*: Yes. You got a piano?⁶

(Susan herself comments perceptively at the end of her narration: 'Perhaps I should never have sung for Charlie that first evening.') The glass paperweight is visible on Susan's dressing table, to the left-hand side of her reflection in the mirror. No one draws attention to it, nor does the camera pay it any special attention, but there it sits, like a narrative time bomb awaiting its moment, for the observant spectator to pick up and take note.

These are just some instances of the way in which the film links motifs through objects. The 'semiology' of the objects offers the spectator an aesthetic opportunity to return to, and reread, the text and puzzle out its configurations retrospectively. The end returns you to the beginning; there is both a formal symmetry (the camera's exit through the fence) and the unanswered questions that are left hanging in the smoke rising from Xanadu's chimney.

Psychoanalysis and History: Narrative Structure

The personalised nature of the flashbacks, and their general adherence to chronology, overshadow and disguise the film's underlying dramatic structure which divides into two parts cutting across the chronological biography and the narrations of the different witnesses with a broad, dominating binary opposition. Kane's rise and decline separate the two parts narratively, but his relation to male and female worlds separate the two parts thematically. The first two flashbacks, narrated by Thatcher and Bernstein, tell of Kane's dramatic rise to triumphant success; the last two, Susan's and Raymond's, tell the story of his disgrace and withdrawal. The first two are set in the competitive, public, all-male world of newspaper reporting; Susan's and Raymond's are set in the spectacular, cultural and feminised world of the opera and Xanadu. The turning point comes in Leland's narration which deals with Kane's love life and political life and the increasingly inextricable relationship between the two. The turning-point effect is accentuated by the fact that the world of politics is sandwiched in between Kane's meeting with Susan and their marriage.

Kane's defeat in his campaign for Governor marks the apex of the rise and fall structure and switches the movement of the story. Kane invests all his financial and emotional resources into Susan's career in opera, so that, in terms of the film's symmetry, the opera production, *Salammbô*, balances that of the newspaper, *The Inquirer*. While *The Inquirer*'s triumph led to Kane's first marriage and to politics, *Salammbô*'s collapse leads to the claustrophobic grandeur of Xanadu. Kane's massive enterprise is concentrated on buying and importing art treasures to construct an appropriate environment for his retreat into an isolated domesticity with Susan.

The scene of Kane's childhood separation from his parents could be described as the film's 'primal scene'. It enacts, in dramatic form, the two psychoanalytic motifs that determine the later development of the plot and divide it into its two parts: the child's closeness to his mother, his instinctive aggression against his surrogate father. The first, male-dominated, section of the film tells the story of the radical, Oedipal Kane continuing to battle against his surrogate father. The second, Susan-dominated, section of the film shows him isolated from public life and fetishistically amassing things, attempting to fill the void of his first loss, his separation from his mother.

The Thatcher flashback covers, in three scenes, the whole span of Kane's career, from the first meeting in the snow, to Thatcher's rage at Kane's campaigns against capitalist corruption, to the crash and Kane's bankruptcy. The last lines in the sequence are:

> *Thatcher*: What would you like to have been?
> *Kane*: Everything you hate.[7]

When Kane, as an old man, gives his uncompromising answer to Thatcher's question ('Everything you hate') this one line suddenly illuminates the Oedipal element in his political behaviour. This last line of the Thatcher episode links back not only to Kane's violent reaction against him at their first meeting but also to the *Inquirer*'s campaigns against everything he stands for. To fight against Thatcher, the banker and old-fashioned capitalist, Kane espouses the cause of those who suffer at the hands of privilege, using as his weapon a new form of capitalist enterprise, that is the mass circulation newspapers known in the United States as the 'yellow press'. But, in implying that this radical stand has an unconscious Oedipal origin, the film throws doubt on the altruism of Kane's politics and implies a personal agenda concealed behind the overtly political principles.

When Kane first attacks Thatcher, he uses the sled as a weapon; and his aggression is directed at the adult male who is threatening to, and who will, separate him from his mother.

> *Mother*: Mr Thatcher is going to take you on a trip with him tonight. You'll be leaving on number ten.
> *Father*: That's the train with all the lights on it.
> *Charles*: You goin' Mom?
> *Thatcher*: Oh no. Your mother won't be going right away, Charles, but she'll ...
> *Charles*: Where'm I going?[8]

The scene is credible only from a psychoanalytic point of view. The characters' motivations and attitudes are not rational or explicable. Only the threatening nature of the doubled fathers, and their incompatible violences, gives the scene cohesion. This scene splits the image of the father into two opposed aspects, but both pose a threat to the child. While the biological father threatens the son with physical violence, the surrogate father threatens him with separation from his mother. The scene ends with the mother and son clinging to each other, the mother protecting her child against his father's violence, the child holding onto her love and staring resentfully off screen at his substitute father who proposes to introduce him to a new cultural and symbolic order. The child is suspended between two psychological phases, on the threshold between a pre-Oedipal love for his mother and rivalry with his father and the post-Oedipal world in which he should take his place within society, accepting separation from his mother and acknowledging the authority of his father. The scene is played with the irrationality and condensation of the unconscious, the characters act out their psychic roles without regard for verisimilitude, and the snow-covered landscape with its remote log cabin is an appropriate setting for this psychic moment. Kane never crosses the threshold between the pre- and post-Oedipal, remaining frozen at the point of separation from his mother and, from then on, directing his Oedipal aggression at his surrogate father. The child, from then on, is in conflict with the Symbolic order.

The Symbolic father, in the terms of Lacanian psychoanalytic theory, represents the demands of culture and society and necessarily disrupts the mother and child's unity. A child's closeness to its mother creates a sphere of physical and emotional completeness, simultaneously an Eden and a strangulation, a place of safety to escape from, and, once escaped, a place of longing that cannot be regained. There is a before and an after. The sphere of maternal plenitude gradually gives way to social and cultural aspirations represented by the father's social and cultural significance. This process may never, as in the case of Charles Foster Kane, be satisfactorily achieved. If Mr Kane represents a pre-Oedipal father, Thatcher personifies the father who should teach the child to understand symbolic systems on which social relations rest and which replace the physical, unmediated bond between mother and child. Both money and the law are products of a social order based on abstract principles and symbolisation. Money transcends the physicality of a literal exchange of objects and substitutes an abstract system of value. The law transcends the literal and physical relations between people and places them within a timeless system of morality. The scene inside the log cabin polarises Kane's split father figures on each side of these symbolic systems. One represents poverty, failure and ignorance, the other represents wealth, success and education. When Mrs Kane signs her son away to the world of culture and social advancement, with a legal agreement and in return for money, she seems to acknowledge the inevitability of a transition that only the mother, she seems to imply, can ever understand and, then, only mourn. The child's mourning returns, in the manner of the repressed, through symptoms which perpetuate an original trauma. He will become fixated on *things* and the accumulation of objects, rejecting the abstractions of capital, exchange and the circulation of money.

The real father, who is left behind in the 'before' that the log cabin stands for, complains: 'I don't hold with signing away my boy to any bank as guardeen just because we're a little uneducated.'⁹ His speech and dress are rough, and diametrically opposed to Thatcher's, whose clipped legalistic language and dark suit come from a world without room for emotion. That world is about Order, in the sense of both regulation and hierarchy, without which money cannot become capitalism. Mrs Kane's correctly grammatical speech and her dark dress are iconographically closer to Thatcher than to her husband. She understands this abstract cultural necessity while her husband ('I want you to stop all this nonsense, Jim') in his naiveté does not. The scene in the log cabin places Thatcher and Mrs Kane together on the right-hand side of the frame, sitting at the table with the documents, while Mr Kane hovers anxiously, and unstably, across the left side. Charlie, in this famous scene of deep-focus photography, is playing outside, seen through the window, between the divide. Within the Oedipal conflict, it is the mother's role to give up her child. To hold on to him would be to keep him in the netherworld of infancy, cultural deprivation, impotence, and prevent his departure on the journey towards greatness, towards the White House, as it were. In *Citizen Kane*, the separation is too abrupt and painful, and the transition is never resolved.

The last shot of the separation scene holds for a long time on the abandoned sled now covered by the snow and a train's whistle sounds in the distance. As I said earlier, in Freud's theory of the unconscious, a memory that is apparently forgotten is also preserved, to return, if called on, at a later date. The snow, with its connotations of both burying and freezing, perfectly evokes this metaphor. The memory can be recovered when something happens to make the mind delve down into those depths of time and the unconscious, just as the memory of 'Rosebud' is revived for Kane by the little glass snowstorm and log cabin he finds when Susan leaves him. The *mise en scène* is no more rational than the characters' actions. The remote snow-covered countryside and the little log cabin create a phantasmatic landscape which introduces American myth into the psychoanalytic metaphor, just as the action combines melodramatic gesture with the rudimentary elements of Oedipal drama.

When the serial father figures who stood in his way, Thatcher, Carter and the *Chronicle* (the lawyer/banker, non-populist/liberal journalist, the yellow press magnate), have been defeated by the Kane *Inquirer*, there is a party/celebration that also marks Kane's passage from youth to maturity. At this point, towards the middle of the story, a triumphant happy end seems to be a foregone conclusion. Happy endings are, in popular culture, immediately preceded by marriage, as the rite of passage that should mark a transition from youthful irresponsibility to patriarchal authority. The party (almost like a stag party, especially as the original script included a brothel scene that was cut at the request of the Hays office) leads immediately to Kane's engagement, and when he then appears with Emily Monroe Norton, Bernstein's narration ends on a triumphant note. He understands that Kane's marriage opens the way for his next step up the ladder towards the Presidency:

Miss Townsend (awestruck): She's the niece of the President of the
United States!
Bernstein: President's niece, huh! Before he's through she'll be a
President's wife! [10]

Kane's campaign as Independent candidate for the Governor of the State
of New York is a stepping stone on the way to the White House (as is made
clear in the segment of *The March of Time*: 'The White House seemingly
the next easy step'). In American mythology, the iconography generated
by the White House complements the iconography of Kane's childhood. In
his trajectory from the poverty and obscurity of a remote Colarado log
cabin to fabulous wealth and one step from the White House, Kane encapsulates a populist cliché of the American political dream. Like a version of
the old, Whittingtonesque, folk-tale of class mobility, 'from a log cabin to
the White House' is a story-cum-icon of American mythology. The United
States, as the land of equality and opportunity, promised to put the old
folk-tale within reach for all the European rural and urban poor who
crossed the Atlantic. William M. Thayer called his biography of President
James Garfield *From Log Cabin to White House*[11] to emphasise the parallels between his trajectory and that of President Lincoln, both born to poor
pioneer families 'in the wilderness', both called to the highest office in the
United States. Freud suggested, in his short article about creative writing
and the day-dream,[12] that the story of a young man's journey to seek his
fortune could be the basic model for the day-dream; but he also points out
that it integrates an erotic fantasy with an ambitious fantasy. The young
man achieves power and/or riches through marriage to the daughter of a
an important man who will pass on his position to a worthy son-in-law.
Kane's first marriage illustrates the close ties between the love or erotic
element of this day-dream and the theme of power through marriage and
inheritance through the wife. His marriage to Emily Monroe Norton, the
President's niece, puts him, as it were, in line to succeed the President, just
as, in Freud's bourgeois version, a father-in-law leaves a business to his
daughter's husband or, in the folk-tale version, the hero is rewarded for
his heroism with the princess's hand in marriage and inherits her father's
kingdom.

But Kane himself or, perhaps more precisely, Kane and his unconscious
sabotage the 'happy end'. So, ruined by the success of his Oedipal struggle
with his surrogate fathers, his future narrative path leads, not from a log
cabin to the White House, but from a log cabin to Xanadu. As President of
the United States he would have become the ultimate Father, personifying,
but also subordinate to, the Symbolic order and the Law. Kane's psyche
retreats into a new scenario with Susan, and fetishism replaces Oedipal
struggle. And although Kane tries, for a while, with an increasingly rhetorical and empty sense of desperation, to turn Gettys into a father/mon-
ster, he lapses back into the personal, unable to come to terms with the
symbolic implications of political, and thus, patriarchal power. The

Inquirer and its campaigns fall into the background when Kane's personal struggle against Thatcher becomes subsumed into a circulation battle against the *Chronicle* which, in turn, is subsumed into political ambition. In the sixteen years covered by the breakfast-table montage, the fairy-tale promises of Bernstein's narration fade away. The film and Kane's life then both reach a crossroads. By the time he starts on his political campaign, Kane's radical, Oedipal, populist politics are a thing of the past and slogans about the 'cause of reform' against Tammany Hall look increasingly like an investment in dictatorial personal and non-symbolic power. Both Leland, explicitly, and Gettys, implicitly, accuse him of not being able to distinguish between the personal and the political.

It is during the 'stag' party that Kane's collecting mania is first mentioned. Hitherto, the Oedipal struggle that started when he attacked Thatcher with the sled had kept Kane in touch with that traumatic moment. His new symptoms, which in the future will take on manic proportions, appear chronologically before his relationship with Susan and before his self-exile, out of the male world of power and politics into the female world of fantasy and fetishism. This massive accumulation of 'things' relates back, metonymically, to the original lost object, the sled, and the traumatic loss of his mother that the sled stands in for. Bernstein mentions, for the first time, Kane's new habit of collecting statues:

> *Bernstein*: Say, Mr. Kane, so long as you're promising there's a lot of statues in Europe you ain't bought yet.
> *Kane*: You can't blame me Mr. Bernstein. They've been making statues for two thousand years and I've only been buying for five.[13]

There is an Oedipal as well as a fetishistic element here. Kane's collecting obsession fits in with his rebellion against the frugal principles of careful investment and return that Thatcher stands for. The third, and last, scene between Kane and Thatcher (which is in the film and not in the original script) includes this dialogue:

> *Thatcher*: Yes, but your methods. You know, Charles, you never made a single investment. You always used money to ...
> *Kane*: To buy things. To buy things. My mother should have chosen a less reliable banker.[14]

The 'Protestant ethic' of productive capitalism stands in diametrical opposition to the wasteful consumption of capital through the accumulation of useless things. Kane is not interested in productive capital ('Sorry, but I'm not interested in goldmines, oil wells, shipping, or real estate') and the abstract, symbolic, concepts of money and exchange. He cashes in his capital and turns it into concrete objects. In the second part of the film, and especially around the construction of Xanadu, Kane takes spending to obsessive levels, unable even to unpack the vast amount of stuff he accumulates. At the same time, evidenced in the last scene at Xanadu, he has never thrown any object away. The 'things' of a lifetime lie strewn about, higgledy-piggledy, and the camera tracks across them, allowing the audience to recognise particular objects that have figured in earlier scenes, to find the original object, the sled 'Rosebud'. This massive accumulation of 'things' is set in the context of a lifetime that has attempted to freeze and preserve a traumatic moment of loss. Held in the timelessness of the unconscious, the things relate to each other metonymically, reaching back, longingly and through displacement, towards the original lost object, which screens the memory of loss itself. Into the midst of these fetishised objects, the film introduces a personification of fetishism into its storyline.

The film does not construct the spectator's look at Susan, the hero's object of erotic desire, into voyeuristic complicity. When Susan's erotic qualities and performing abilities enter the scene, the audience is not involved with or into Kane's gaze. Susan produces a distanciation effect. Kane's estimation of his love object is wildly at odds with reality. From the first moment that Susan sings at the parlour piano, the audience finds listening to her painful. But for Kane her voice is the source of true fascination. As he fetishises Susan's inadequate voice into a precious and valued object, he blinds himself to what he knows, and invests all his emotional and financial resources in a deluded belief. He transforms Susan into a highly stylised and produced object. For the opera, her small inadequate singing voice is dressed up and embellished in an elaborate costume and crowned with two enormous blonde plaits and a top-heavy head-dress. Her legs move across the stage, incongruously vulnerable and detached from her body. Confusion swirls around Susan, the presentation of the opera itself, and the culture it attempts to mimic.

At the same time, the review Kane finishes for Leland indicates that, in some way, he knows. Fetishism, according to Freud's theory, bears witness to the human psyche's ability to maintain knowledge and belief simultaneously. The mother's body is traumatically misperceived as castrated, knowledge of sexual difference itself is disavowed, and the missing 'object' can be represented and preserved by a substitute idealised object. However, psychoanalytic theorists have since argued that fetishism is a structure of which the castration model need only be one example. Fetishistic disavowal and substitution can represent the trace of other kinds of traumatic loss. In the Kane 'case study' the child's separation from his mother is traumatic and need not be literally or mechanically tied to castration anxiety. However, the substitution of an object, the sled, for the mother and subsequent objects, Kane's 'things' and, finally, Susan, all bear witness to the structures of disavowal, substitution and displacement.

Fetishism holds time in check. It is fixated on a thing that artificially resists the changes that knowledge brings with it. The object links back to the original scene and substitutes for it. Freud argues that the fetish functions as a screen memory. The fetish interjects an object between memory and the actual traumatic moment. At the same time, the object also marks the place of the lost memory it masks. Freud describes a screen memory as a witness, simultaneously precious and insignificant, where something that must never be lost may be hidden and preserved.[15] This image evokes the little sled (simultaneously precious and insignificant) buried in the snow (hidden and preserved).

The fact that Kane's collecting is directed, exclusively, towards European things brings a wider cultural and historical metaphor into the scene. The statues are European in origin and imported into Kane's collection. They prefigure the opera, and its European origin, by means of which Susan is transformed into a living item, fetishised fantasy. Everything is then concentrated in Xanadu itself. And the scenario of the opera and the scenario of Xanadu, while being constructed out of culture and antiquity, end up as pastiches. While having a veneer of European antiquity and culture, they are empty, shell-like constructions that Kane never even attempts to understand. Kane retreats into a pseudo-Gothic castle and its space sets up a grotesque caricature of the little log cabin that was his first home. In the opening sequence of the film the castle is located within the uncanny and its grounds are filled with objects as incompatible as gondolas and spider monkeys. Xanadu bears witness to the archaic, Old World space of the mother/Europe but also introduces a heterogeneity of historical reference that prefigures post-modern citation.

Psychoanalysis and History: the Political Context

It is here that the figure of William Randolph Hearst arises with full force as the main object of Orson Welles's attack. The question of Hearst, of course, added a further level of enigmatic encrustation to the film. And Hearst himself contributed the first dramatic public chapter of *Citizen Kane*'s extra-cinematic history in the vendetta waged by the Hearst press against the film just before and after its release. *Time* described the first, private and specially commanded, screening of the film in the following way:

> Lolly Parsons nearly fell out of her chair. On the preview screen before her, Orson Welles, the bearded boy, was playing Citizen Kane, a corrupt newspaper magnate, in a manner that reminded columnist Parsons irresistibly of her boss William Randolph Hearst. ... With her she had brought her chauffeur and two lawyers. ... She rose like a geyser. As the lights went on Miss Parsons and lawyers steamed out. Only the chauffeur had enjoyed the film. ... The result was that no more mention of RKO pictures appeared in Hearst papers.[16]

Hearst not only attempted, indirectly, to sabotage the release of the film, but attacked Orson Welles politically. Coincidentally with the release of *Citizen Kane*, Welles's radio programme, 'His Honour the Mayor', in

CBS's *Free Company* series, was reported in the Hearst press to have been condemned by the American Legion as 'an appeal for the right of all subversive fifth-column groups to hold anti-American meetings in the public hall of an American city'. And: 'The name itself, *Free Company*, sounds suspiciously Communistic.' Frank Brady, in his book *Citizen Welles*, describes the subsequent surveillance:

> Welles never knew that a number of Hearst sympathisers began reporting Orson's activities to the FBI as potentially dangerous to the national interest. ... In a report by a special FBI agent to J. Edgar Hoover it was noted: 'It should be pointed out that this office has never been able to establish that Welles is an actual member of the Communist Party; however, an examination of Welles's activities and his membership in various organisations reflects that he has consistently followed the Communist party line and has been active in numerous "front" organisations.'[17]

Welles fought back with reiterated denials that Hearst was the model for Kane, attacking back politically in response to political attacks, through psychoanalytic explanation in response to economic sabotage, later through anecdote and humour. One of the last denials appeared, strangely, in his introduction to Marion Davies's autobiography published in 1975:

> Xanadu was a lonely fortress and Susan was quite right to escape from it. The mistress [Marion Davies] was never one of Hearst's possessions ... she was the precious treasure of his heart for more than thirty years until the last breath of life. Theirs was truly a love story. Love is not the subject of *Citizen Kane* ... if San Simeon had not existed it would have been necessary for the authors to invent it.[18]

In the face of the Hearst campaigns, and their undoubted power to damage Welles professionally, and to damage him through political innuendo, there is no doubt that he had to deny the importance of the Hearst model for Kane 'after the event'. Debate, however, continued over the origin of the Hearst model in the context of rival claims over the authorship of *Citizen Kane*. John Houseman describes the scriptwriter Herman Mankiewicz's interest:

> Total disagreement persists as to where the Hearst idea originated. The fact is that, as a former newspaper man and an avid reader of contemporary history, Mank had long been fascinated by the American phenomenon of William Randolph Hearst. Unlike his friends on the left, to whom Hearst was now an archenemy, fascist isolationist and a red baiter, Mankiewicz remembered the years when Hearst had been regarded as the working man's friend and a political progressive. He had observed him later as a member of the film colony – grandiose, aging

and vulnerable in the immensity of his reconstructed palace at San Simeon.[19]

In the years before Welles went to Hollywood, Hearst's vast empire was barely staving off financial collapse. In 1937 his financial affairs were removed from his direct control and put in the hands of a 'Conservation Committee', and he was forced to auction off some of his art collection. In March 1939 his financial difficulties were the subject of a *Time* magazine cover story, and around the same time Aldous Huxley's Hearst novel, *After Many a Summer,* was published. In *Citizen Welles,* Frank Brady describes a dinner, at which Welles was present, to celebrate the publication of the book where the model for the portrait and the consequent impossibility of turning it into a film were discussed. Hearst was, therefore, in the news in the months before the conception of *Citizen Kane.* It was when 'the miraculous contract had three and a half months to run and there was no film in sight' (in John Houseman's words) that the Hearst idea was floated somewhere between Welles and Mankiewicz. But when Welles, who was definitely on the Left, decided, in 1940, to use Hearst as the basis of his first film, he was interested in more than the story of a grand old man of capitalism who was running out of time and money.

Welles had come of age and risen to be an outstanding figure in American theatre at a time when extraordinary opportunities had been created by the New Deal's cultural policy orchestrated through the Works Progress Administration. Orson Welles first attracted widespread attention with his production of *Macbeth* for the Negro Theater Project in Harlem, of which John Houseman was, at that time, a director. Welles and Houseman were later commissioned by the Federal Theater to run their own company which they named after its WPA number, Project #891. Welles, returning to the United States from Europe in 1934, at the age of nineteen, was formed intellectually, politically and professionally by the Popular Front and the theatre of the New Deal. Welles and Houseman founded their own, independent, Mercury Theater and published their manifesto in the Communist Party newspaper *The Daily Worker.* Welles's growing reputation as an actor and director was established at a new level by his Mercury productions. Their success brought offers from CBS radio, for which Welles was already working, and the formation of the Mercury Theater of the Air. One of their regular Sunday evening radio adaptations, broadcast for Hallowe'en 1938, *War of the Worlds,* put Welles on the front pages of newspapers across the United States, and led George Schaeffer of RKO to invite him and the Mercury company to Hollywood. In spite of his outstanding qualities as an actor and director, it is always possible that his career would not have taken off in such meteoric style if it had not been for the unprecedented and never-to-be repeated opportunities offered by the WPA. And this would add a personal element to Welles's longlasting political commitment to Roosevelt which the President publicly acknowledged. In 1944 Roosevelt chose Welles to run a radio campaign to sell war bonds and Welles devoted himself, that year, to campaigning for the President's re-election. He was invited to the White House for the re-election celebration. In 1944 Roosevelt also encouraged Welles to stand as candidate for the Senate in California.

During the 30s, Hearst had moved from reluctant support for Roosevelt as the Democratic candidate in 1932 (only at the last moment and under enormous pressure when it became clear that his candidate, John Garner, had no hope of victory) to outright denunciation. Unlike the fictional Kane, Hearst was far from in retreat from politics during the New Deal period. His hostility to Roosevelt escalated critically around new tax legislation on the super-rich in 1935 and union protection legislation which led to conflicts with his own editorial staff during the mid-30s, after they organised through the American Newspapers' Guild. Hearst's increasingly vituperative move to the Right was also a symptom of a generalised political polarisation during this period, instanced not only by Upton Sinclair's candidacy for the Governorship of California but by the longshoremen's strike in 1934. Hearst contributed to the defeat of both by means of behind-the-scenes politics as well as newspaper pressure. But polarised American politics was also marked by international association, both on the Left and the Right. Towards the end of 1934 the *San Francisco Examiner* published, without editorial comment or disclaimer, three articles by Goebbels. And the Hearst papers' red-baiting campaigns, proto-typical of anti-communist McCarthyism of the postwar period, took off throughout the same year. In 1936 his antagonism to Roosevelt took Hearst back into the Republican camp. He contributed $30,000 to the Republican campaign and said: 'The race will not be close at all, Landon [the Republican candidate] will be overwhelmingly elected and I'll stake my reputation as a prophet on it.'[20]

The Hearst papers were instructed to refer to the New Deal as the 'Raw Deal'. William Stott describes how the newspapers reached a low ebb of credibility:

> Throughout the early thirties the press managed to ignore or belittle evidence of a depression. In the 1936 Presidential campaign, more than 80 per cent of the press opposed Roosevelt, and he won by the highest percentage ever. During the campaign and for years after, many newspapers, including major syndicates, went beyond all legitimate bounds in an effort to disparage the President and the New Deal. And, as Roosevelt warned the editors, the press lost by it. Public opinion polls in the late thirties suggested that 30 million Americans, nearly one American in three, doubted the honesty of the American press.[21]

Hearst's deep involvement with public and political affairs during the 30s, and his active support for the Right, presents a problem for any attempt to analyse *Citizen Kane* systematically in terms of his actual biography. Kane retires from politics after his personal disgrace and political defeat, and the film thus avoids almost any reference to the contemporary political scene and its immediate antecedents. However, this apparent lapse has important implications. It allows the Hearst model to be moulded into a narrative that has its own self-sufficiency, its own symmetries and wider metaphorical significance. The split in the narrative between male and female spheres achieves sharp relief as an aesthetic structure in its own right; Kane retreats from public life into a private world of his own making. Furthermore, the psychoanalytic and metaphoric aspects of the film's themes gather a strength that moves beyond the individual into wider mythological issues. The Hearst model is, thus, of importance for *Citizen Kane* not only in its accuracy but in its deviations. In its accuracy it comments on a major and recognisable political figure of the far Right from the political perspective of the liberal Left. Mankiewicz's source material was derived so precisely from the hostile biography *Imperial Hearst* that its author, Ferdinand Lundburg, brought a suit for plagiarism against *Citizen Kane* in 1948. The accuracies are obvious. They include the silvermine fortune, concentration on political power through a popular press which exploited jingoism, sex and violence, the Hearst papers' part in the Spanish–American war, Hearst's aspiration to the Presidency and tangles with Tammany (especially Al Smith whose trace appears in Gettys), his collecting mania and his construction of San Simeon, his poaching of his arch-rival Pulitzer's staff from *The World,* his relationship with Marion Davies. The deviations are concentrated particularly at the beginning and end of *Citizen Kane*: that is, in Kane's humble birth in a log cabin, his separation from his mother and his relation with, and separation from, Susan Alexander. There was no precedent in the Hearst/Davies model for Susan's humiliating failure as an opera singer and attempted suicide, nor for the breakdown of their relationship. Hearst and Davies lived happily together, unmarried, until his death in 1951. These deviational elements are the basis for a psychoanalytic reading of the film.

The insertion of a psychoanalytic explanation for the famous Hearstian puzzle makes *Citizen Kane* seem particularly iconoclastic. The fictional unconscious that the film constructs may well amount to nothing much more than sophisticated mischief making on the part of the screenwriter and the director. It could be that it seemed amusing to find unconscious motivations for the eccentricities of a recognisable, ageing and reactionary public figure. After all, the political 'puzzle' that Hearst represented for Mankiewicz – that radical youth gives way to conservative old age – is a cliché in a society that more or less invented adolescent revolt as a rite of passage into responsible citizenship. But the war in Europe and the alignment of Left and Right in the United States around isolation or intervention throw light both on the appeal that a Hearst-based script would have for Welles and on the wider implications of its psychoanalytic undertone.

By the time Welles and the Mercury players arrived in Hollywood, Hearst was a major opponent of the entry of the United States into the war in Europe. For the Left, the threat of fascism was actual and urgent. The Mercury Theater had staged *Julius Caesar*, portraying Caesar as a contemporary fascist surrounded by blackshirts, the production lit to create a Nuremburg look, in the aftermath of the Nazi rally. In the eyes of the Left, the powerful tycoon's press campaigns to keep America from joining the struggle against fascism was tantamount to support for fascism. When he was holidaying in Germany in 1934, Hearst had visited Hitler and the German press had quoted his approving and friendly remarks, or as Hearst later claimed, misquoted. But the famous lines spoken by Kane during an interview included in *News on the March* are the only trace of contemporary politics in *Citizen Kane*: 'I have talked with the responsible leaders of the Great Powers – England, France, Germany, and Italy. They are too intelligent to embark upon a project that would mean the end of civilisation as we now know it. You can take my word for it, there will be no war.' And alongside the commentary: 'No public man whom ... Kane himself did not support ... or denounce. Often support ... then denounce.'[22] The fictional newsreel shows Kane appearing on a balcony, first with Roosevelt, then with Hitler. The last but one draft of *Citizen Kane* links Kane more explicitly to fascism through his son, who grows up to become a Nazi and is killed in a raid on an armoury in Washington.

Although the film avoids contemporary politics, Hearst was still a politically relevant figure in the late 30s. The right-wing opposition to Roosevelt had emerged as a new and real threat in the context of fascism. The film, however, draws attention to an earlier war, the Spanish–American war in Cuba, which had been manufactured by the Hearst press. Hysterical and completely fictional headlines, that would make today's gutter press blush, forced the United States into ultra-nationalism and an unnecessary war. The *Inquirer* scene in the Thatcher narration reproduces the famous exchange between Hearst and the artist/illustrator F. Remington: 'Dear Wheeler, you provide the prose poems, I'll provide the war.'[23] Just as significant as these signs of gutter-press populism is the essential instability of the political portrait drawn. There is no solid line of conviction, only the zigzags of opportunism.

From the perspective of New Deal and anti-fascist politics, Hearst presented an appropriate subject for the first Mercury production in Hollywood. However, the political references to Hearst are overshadowed by the psychoanalytic undertones of the fictional character Kane. But the condensation of the two factors, the real-life political and the fictional psychoanalytic, carry their implications into a psychoanalytic attack on the politics of right-wing populism. This is where the film is daring. And it could be that the furor over the question of whether or not the film was a portrait of Hearst distracted critics and commentators from what the film was implying about the political and personal bankruptcy of the American Right. It continually reaches out towards a mythological level, appro-priating quite obvious, even hackneyed, psychoanalytic tropes to cut the corners between character and metaphor.

The image of Kane at the end of the film is an allegorical warning about the fate of European/American relations. As I said at the beginning of this chapter, the film was made during the bleakest period of the war when Roosevelt was becoming more and more convinced of the need for America to get involved in the fight against fascism. Welles's portrayal of Kane is an apt image of the destiny that isolationism would bring in its wake. He is shown as an old man, lonely and alone, literally isolated in the enormous, claustrophobic castle he had constructed as a fantasy world against the reality outside with which he was no longer involved, incarcerated inside his own mausoleum. Welles himself in his press conference justified the San Simeon reference as an 'ivory tower'. More precisely, this image seems to represent the isolationist policies of the Hearst press, and Xanadu, through its blatant similarity to San Simeon, is one of the most transparent references to Hearst in the film.

In *The Making of Citizen Kane* Robert Carringer analyses the RKO art director Perry Ferguson's designs for Xanadu, showing that its Great Hall was based closely on a photograph of the Great Hall at San Simeon: 'The Hearstian element is brought out in the almost perverse juxtaposition of incongruous architectural styles and motifs – Gothic along the far wall, Venetian Baroque in the loggia, Egyptian on the landing (including a sphinx on a plinth!), vaguely Far Eastern along the staircase.'

Such a confusion of culture points to a confusion of history and the ordering of time; and also to the confusion of populist politics. If Kane, and by implication Hearst, is stuck in a fetishistic inability to understand or acknowledge the processes of history, the film seems to hint that this disorder has a psychoanalytic origin. And, also by implication, the isolationist stance is a sign of a repressed, unresolved Oedipal trajectory that has been prematurely broken off, leaving the subject tied to a 'frozen' memory of loss. In Freudian terms, a child's Edenic relation to its mother may be represented metaphorically by antiquity, the place of ancient origin, the Old World. It is striking that no Hollywood genre, and extremely few individual films, deal with migration across the Atlantic. It is almost as if this passage, from the Old to the New World, was a taboo subject in American popular culture. In *Citizen Kane*, however, the Old World is presented metaphorically and ambivalently. It contains a threat of paternal violence within the 'before' of the before/after divide between the mother's exclusive and dependable love and the child's Oedipal journey into the outside world of ambition. For both these reasons the Old World is in danger of lying outside history, subject to repression. At the moment of fascist threat, Welles seems to suggest a psychoanalytic metaphor to explain the dilemma facing the Euro-American collective psyche. At the same time, the film's address cuts across a purely psychoanalytic rhetoric. It also appeals to the discernment of those spectators who can figure out an enigma without the help of a narrator/commentator. The spectators, in the last resort, will piece together the history of the film's protagonist in its closing moments and then, if their curiosity has been really engaged, will re-view and retell the film by tracing and linking together the clues and symptoms that conceal, but preserve, its meaning. In doing so, they would not only be directed towards the figure of the newspaper magnate and his hold over national narrative, but also towards their own ability to read cinematic images and even, perhaps, towards the entanglement of contemporary politics with past, historical, trauma.

The scene of separation and loss, which stands metaphorically for the 'Old World' and the lost mother, has been fetishistically buried under the accumulation of 'things' in the New World. To decipher the meaning of the fetish would be to regain a historical and political relation with the political and historical crisis taking place in contemporary Europe.

There is a kind of poetic justice in Welles's and the cinematographer Greg Toland's use of deep focus in a film which attacks Hearst. The magnate of newspapers and old-style movies is depicted in a new-style cinematography pioneered by the newspapers' new rival, the photo-magazines. And, on the level of sound, Welles made maximum use of his own experience of radio, the medium beloved by Roosevelt, to create a texture that had never been heard before in the Hollywood cinema. And although the deep-focus look had been previously pioneered in Hollywood, the politics of *Citizen Kane* juxtaposes it, perhaps even coincidentally, with the cinematic aesthetics of other Left cinemas of the 30s and 40s. In the view of André Bazin, the deep-focus cinematography of Jean Renoir's Popular Front movies in the 30s in France returned in the Italian neo-realist and leftist cinema of the postwar period. For Bazin, engagement between spectator and screen in *Citizen Kane* was an effect of its composition in depth and formed a triptych with the Popular Front cinema on the one hand and that of neo-realism on the other. Dramatic juxtapositions are composed within the frame and a shot then lasts long enough for the spectator to work out the relationships between the characters, and extract the poetic and emotional implications of the scene. Bazin argued that this kind of composition gave the spectator's eye and mind an autonomy that both montage and the cutting conventions of commercial cinema (especially after the coming of sound) denied: 'Classical editing totally suppresses this kind of reciprocal freedom between us and the object. It substitutes for a free organisation, a forced breaking down where the logic of the shots controlled by the reporting of an action anaesthetises our freedom exactly.'[24]

From my own, European, point of view, Bazin's inclusion of *Citizen Kane* in his political/aesthetic argument seemed to privilege aesthetics over politics. However, looking again at *Citizen Kane*, in the context of the New Deal in the United States, and the conflict between an extreme Right and an attempted Popular Front in both the United States and Europe, Welles's perhaps intuitive choice of cinematic style finally seems to fit with the politics of Bazin's, perhaps intuitive, triptych.

Chapter 8

The Carapace That Failed: Ousmane Sembene's *Xala*

The film language of Xala *can be constructed on the model of an African poetic form called 'sem-enna-worq' which literally means 'wax and gold'. The term refers to the 'lost wax' process in which a goldsmith creates a wax form, casts a clay mold around it, then drains out the wax and pours in pure molten gold to form the valued object. Applied to poetics, the concept acknowledges two levels of interpretation, distinct in theory and representation. Such poetic form aims to attain maximum ideas with minimum words. 'Wax' refers to the most obvious and superficial meaning, whereas the 'gold' embedded in the art work offers the 'true' meaning, which may be inaccessible unless one understands the nuances of folk culture.*

Teshome H. Gabriel [1]

This quotation illustrates the intense interest that recent African cinema holds for any film theory concerned with the 'hieroglyphic' tradition, and potential, of cinema. The catch-all phrase 'hieroglyph' is useful in that it evokes three processes: a code of composition, the encapsulation, that is, of an idea in an image at a stage just prior to writing; a mode of address that asks an audience to apply their ability to decipher the poetics of the 'screen script'; and, finally, the work of criticism as a means of articulating the poetics that an audience recognises but leaves implicit. My critical perspective cannot include the 'nuances of folk culture' or, indeed, other important aspects of African culture and history but attempts to present *Xala*'s significance for film theory beyond its immediate cultural context. While as a critic I would like to fulfil the third deciphering function, that of 'articulation', my critical process does not aspire to go beyond making explicit the first two hieroglyphic processes, that is the 'screen script' and its mode of address to an audience. African cinema should no longer be seen as a 'developing' cinema. It has already made an original and significant contribution to contemporary cinema and its cumulative history and aesthetics.

The germinal ground in which the African cinema developed in the post-colonial period was the francophone sub-Sahara, above all Senegal and Mali, and first of all with Ousmane Sembene. Geographically, this area has its own cultural traditions dating back to the old Mande empire founded by Sundiata in the 11th century, and revived in resistance to French colonialism as the Dyula Revolution led by Samoury Toure in the late 19th century. It was not until independence in 1960, when the French were abandoning most of their African colonies in the hope of holding on to Algeria, that the conditions for an African cinema came into being. Sembene's work, first as a writer, then as a film-maker, crosses the 1960 divide and is also divided by it. During the 50s, he had made his name as an African writer, writing, of course, in French. His first novel, *Le Docker noir* (1956), was written while he was working in the docks and as a union organiser in Marseille. *Les Bouts de bois de Dieu* was published in 1960 (after a number of others) based on his experiences during the famous 1947–8 strike on the Bamako–Dakar railway. Then, in 1961, immediately after Senegal achieved independence, he went to the Soviet Union to study at the Moscow Film School and his first short film, *Borom Sarret,* was shown at the Tours film festival in 1963. *La Noire de ...* , released in 1966, was the first full-length feature from the sub-Sahara.

Sembene's novels were written during the period in which African poets, novelists, Marxist theorists and intellectuals in Paris were grouped around the journal *Présence Africaine*. Sembene was critical of the *négritude* [2] movement with which they were identified. He considered the concept to be irrelevant to the popular resistance that grew into the independence movement, and he identified himself with, and was part of, the anti-colonial struggle in Senegal rather than intellectual circles in Paris. While he wrote novels in French during the colonial period, the cinema offered Sembene a means of contact with popular traditions and his films are directed towards the cultural needs of the ordinary people, who had no access either to the French language or to traditions of written culture:

> Often the worker or the peasant don't have time to pause on the details of their daily lives; they live them and do not have time to tie them down. The film-maker, though, can link one detail to another to put a story together. There is no longer a traditional storyteller in our days and I think the cinema can replace him. [3]

This last observation is characteristic of Sembene's commitment to promoting and transforming traditional culture, to using the technological developments of Western society in the interests of African culture. Sembene was more interested in finding a dialectical relationship between the two cultures than in an uncritical nostalgia for pre-colonial pure Africanness. This position is underlined by his background as a worker and his Marxism.

The cinema can speak across the divisions created by oral tradition and written language and is, therefore, a perfect mechanism for a cultural dialectic. It can perpetuate an oral cultural tradition as the spoken language plays a major role in cinema; and it can bring oral traditions into the modernity of the post-colonial. Sembene himself was the son of a fisherman and self-educated into French literacy. His own Wolof language, like the Mandinke, had no written equivalent. In the social structure of the Mande tradition, the task of maintaining and creating oral culture devolved onto a specific social grouping, the *griots*, dependent on the nobility in pre-colonial times. They functioned as the repository of historical memory, traditionally that of the kings and their families, and as creators, among other things, of poetry and music. African culture has had to negotiate a contemporary *modus vivendi* between writing in French, its own traditional oral forms and the facts of post-colonial cultural life. While the figure of the *griot* may evoke the oral culture of the pre-colonial past, he (and, sometimes, she) spoke primarily to an elite. The cinema economically and politically had to address a mass audience in post-colonial Africa.

In *Xala* the question of language is at the political centre of the drama. The economic division between the indigenous entrepreneurial elite and the impoverished people is reflected in a division between French and Wolof. The elite use French exclusively to communicate among themselves and as their official language. They speak Wolof only across class and gender lines and treat it as inferior and archaic. In the novel *Xala,* which Sembene wrote up from his script while searching for funds for the film, the young people on the Left have developed a written equivalent for Wolof and are publishing a journal in their native language for the first time. In the film, Sembene sets up a parallel between two figures who are quite marginal to the story but significant for its politics. One is a young student selling the new journal; the other is a peasant, robbed of his village's savings which he had brought to town to buy seed. Both get caught in the police round-up of beggars that forms the film's central tableau, and become integrated into the beggar community. Any moves by the people towards cultural and economic advance and self-sufficiency are dashed in the polarisation between the entrepreneurial elite and the underclass it creates.

Although the cinema has often been evoked as a continuation of the *griot* tradition, there are important points of difference besides those of class. The oral tradition of the *griot* was based on verbal language as such. The cinema sets up a dialectic between what is said and what is shown. One can undercut, or play off, the other. In *Xala*, Sembene uses the language of cinema to create a poetics of politics. He gives visibility to the forms, as opposed to the content, of social contradiction and then, through the forms, illuminates the content. He forges links between underlying structures, or formations, and the symptoms they produce on the surface, stamped, as it were, onto everyday existence, across all classes. This is an aesthetic that depends on making visible those aspects of economic and political structure that are either invisible or repressed in articulated language. It is a cinema of what cannot be said. Underlying structures mark the lives of the ruling elite as well as the people, and as the story unfolds signs and symptoms signal an insistent return of the repressed. The repression is both political, of the people by the ruling elite, and psychoanalytic, of the ruling elite by their relation to Frenchness, its consequent phobias and fetishims. The two spheres become increasingly interlinked throughout the film. While Sembene's analysis of signs is always historical and, in the last resort, materialist, he also acknowledges the place of sexuality and the structure of the psyche in the symptomology of neo-colonialism. There are shades of Frantz Fanon's *Black Skin, White Masks*.

Xala is set in Senegal after independence when the presence of the colonial power is concealed behind a façade of self-government. The story's premise is that independence politics had become inextricably compromised with colonial financial structures. The opening, pre-credit, sequence of *Xala* shows a crowd celebrating as a group of African businessmen expel the French from the Chamber of Commerce and take control of their own economy. The people in the crowd are depicted in such a way as to evoke 'Africanness', with bare breasts, dancing and drums. These connotative images never appear again in the film; (thereafter the characters' clothes and appearance are appropriate for the Islamic sub-Sahara). The businessmen are dressed in loose shirts and trousers made out of 'African'-type materials. They appear at the top of the steps, ejecting a few objects that evoke the colonising culture (including a bust of Marie-Antoinette). The camera is placed at the bottom of the steps. As the men turn to go into the building, the camera dips slightly to change its angle and the steps suddenly resemble a stage on which a performance has just taken place. When the camera joins the men back in the Chamber, they are dressed in the dark European business suits that they will wear for the rest of the film. While the crowds still celebrate, a posse of police arrive and, under the command of one of the recently expelled Frenchmen, push the people back from the central space in front of the Chambre de Commerce, literally enacting the process of domination and repression. The other two Frenchmen then enter the Chambre and place an attaché case in front of each African businessman. Each case is full of money. The two men step backwards with the silent subservience they maintain, as 'advisers', for the rest of the film. The sequence closes as El Hadji Abdou Kader Beye invites his colleagues to the party celebrating his marriage to a third wife. All the speeches are in French.

I have chosen the word 'carapace' to evoke the central poetic and political themes in *Xala* in order to convey an image of vulnerable flesh covered by a protecting shell. The carapace doubles as a mask behind which the ruling elite camouflages itself, adopting the clothes, language and behaviour of its former colonial masters. The carapace also evokes the social structure of neo-colonialism. The entrepreneurial bourgeoisie live the life of an upper crust, floating and parasitical on the lives of the people. In *Xala* the carapace conceals not simply vulnerable flesh, but flesh that is wounded by class exploitation. Whereas a scab indicates that a wound has developed its own organic means of protection, the carapace of neo-colonialism denies and disavows the wound and prevents healing. The elite encase themselves in expensive Western cars, while the beggars' bodies are crippled by deformed or missing limbs. Concealed corruption at the top of the social hierarchy manifests itself on the wounded bodies of the dispossessed. During the film, the gap between the two groups, the beggars and the elite, narrows until the final scene which brings them together. The central character is El Hadji, a member of the entrepreneurial elite, who finds he is impotent when he marries his third wife. A tension then runs through the film between the vulnerability of his body, his failed erection, on one side and, on the other, his outward carapace made up of European props. In the end, his sexual vulnerability has brought him to realise that the carapace has failed and he exposes his own body, naked and covered in spit, to the beggars' ritual of humiliation and salvation.

During a climactic scene just before the end of the film, El Hadji is being hounded out of the Chamber of Commerce by his equally corrupt colleagues. His most vindictive antagonist seizes his attaché case, and opens it to find it empty except for the magic object with which El Hadji had attempted to ward off the curse of impotence, the *xala,* that has afflicted him. His enemy holds it up for public ridicule. El Hadji seizes it and waves it defiantly in the faces of the others, shouting: 'This is the true fetish, not the fetishism of technology.' At this moment, Sembene brings into the open the theoretical theme of his film, that is the different discourses of fetishism. Up until that point, these different discourses had been woven into the story implicitly, creating the complex semiotic system that makes special demands on the spectator's reading powers. Suddenly the three strands are condensed together in one object. The object acts simultaneously as a signifier of religious belief that predates Islam and colonialism, as a signifier, in the context of the story, of El Hadji's sexual impotence, and it is enclosed, concealed, in the attaché case, a key signifier of financial corruption and the commodity fetishism that corruption breeds.

Sembene weaves a series of reflections on fetishism across the film. As something in which are invested a meaning and a value beyond or beside its actual meaning and value, a fetish demands the willing surrender of knowledge to belief. The fetishist overrates his object, and ignoring the commonsense value attributed to it by society, secretly attaches mysterious powers to it. But, however intensely invested, this secret belief is vulnerable, acknowledging, even more secretly, what it simultaneously disavows. For an individual, the fetish object may be invested with private magical or sexual significance, but distortions of value and attributions of inappropriate meaning may also be shared by social groups in a kind of collective fantasy. The fetish thus acts, either individually or collectively, as a sign, signalling the intervention of fantasy into the normal course of the reality principle. And the intervention of fantasy signals a point of anxiety which cannot face the possibility of knowledge, and in the process of avoiding it, erects a belief in an object that, in turn, denies knowledge of its actual value. While supporting the suspension of disbelief, the fetish also materialises the unspeakable, the disavowed, the repressed.

The cinema, too, appropriates objects, turns then into images and wraps them in connotations and resonances that are either collectively understood, or acquire specific significance within the context of a particular story. Sembene makes use of the language of cinema, its hieroglyphic or pictographic possibilities, and creates a text which is about the meaning of objects and objects as symptoms. His use of cinematic rhetoric is the key to *Xala*. The form of the film engages the spectators' ability to read the signs that emanate from colonialism and its neo-colonialist offspring. And, because the film shows an African ruling elite accepting and appropriating the fetishisms of European capitalism, it allows a double reading. As a comedy of fetishistic manners *Xala* uses signs, objects and the rhetoric of cinema to allow its audience direct engagement with, and access to solving, the enigmas represented on the screen. But *Xala* also sets off a kind of chain reaction of theoretical reflections on fetishism, linking together otherwise diverse ideas, and highlighting the age-old function of fetishism as a conduit for the to and fro of cultural and economic exchange between Europe and Africa.

I

There is a double temporality hidden in Sembene's use of the discourses of fetishism in *Xala*. Behind, or beside, the thematic strands of the story, lies another, extra-diegetic, history. This history, quite appropriately, is not visible in the film. But any consideration of fetishism in Senegal today raises 'ghosts' from the past. These are reminders that the word first came into existence in the proto-colonial exchanges, beginning in the mid-15th century, between Portuguese merchant traders and the inhabitants of the West African coast, part of which is now Senegal. Sembene depicts an entrepreneurial, pre-capitalist economy in contemporary Senegal and the film is about the function, within that economy, of fetishised objects as signifiers of unequal exchange. The attention of anyone interested in the history of the concept of fetishism is drawn to its origins in that earlier period of pre-capitalist, mercantile, economic exchange.

Before analysing the theme of fetishism in the film itself, I would like to use it as an excuse to raise some of these ghosts and make some introductory points about the history of the concept of fetishism. Marcel Mauss first pronounced the epitaph on the anthropological use of the word 'fetishism' as a compromised relic of nineteenth-century imperialist ethnography:

When the history of the science of religions and ethnography comes to be written, the undeserved and fortuitous role played by concepts such as fetishism in theoretical and descriptive works will be considered astonishing. The concept represents nothing but an enormous misunderstanding between two cultures, the African and the European, and is based purely on a blind obeisance to colonial usage.[4]

The recent revival of interest in the origins of the term 'fetishism' has drawn attention to its conceptual contribution to the European polarisation between primitive and civilised thought and consequent moral and intellectual justifications for imperialism. In other words, the concept of fetishism cannot be dismissed because of its compromised place in exploitative exchange and imperialist ethnography. On the contrary, the concept and its history can throw light on the 'enormous misunderstandings' between Europe and Africa.

William Pietz has discussed the origins of both the word and the concept in a series of articles in the journal *Res*.[5] He shows how the word emerged in the encounter between West African and European Christian cultures in the 16th and 17th centuries. It was a 'novel word that appeared as a response to an unprecedented type of situation',[6] of relations between 'cultures so radically different as to be mutually incomprehensible'.[7] Pietz argues that the term bears witness to its own history. To reject the term completely, as purely and simply a relic of colonialism and imperialist anthropology, is to ignore its historical specificity and the cultural implications that go with it. Pietz demonstrates that fetishism is a debased derivation of the Portuguese *feticio*, which means witchcraft, in turn derived from the Latin *facticium* which means artificial, something made up to look like something else. *Feticio* was applied by the Portuguese wholesale to beliefs and practices which they neither could nor would interpret, but encountered in their commercial relations. In the pidgin of middlemen who settled in West Africa and became *soi-disant* experts on native customs, the word became *fetisso*. Pietz notes: 'It brought a wide array of African objects and practices under a category that, for all its misrepresentation of cultural facts, enabled the formation of more or less non-coercive commercial relations between members of bewilderingly different cultures.'[8]

The lore and practices that developed around the concept of the *fetisso* were then inherited, wholesale and to a second degree, by the Dutch traders who arrived on the West Coast in the very late 16th century and had gradually ejected the Portuguese by 1641. The Dutch Calvinists brought the Reformation's deep hatred of, and anxiety at, the superstitious and idolatrous practices of Catholicism. To them, the idolatry of the Portuguese and the fetishism of the Africans were six of one and half a dozen of the other. It was the Dutch merchants of this period, Pieter Marees and William Bosman in particular, who wrote down their experience and observation of African customs. Pietz argues that the implications of the concept 'fetishism' took shape during this period. It was during the late 17th century, with West African trade efficiently organised by the Dutch East India Company, that conceptual problems of value began to be theorised as a problematic concerning the capacity of the material object to embody values. The concept of fetishism, as an inappropriate attribution of value to an object, emerged alongside and in conjunction with the emergent articulation of the commodity form. It was, for instance, during the second part of the 17th century that William Petty, an influence on Adam Smith and described by Marx as 'the father of Political Economy and to some extent the founder of statistics', was evolving an early version of the labour theory of value.[9] At the point when trade in commodities became a 'market', not only did the question of attribution of value become crucial, but also how value could be marked by a shared and recognised 'general equivalent'. A coinage, money, with value represented in quantities of silver and gold, translated value into something that could represent the same for everyone involved in the process of commercial exchange. The abstract, symbolic nature of the money form seemed, to the European mind, to emerge from the same thought processes that could conceptualise the abstract, symbolic nature of God.

To the European traders, the Africans' attribution of talismanic and prophylactic powers to inanimate objects was the basis for their false economic valuation of material objects. They would exchange gold for what the Europeans considered to be worthless 'trifles'. Overestimation of the trifles, on the one hand, underestimation of the standard value of gold, on the other, blocked 'natural reason' and 'rational market activity'. Although there were examples of a proto-money form in Africa at the time (iron bars, for instance, in Senegambia), although a developed network of commercial trade and exchange existed between sub-Saharan Africa and the Arab North, although Islam, a religion of monotheism and the written word, had spread into Africa, European observations only confirmed their preconceptions. At the same time, the *fetisso* became deeply imbricated in commercial relations. It was the practice to guarantee transactions by getting Africans to take 'fetish oaths', which, while ensuring the efficacy of the transactions, also seemed to confirm the innately superstitious nature of the indigenous people.

For the European merchant, the Fetisso posed a double problem, a double perversion. First, the status of commercially valuable objects as Fetissos complicated his ability to acquire them as commodities and seemed to distort their relative exchange value. This often led to transactions with an exceptionally high rate of profit, but it also caused difficulties since the locals regarded the desired objects in a personal, social or religious register rather than an economic one. Second, to effect economic transactions merchants had to accept the preliminary swearing of oaths upon Fetissos – a perversion of the natural processes of economic negotiation and legal contract. Desiring a clean economic interaction, seventeenth-century merchants unhappily found themselves entering into social relations and quasi-religious ceremonies that should have been irrelevant to the conduct of trade were it not for the perverse superstitions of their trade partners. The general theory of fetishism that emerged in the 18th century was determined by the problematic specific to this novel historical situation.[10]

The beliefs and practices surrounding *fetissos* were described, exotically and derogatorily, by travellers, merchants and priests above all, during the 17th and early 18th centuries, culminating in the publication of William Bosman's *New and Accurate Account of the Coast of Guinea* in 1704. It was this descriptive work that was used as the basis for President de Brosses's general theorisation of fetishism published in 1760. De Brosses used the concept of fetishism to describe the culture of Africa as essentially childish, also stating that 'what is today the religion of African negroes and other barbarians, was once upon a time the religion of the ancients, everywhere on earth.'[11] De Brosses's account of fetishism influenced some thinkers of the Enlightenment and the concept of fetishism began to become integrated into intellectual discourse. Pietz comments: 'This sanctioning power through magical belief and violent emotion was understood to take the place of the rational institutional sanctions that empowered the legal systems of European states ... social order was dependent on psychological facts rather than political principles'.[12]

It is in this sense that the concept and discourse of fetishism has itself played an important part in justifying the colonisation, exploitation and oppression of Africa. The European extrapolation of the concept of fetishism, the fetishisation of 'fetishism', seems like an enormous blindfold, one that was necessary to justify the colonisation of African people. Auguste Comte took one stage further de Brosses's theory that fetishism constituted an infancy in the history of human spiritual belief, a moment through which, once upon a time, all religions have passed. Comte argued that the lack of priests as intermediaries and the personal and domestic nature of the cults blocked the development of belief in an invisible, abstract godhead:

It is above all a belief in the invisibility of the gods and their essential distinction from the bodies under their discipline, that must determine, in the polytheistic period, the rapid and significant development of a true priesthood, able to acquire a high social authority, constituting, in a permanent and ordered manner, an indispensable intermediary between the worshipper and his god. Fetishism, on the other hand, does not involve this inevitable intervention, and thus tends to prolong indefinitely the infancy of social organisation, which must depend, for its first step, on the distinctive formation of a class of speculative thinkers, that is to say, a priesthood.[13]

Jean Pouillon argues that Hegel, however, saw the fetishism of the African not as a stage on the path towards civilisation but as inherent, the 'African' being unable to 'move beyond a first antithesis between man and nature'. From the perspective of this logic, colonisation and civilisation become synonymous. Pouillon comments 'Le fétichisme ne débouche sur rien et les colonisateurs pourront avoir bonne conscience.'[14]

The concept of the fetish provided an antinomy for the rational thought of the Enlightenment. It gives a new form and historic twist to the long-standing and familiar spirit/body and abstraction/materiality polarisations. It coincides with the iconoclastic purification of Christianity from the trappings of idolatrous Catholicism, in which a return to the Old Testament and the precedent of the Jewish, monotheistic rejection of Egyptian iconology was influential. Pietz emphasises that the coming into being of the concept of the fetish was necessarily in conjunction with 'the emergent articulation of the ideology of the commodity form'.[15] W.J. Mitchell points out: 'If Adam Smith is Moses he is also Martin Luther.'[16] It was this discourse of fetishism ('the mist-enveloped regions of the religious world') that Marx turned back onto his own society and that Freud used to define the furthest limits of the psyche's credulity. Both analogies gave the concept of the fetish a new pertinence, turning it away from its anthropological roots towards questions of signification. The fetish raises questions of meaning quite apart from its constructed antinomy with abstraction. It epitomises the human ability to project value onto a material object, repress the fact that the projection has taken place, and then interpret the object as the autonomous source of that value. The process becomes invisible; as the object acquires exchange value, its historical specificity drops into obscurity. The enigma, then, challenges the historian or analyst. The fetish is a sign rather than an idea and it can be analysed semiologically rather than philosophically. This process is central to *Xala*.

II

After the credits the film proper opens with El Hadji collecting his two other wives to go to the party. The elder, Adja Awa Astou, is traditional and religious. In the interview cited earlier Sembene says 'He got his first wife before becoming a somebody.' The second, Oumi N'Doye, is Westernised and mercenary. Sembene says 'Along with his economic and social development, he takes a second who corresponds, so to speak, to a second historical phase.' Awa's daughter Rama, who stands up to her father throughout the film, synthesises progressive elements in both African and Western cultures. She has posters of Amilcar Cabral and Charlie Chaplin in her room; she dresses in African style and rides a motor scooter; she is a student at the university and will only speak Wolof. N'gone, El Hadji's new wife, is dressed for a Western white wedding and her face is covered with a bridal veil. Sembene says: 'The third, his daughter's age but without her mind, is only there for his self-esteem.' Then, on the wedding night, El

Hadji finds he is impotent. During the rest of the film he tries to work out who could have cursed him and visits two *marabouts* to find a cure. His financial affairs unravel, unable to sustain the cost of three households and the lavish wedding, until he is finally expelled from the Chamber of Commerce.

The central enigma in *Xala* cannot be deciphered until the very last scene, when the beggars, who at the beginning of the film are marginal to the story but gradually come to occupy its centre, invade El Hadji's house. Then the different clues that have been signalled by Sembene throughout the film fall into place and complete the picture. El Hadji does not function as a knowing narrator and the only character with whom the spectator is given any identification, personally and ideologically, is Rama, who plays only a small, though important, part in the film. El Hadji is a didactic hero. He is made into an example, rather as Brecht makes an example out of Mother Courage. He only engages sympathy through the disaster he has brought on himself, and, like a tragic hero of the cathartic theatre, he is stripped literally to nakedness. On a more significant level, he cannot command the narration because he is unable to understand his own history and the audience are thus deprived of the safety and security of a hero who will guide them through events, and provide them with an appropriate moral perspective. And the spectator realises, at the end, that the film itself has held the clues to the enigma of El Hadji's *xala*, and these linked images and figurations can, retrospectively, be deciphered. Sembene's use of cinema demands a spectator who is actively engaged with reading and interpreting the sounds and images unrolling on the screen.

There are certain parallels between *Xala*'s narrational strategy and that of *Citizen Kane*. Both films also tell the story of a man's relationship to money, fetishised objects and sexuality. Both films are constructed around a central enigma. In *Citizen Kane,* the audience's investigation of the enigma is conducted by a surrogate, the journalist, Thompson. However, he is unable to see or interpret the clues contained in the visual discourse of the film. The pieces finally fall into place when the camera allows the audience a privileged look at the little sled as it is thrown on the flames. Thompson cannot see how these signifiers link together like the rings of a chain and mark the movement of associated ideas, objects and images that map out the process of displacement. The camera, or rather the rhetoric of the cinema, assumes the position of master narrator, and directly addresses the audience.

As in *Xala*, the audience of *Citizen Kane* then has to think back over the whole course of the film to translate the 'sensitive areas' retrospectively, and solve the enigma by deciphering the sliding of the signifiers. Just as the glass snowstorm allows a 'reference back' to the log cabin, so the name on the sled at the end of the film returns the missing signified to the enigma, seeming to halt and restore order to the slippage of the signifiers. But the signified 'Rosebud' then sets off on another journey, as a signifier for the lost mother and a memorial to that loss. As Jacques Lacan points out in his essay 'Agency of the Letter in the Unconscious', a signifier's ability to suggest multiple signifieds creates the leap of association that allows the unconscious mind to displace one idea onto another. Where the conscious mind has set up an impenetrable wall of censorship, the unconscious disguises its ideas through displacement, but not so completely that the link between the original idea and the disguised idea will be lost. Psychoanalysis tries to trace the process backwards, following the links and deciphering the clues in reverse, restoring the links between the signifiers lodged, but indecipherable, in the conscious mind and the unconscious idea they represent. Describing the language of dreams, Freud used the image of a rebus and compared dream interpretation to the decipherment of the clues in a pictogram.

In *Xala* the visual coding of ideas is even more marked and further emphasised by the absence of a surrogate narrator. This mode of cinematic address is perfectly suited to the film's subject matter: fetishism. El Hadji and his colleagues have lost touch with their own history and society through adopting Frenchness as a sign of superior class position. There is an unbridgeable gap between the elite's own origins, their present masquerade of Westernised commodity culture and the condition of the people. The gap is demonstrated by the elite's use of French rather than Wolof, and safeguarded by a fetishisation of European objects. These things, for instance El Hadji's Mercedes, are the literal materials of the carapace, his defence against political and economic reality, and the outward manifestations of a corruption that sucks the life blood of the people. When the Mercedes is repossessed, Modu, the chauffeur, carries a wooden stool as he guides his employer along the street. The stool is like a shrunken or wizened version of the proud object of display. It is a trace of, or a memorial to, the Mercedes and its meaning for El Hadji. Because Modu has been so closely identified with the car and its welfare, his presence links the two objects ironically together. Sembene consistently links people with things, things substitute for people or for each other, things acquire associations and resonances that weave like threads of meaning through the film. At the same time, he raises the issue of substitution and exchange in a social and economic sphere. The *marabout* who cures El Hadji's *xala*, Sereen Mada, restores it when the cheque that El Hadji gave him in payment is bounced by the bank.

As the members of the Chamber of Commerce arrive at El Hadji's wedding party, the camera is positioned so that, as each man walks past, his attaché case is framed in close-up. On the outside, the attaché case is emblematic of the power of the international business community, but inside, as only the audience can know, is the secret evidence of corruption and collaboration with the old colonial masters. While seeming to be signs of power and authority, the attaché cases represent the real impotence of the entrepreneurial elite in relation to neo-colonialism. Once the film has established these associations, the image of the attaché case evokes them whenever it appears. So that when El Hadji walks dejectedly away, carrying his attaché case, from N'gone's house after his failed wedding night, he seems to be bowed down with a double impotence. And, in his final confrontation with his colleagues, his case is empty apart from the fetish given him by the phoney *marabout*. The failed fetish is found in the place formerly occupied by the colonialists' banknotes.

Although the particular discourse of sexuality, on which Freud's theory of fetishism depends, cannot be imposed carelessly on another culture, Sembene's juxtaposition of the psycho-sexual with the socio-economic is explicit. He uses the sexual as the point of fissure, or weakness, in the system of economic fetishism. El Hadji's impotence is a symptom of something else, a sign of the eruption of the unconscious onto the body itself. In Freud, the fetish enables the psyche to live with castration anxiety; it contributes to the ego's mechanisms of defence; it conceals the truth that the conscious mind represses. When the fetish fails to function effectively, the symptoms it holds in check start to surface. In *Xala*, the fragile carapace collapses under pressure from class politics and economics but these pressures are expressed through, and latch onto, sexuality and work on the body's vulnerability to the psyche. For Sembene, class politics determine over and above sexuality. Sexuality plays its part in the drama as the site of the symptom, the first sign of a return of the repressed. In his representation of repression, Sembene makes full use of the *double entendre* that can condense its political and psychoanalytic connotations.

The morning after the wedding El Hadji's secretary opens his shop. Modu delivers El Hadji in the Mercedes. El Hadji asks his secretary to telephone the President of the Chamber of Commerce who comes over to see him at once. Interspersed and separate from these events, the beggars are slowly collecting and taking up their usual positions outside in the street. As the local women empty their slops into the drain outside the shop, the secretary runs out with her disinfectant spray to ward off infection. As El Hadji's car appears, so do the beggars and their music; as the President's car appears, so do the cripples. In the back office, El Hadji tells the President about the *xala*. The President reacts with horror saying 'Who? Who could have done this to you?' At that moment the beggars' music drifts into the room. El Hadji gets up from his chair without answering and goes through to the front office and closes the window. He asks the President to call the police and remove this 'human refuse', adding that 'it's bad for tourism'. The police arrive, and under the direction of their French commander, load the beggars and cripples into a lorry and drive them out of town. They are left miles away, in the middle of nowhere, and start their slow, painful, trek back into town.

When watching this scene, the spectator cannot but be conscious of a figuration of 'repression'. The President orders that the beggars be removed from sight and from consciousness. And their return then figures a 'return of the repressed'. To the mutilated limbs of the cripples is now added a baton wound on the head of the boy who guides the blind man and whom Modu employs to clean the car. The repression is both physical and social, and the bodies of the beggars are symptoms of social and economic injustice. But this scene also contains a clue to the enigma, to the source of the *xala,* to its source in El Hadji's social and historical position. This other, psychic, dimension is not revealed until the final scene in the film. El Hadji's fall is complete: Oumi has left him, N'gone's Badyen (her father's sister) has repudiated the marriage, his cheque to the *marabout* had bounced so the *xala* has returned, his bank has refused to extend his loans, and his colleagues have voted unanimously to expel him from the Chamber of Commerce for embezzling 30 tons of rice destined for the country people. As Modu takes him to Awa's house, he tells El Hadji that the blind man can cure the *xala.* The scene builds up to the final revelation as the beggars invade the house under the blind man's leadership. While some of the beggars loot the kitchen, the blind man sits in judgment. He says to El Hadji:

'Do you recognise me? ... Our story goes back a long way.' He tells how El Hadji had taken his clan's land. 'What I have become is your fault. You appropriated our inheritance. You falsified our names and we were expropriated. I was thrown in prison. I am of the Beye family. Now I will get my revenge. I arranged your *xala.* If you want to be a man you will undress nude in front of everyone. We will spit on you.'

It was this first act of expropriation that had set El Hadji on the road towards entrepreneurial success and had taken him from the country to the town, away from loyalty to family and towards individualism, from traditional modes of inheritance towards falsified written legal documents, away from the continuity of his own history and into a charade of Frenchness. His failure to recognise the beggar indicates that he had covered his tracks by 'forgetting'. But when the President asked who had cursed him, his response was to shut out the sound of the beggar's song. This gesture signified both an acknowledgment of the truth and the need, quickly, to re-enact its repression.

During the final scene with the beggars, the tailor's dummy with N'gone's wedding veil, returned contemptuously to El Hadji by the Badyen, stands clearly visible in the corner. The presence of these objects sets off a chain of associations that run back through the film as the links between them begin to emerge. N'gone acts as a pivot between the two fetishistic systems: the economic and the sexual. She is woman as commodity, woman as fetish and woman as consumer of commodities. This sphere of capitalist consumption has been traditionally the province of women; Luce Irigaray, in her essay 'Women on the Market', traces the development from the anthropological exchange of women to the emergence of women as both consumers and consumed in modern, urban society. N'gone's marriage to El Hadji was based on exchange. At the wedding his gifts are displayed including, most prominently, a car key. The car, which stands decked out with ribbons outside the gate of the villa on the back of a truck, is El Hadji's present to her in exchange for her virginity. As he leaves the villa after his unconsummated wedding night, he stops by the car and touches it mournfully, so that it seems to substitute for N'gone's unattainable sexuality. The car's fetishistic quality, its elevation out of ordinary use, the ribbons, are displaced onto her figure. She is first seen concealed behind her wedding veil, packaged like a valuable commodity, and she speaks only once throughout the film. To emphasise this 'thingness' and 'to-be-looked-at-ness', Sembene places her next to a large, nude but tasteful, photograph of her as the Badyen prepares her for her wedding night. As she is undressed and her wedding veil placed on the tailor's dummy, the camera pans up from her naked back to her body in the photograph. In a later scene the same camera movement reiterates this juxtaposition.

N'gone's fetishised erotic appearance contrasts with Oumi's immediate, vital, demanding and corporeal sexuality. N'gone is image and commodity and, half concealed behind the wedding veil, she evokes the double nature of commodity fetishism. The commodity, to circulate and realise the capital invested in it, must seduce its consumer and, in its very seductiveness, its 'packagedness', disguise the secret of its origins. That is, the inherent unglamorousness of the production process should be invisible and, most of all, class relations, the extraction of surplus value, must be concealed by seductive surface. N'gone's image as fetish evokes the processes of veiling, disguise and substitution necessary to commodity fetishism and it is perhaps significant that when El Hadji, temporarily cured of his *xala* by Sereen Mada, goes triumphantly to his new bride she has her period and is 'not available'. Her perfect surface is tarnished by menstrual blood. Although the depiction of N'gone suggests links with the appearance and circulation of the commodity under capitalism, the story is taking place in a non-industrialised and 'underdeveloped' country. The money El Hadji needed to acquire her as commodity, in the specific economic conditions of neo-colonialism, came from financial corruption and exploitative entrepreneurial capitalism. He paid for the wedding and N'gone's gifts by embezzling and illegally selling the quota of rice intended for the country people. The secret corruption is displaced onto the little car that N'gone will receive in exchange for her virginity; the car's fetishistic qualities are displaced onto N'gone for whom a photograph and a tailor's dummy become substitutes and metaphors.

Marx evolved his theory of commodity fetishism in the process of developing his theory of value. The problem Marx perceived to be at stake in the theory of value is connected to the question of visibility and invisibility of labour power and of value. Here the question of materiality and abstraction returns, in the context of a capitalist system of thought that Marx can show to be deeply imbricated with fetishism, its phobic other. W.J. Mitchell says: 'Marx's turning the rhetoric of iconoclasm on its principal users was a brilliant tactical manoeuvre; given nineteenth-century Europe's obsession with primitive, oriental, "fetishistic" cultures that were the prime object of imperialist expansion, one can hardly imagine a more effective rhetorical move.'[17]

Marx identified commodity fetishism as emerging out of the gap between a belief in the commodity as its own autochthonous source of value and knowledge of its true source in human labour. This gap is finally papered over and disguised under capitalism, as the labour market necessary for mass industrial production can only function by transforming individual labour power into abstract and generalised wage labour. The commodity's glamour, verging into sex appeal, seals these complicated processes into a fixation on seeing, believing and not understanding.

Money, the means of expression of value as a symbolic equivalent, is comparable, Marx said, to language. The disavowal characteristic of fetishism is due to misunderstandings of the complex stages inherent in an abstract, symbolic system and the political need to disavow the worker's labour power as source of the commodity's value. Just as a religious believer refuses to accept the human origin of his object (either physical or abstract) of worship, so capitalism refuses to accept that value originates in the labour of the working class. The more abstract the process, the more utterly fundamental is the denial of human origin. While belief in a fetish may be obviously a disavowal of its intractable materiality, belief in an abstract god creates a gap between man and spirit that is harder to materialise. 'A commodity is therefore a mysterious thing, because in it, the social character of men's labour appears to them as an objective character stamped on the product of that labour.'[18] It was at this point that Marx evoked, in his famous phrase, 'the mist-enveloped regions of the religious world' where 'the productions of the human brain appear as independent beings endowed with life and entering into relations both with one another and the human race'. Then

> value does not stalk about with a label describing what it is. It is value that converts every product into a social hieroglyphic. ... The determination of the magnitude of value by labour time is therefore a secret, hidden in the apparent fluctuations of the relative values of commodities. ... it is the ultimate money form of the world of commodities that actually conceals instead of disclosing the social character of private labour and the social relations between the individual producers.[19]

The hieroglyph of value is like a *trompe-l'oeil*. It appears on the surface to be intrinsic to its commodity but, with a move to another perspective, from the visible to the theoretical, its structure may be made accessible to knowledge. The commodity thus seals its enigmatic self-sufficiency behind a masquerade, a surface that disavows both the structure of value and its origin in working-class labour. Instead it is inscribed with a different kind of semiotic, one that is directed towards the market place, which further disguises, or papers over, the semiotic that originated in its production. Baudrillard argues in 'The Political Economy of the Sign' that increasingly in the consumer societies of advanced capitalism, both the object form (use value) and the commodity form (exchange value) are transfigured into sign value. This is partly the function of advertising, which is expert in the creation of sign values, weaving an intricate web of connotation, as Roland Barthes describes in his analysis of the Panzani advertisement in the essay 'The Rhetoric of the Image'. Baudrillard then argues that spending, or perhaps one should say 'shopping', elevates the commodity form into sign value, so that the economic is then transfigured into sign systems, and economic power becomes visibly transmuted into the trappings of social privilege. Consumer objects can then create needs in advance of the consumer's awareness of a need, bearing out Marx's point that 'production not only produces goods but it produces people to consume them and corresponding needs.'

The circulation of European commodities, in a society of the kind depicted in *Xala*, caricatures and exaggerates the commodity fetishism inherent in capitalism. Rather than representing an enigma that may be deciphered, politically and theoretically, to reveal its place in the historical and economic order of things, the commodity's ties with history have been effectively severed. The chain of displacements that construct the concept of value is attenuated to the point that all connection with the source of value is irredeemably lost in the movement from capitalism to colonialism. Floating freely outside First World economy, the gulf between luxury objects monopolised by a Third World elite and the labour power of the working class in the producing country seems vast. Belief in the commodity's supposedly self-generated value does not demand the process of disavowal it depends on at home so that it can live out its myth as an object of cult. In *Xala*, Sembene uses the neo-colonial economy to show the capitalist commodity 'superfetished'. Modu, for instance, only puts imported bottled water into the Mercedes. These things take on pure 'sign value' (as Baudrillard would put it). However, the objects enable another process of disavowal. Sembene suggests that these fetishised objects seal the repression of history and of class and colonial politics under the rhetoric of nationhood. His use of the concept of fetishism is not an exact theoretical working through of the Marxist or Freudian concepts of fetishism, however; his use is *Marxist* and *Freudian*. The interest of the film lies in its inextricable intermeshing of the two.

In its final images, *Xala's* class and psychoanalytic themes are suddenly polarised into a new pattern. Sembene invokes horror of the body and its materiality through the desperate and degraded condition of the beggars and cripples. As El Hadji is denounced by the blind man, their wounds and their missing limbs demonstrate the political fact that financial corruption and profit are manifested on the bodies of the poor. The Western objects that the entrepreneurial elite fetishise inflict not impotence but castration on those they impoverish. The wounded body, the source of horror in the Freudian concept of castration anxiety, returns in the wounded bodies of the beggars and the hunger of the peasants. These bodies break through the barriers maintained by the French language and symbolised, for instance, by El Hadji's cult of Evian water. The otherness of Africa which horrified Europeans is perpetuated in colonialism's real horror of the ordinary people, and grotesquely more so, in the irresponsible greed of the new ruling class.

For Freud, the site of castration anxiety is the mother's body. For Julia Kristeva, the mother's body is the site of abjection. The child's relation to its mother was a time of boundarilessness and a time when the body and its fluids were not a source of disgust. For Kristeva, the ego defines itself by a demarcation of its limits through mastering its waste and separating itself from those of the mother. It establishes itself as an individual, in its oneness. This concept of individualism is, it has been extensively argued, a crucial basis for the ideology of entrepreneurial capitalism. And, as has also been extensively argued, the residue of disgust, bodily waste, is the matter of ritual. In the last moments of *Xala,* the beggars take their revenge on El Hadji in a role reversal of power and humiliation. As El Hadji stands naked in front of his wife and daughter, the beggars crowd around and spit on him. This is the price that the blind man exacts for lifting the *xala.* And as the scene seems to continue beyond endurance, the film ends with a freeze-frame.

Sembene's film opens with the theatre of politics, moves through a ceremonial celebration of marriage, closes with a ritual of rebirth. The prophylactic rituals of fetishised manhood fail, both financially and sexually. Teshome Gabriel says: 'The spitting on El Hadji helps reincorporate him into the people's fold. In other words, the ritual becomes a folk method of purgation which makes El Hadji a literal incarnation of all members of the class or group that spit on him and consequently reintegrates him into folk society'.[20]

In submitting to the body, and to everything that fetishism disavows, psychic and political, El Hadji signals a lifting of amnesia and an acceptance of history. The freeze-frame resurrects a man, whole through community, stripped of the trappings of colonialism and fetishised individualism.

Teshome Gabriel draws attention to a scene between El Hadji and Rama in which words, emblems and the film image weave an intricate pattern of meanings at different levels of visibility:

Before Rama stands up to walk out of the frame Sembene makes us take note, once again, of the map of Africa behind her. We notice too that the colour of the map reflects the exact same colours of Rama's traditional boubou, native costume – blue, purple, green and yellow – and it is not divided into boundaries and states. It denotes pan-Africanism:
El Hadji: My child, do you need anything? (He searches in his wallet.)
Rama: Just my mother's happiness. (She walks out of frame as the camera lingers on the map.)

What Sembene is saying here is quite direct and no longer inaccessible. On one level Rama shows concern for her mother ... On another level ... her concern becomes not only her maternal mother, but 'Mother Africa'. This notion carries an extended meaning when we observe the shot of El Hadji – to his side we see a huge colonial map of Africa. The 'wax' and the 'gold' are posited jointly by a single instance of composition. Two realities fight to command the frame, but finally the 'gold' meaning leaps out and breaks the boundaries of the screen.[21]

Chapter 9

Netherworlds and the Unconscious: Oedipus and *Blue Velvet*

There are many different metaphors in which our thinking about cultural change takes place. These metaphors themselves change. Those which grip our imagination, and, for a time, govern our thinking about scenarios and possibilities of cultural transformation, give way to new metaphors, which make us think about these difficult questions in new terms.

Stuart Hall[1]

Western culture has found many such different metaphors for cultural change within the story of Oedipus. Oedipus himself undergoes personal transitions of status, from those of the folk-tale rite of passage (V. Propp) and the monomyth of accession to kingship (J.-J. Goux) to the tragic developments of *Oedipus Rex* and the ultimate spiritual apotheosis of *Oedipus at Colonus*. Deviations from the norm in the early narrative phase indicate that the Oedipus story itself, as myth in its own right beyond the personal tale, stands on the threshold of wider social and symbolic transformations. And, in turn, these transformations acquire a renewed significance following on from the Enlightenment period, when Oedipus became a privileged emblem of tension between rational consciousness and the return of the repressed, the persistence of the irrational unconscious. It was, of course, in the last decade of the 19th century when Freud was writing *The Interpretation of Dreams* that Oedipus acquired his modern persona in the emblematic narrative of psychoanalysis. Now, in the year of the centenary of cinema, the image of Freud in 1995 seems uncannily juxtaposed to the Lumières' first projections. My analysis of *Blue Velvet* (1986) as a site of the strange persistence of the Oedipus myth into twentieth-century popular culture will use the film as a site not only of Oedipal drama but also of the uncanny and the Gothic. My argument focuses, first of all, on the villain as father figure, a trope of Gothic fiction to which my reading of *Blue Velvet* gives an Oedipal origin; and then I go on to consider the Sphinx, a figuration of the marvellous, who can return to the popular imagination through the technologies of projection which first became a popular form in the Gothic period.

The cinema, with its ability to render visible the invisible and conjure up meanings outside the precision of language, creates a cat's cradle of semiotic, symbolic, metaphoric and all the other terms through which human culture has struggled, to work through and find representations for the imprecise and invisible workings of the human mind. *Blue Velvet*, directed by David Lynch, released in 1986, allows a number of these issues to be discussed together. In addition to the references and citations surrounding its Oedipal hero, the themes associated with the myth are given spatial or topographical imagery in *Blue Velvet*. The film exploits the cinema's ability to visualise narrative. The hero undergoes a transformation of status across a social spectrum by means of a vertical, metaphorical, journey into the lower depths of the psyche. A criminal 'underworld' provides the setting for the story's Oedipal drama, in which the 'repressed' of the law and the 'repressed' of consciousness converge. The journey is a movement towards the future, while the vertical descent suggests a return towards the past. Freud used imagery of ruins or the archaic as a metaphor for the insistent pressure of a repressed past on the conscious mind. The Gothic genre is, of course, literally haunted by the past, by its gloomy ruins, its subterranean passages, by its archaic superstitions and the 'returns' that mark its narratives. It is, perhaps, for this reason that it has never been easy to depict the archaic landscape and beliefs of the Gothic within the so-called New World. This is one of *Blue Velvet*'s most significant achievements. Its narrative topographies manage to install a 'nether'world within small-town America, above all through the villain, who, I will argue, acts as a materialisation of the archaic father from the Oedipus legend. The openness of this link, and the use of 'returns' from the past of Hollywood cinema, both in casting and in generic reference, suggest a new figuration for Gothic themes in American popular culture.

Blue Velvet is a film which knowingly uses the interface between persistent popular iconographies and psychoanalytic theory. The critic does not have to 'read in' or 'read against the grain', as the both generic and psychoanalytic references are clearly marked. It is probably only out of the self-consciousness of contemporary, post-modern Hollywood, in conjunction with Lynch's own influences such as Surrealism, and interests such as psychoanalysis, that such a film could appear.

I. Transitions

The transitional, hybrid nature of the Oedipus story, from folk-tale pattern to psychological drama, demands that the figure of the 'villain' should oscillate between the supernatural monstrous (the Sphinx) and an anthropomorphic monstrous, a projection of infantile fears of the father.

My interest in *Blue Velvet* was first aroused by its overt exploitation of the hybrid temporality of the Oedipus story. First, there is the narrative that is patterned around a young man's rite of passage from adolescence into maturity. Second, there is the story of infantile Oedipal desires and conflicts. The two are linked by the hero's curiosity and his fascination with the enigmas of the netherworld, which relates to the detective genre. The first of these stories is resolved by the hero's victory over the villain. *Blue Velvet* psychologises the villain through its embedding of the Oedipal drama. And this, in turn, Oedipalises the Gothic tradition of story telling, with its particular conflation of father figure with villain. At the same time, the film's citation of film noir allows it to use the detective theme in order to create a conflation between infantile curiosity (Sandy's first initiatives and then Jeffrey's illicit voyeurism) and the investigative drive of the law.

The story of a hero's adventures on a journey, which takes him through a rite of passage from youth into maturity, has carried important motifs from the folk-tale into popular cinema. Film theorists, for instance Peter Wollen in his analysis of *North by Northwest,* have used Vladimir Propp's *Morphology of the Folktale* to identify the characters and motifs that are associated with this narrative pattern. The story is one of social transformation, a narrative rite of passage. A young male hero, unmarried, poor, and of low social status, leaves his childhood home to undergo a series of adventures and trials in which he has to prove himself. The crucial phase of transformation takes place around conflict with and the ultimate defeat of a villain. At the end, in the Proppian model, the hero rescues the princess who has fallen into the villain's clutches (a dragon, a giant, a wicked witch). As a reward, he marries the princess, and the king, his father-in-law, bestows upon him half of his kingdom. He thus ends up mature, married, rich and of a higher social status. He is now the owner of a new home, a palace indeed, in which he is the representative of the Law (the power of the king).

Propp himself noticed that the first part of the Oedipus myth conforms closely to the structure that he had identified in Russian folk-tale and he discussed the similarities and divergences of pattern in his article 'The Oedipus Myth as Folk-tale'.[2] He argued that the deviations in the Oedipus story bear witness to a social transformation. Thus, a story which is itself an account of a hero's transition to a new social status reflects a wider, historical, transition. While the old folk-tale pattern is determined by a system of inheritance based on marriage, from father-in-law to son-in-law, the Oedipus story records the traumatic transition to a system of inheritance based on birth, from father directly to son. Oedipus seems, on the face of it, to follow the folk-tale pattern, leaving home, embarking on a journey, conquering a monster, the Sphinx, and being rewarded by the hand of the queen in marriage and the kingdom of Thebes. He has, in fact, returned to the place of his birth, from which he was banished as an infant, and has actually inherited his own father's kingdom, in direct patrilineal descent. And he has, of course, killed his father to make way for this perverse aberration of the folk-tale pattern, which places parricide and maternal incest at the very moment at which patrilineal inheritance is instigated.

Jean-Joseph Goux, in his book *Oedipus, Philosopher*,[3] draws attention to the Oedipus story as version of an initiation rite, analysing its structural similarity to, in his terms, the 'monomyth' of the hero's rite of passage to royal investiture. He considers the Oedipus story to be aberrant in the hero/villain relation. The Sphinx, structurally situated as the creature that must be defeated for the tale to reach its appropriate conclusion, is a female monster and is thus related to the other monsters of Greek legend, the Gorgon and the Chimera who are also defeated by heroes on their way to kingship, Perseus and Bellerophon. Goux argues that the female monsters stand in for a 'monstrous maternal', whose murder is essential for the rite of passage to take place. Thus the heroes' victory represents an act of matricide that necessarily precedes their ascension to kingship and marriage. The male initiate celebrates his separation from the archaic and overpowering mother. The monstrous mother is archaic in that she belongs to an earlier epoch, both in terms of the psychological development of child/subject and the social development of patriarchy. She is also literally monstrous, part animal, part bird, part human, belonging to an ancient realm of myth that would predate the humanoid appearance of the Olympian gods and goddesses.

Feminist film theorists have pointed out that this 'monstrous maternal' persists into contemporary popular culture. Teresa de Lauretis has analysed the topographical significance of the mythic monster figure, who stands, static, in the path of the hero's trajectory as a space that must be crossed.[4] And Barbara Creed has identified the mother alien in the *Alien* trilogy as a return of this figure.[5] However, the Oedipus myth is once again sited on a threshold. The story bears witness to a transformation in the villain function that will be of central importance in later popular cultures. Oedipus fails to kill the Sphinx. He answers her riddle and thus, as Goux points out, omits the initiate's act of matricide, leaving the Sphinx to self-destruct. The maternal monster is thus only present as a weak function; her challenge is reduced to the verbal and her defeat is reduced to suicide.

The Sphinx is placed in the narrative to mark the defeat of the villain by the hero and his reward with the hand of the princess (Queen Jocasta) and the kingdom (Thebes). But placed immediately before this motif of victory/defeat is another which the Proppian narrative cannot acknowledge in its true transformative sense. Oedipus has been confronted, just previously, at the fork in the road, by a terrifying old man who threatened to run him down and kill him. Oedipus, acting as he later claimed in self-defence, kills him instead. Laius and the Sphinx are doubled in the narrative structure. The Sphinx is present as a remnant of an archaic world and belief system. Laius introduces a new psychic element, inaugurating, perhaps, a new personification of villainy that would survive beyond the villain functions of dragons, witches, giants and so on. Thus, the function 'villain', once the maternal as static, archaic monster, is transposed onto a monstrous paternal, human in shape and, rather than static, in competition with the young man for space on the road. It is, in fact, by eliminating the old king that Oedipus is able to marry Jocasta and inherit Thebes, on a level that the story understands only in retrospect.

The Oedipus complex, in Freud's theory, is also a narrative of a rite of passage. It marks the transition from infancy to childhood, from a boundariless attachment to the mother in which her body and the infant's are inextricably intertwined in a complementary duality to the child's assertion of autonomy from the mother, achievement of a sense of self, and an understanding of his/her place in the cultural order of the family. For Freud, this transition was achieved only through a painful and never-to-be erased threat of castration, which emanates from the father. Lacan theorised the castration complex in the Oedipal trajectory more specifically as a traumatic, but necessary, passage on the way to an initiation into the Symbolic order of culture, through acquisition of language and understanding of the Name of the Father as the signifier of Law. In the process, the infant abandons his desiring and deeply erotic feeling for his mother, murderous jealousy of the father, identifying with the 'promise' that he will grow up to take his father's place within the Symbolic order.

Blue Velvet negotiates a merger of the two versions by embedding the Oedipal narrative of transition within the story of passage from youth to maturity. The hero's 'adventures' are not simply those of the folk-tale's triumphant encounter with danger and victory over evil. Following the Proppian pattern, Jeffrey Beaumont is, at the beginning of the story, still a callow youth. By the end of the movie, after his 'adventures', he has acquired a new maturity and is able to claim Sandy as his future wife. He has also, through his struggle with the villain and victory over him, inherited the place of the father and the father-in-law. He has moved into the position of authority, associated with the patriarchal function, and the Law.

However, the doubling, or distribution, of narrative functions between characters indicates the presence of the second, Oedipal, narrative pattern. While Sandy represents the Proppian princess 'to-be-married' as a reward for the villain's defeat, on the Oedipal level Dorothy represents the princess who must be rescued from the villain. The opening sequence gives an Oedipal twist to Jeffrey's father's collapse. And Mr Beaumont's subsequent illness allows two other figures to occupy the place of the paternal. One is literally the representative of the Law, Sandy's father (Detective Williams), while Frank Booth, the villain who focuses the conflict between hero and villain, emerges as a disturbing perversion of the paternal. His iconography conflates the underworld of the criminal, the netherworld of the city at night, with the unconscious of the Oedipal drama.

David Lynch makes use of specific psychoanalytic scenarios and citations in order to give Frank paternal as well as brutal attributes. The film's most famous and most shocking sequence is a vivid rendition of Freud's concept of the 'primal scene'. Jeffrey, hidden in the wardrobe, witnesses Frank's violent sexual attack on Dorothy. According to Freud, when a child first witnesses his/her parents' sexual intercourse, the sight is terrifying and probably traumatic. The child interprets the scene as one of violence, even sadism, in which the father, the stronger partner, carries out a brutal attack on the mother, the weaker. The mother, who is also, of course, the child's own love object, needs to be rescued. Within the perspective of the primal scene, Frank personifies all that is perceived as brutal in the father, and Dorothy personifies the mother's vulnerablity. In the child's fantasy, the mother would infinitely rather 'be married' to him/her than persecuted by such a monster, and she only undergoes such horrific humiliation to protect him/her from the father's attack. Jeffrey is the horrified witness of the primal scene, but its emotional impact and implications are extended and reiterated into the story as a whole. Jeffrey understands Frank's hold over Dorothy to be the direct result of her need to protect little Don, her son. And Dorothy sometimes calls Jeffrey 'Don'.

Jeffrey's hiding place, the wardrobe, accentuates his status in the scene as both infant and 'infantile voyeur'. The scene therefore condenses a fantasy enactment of the primal scene with a fantasy of desire for the mother. Before Frank arrives, Dorothy has entered her apartment, and started to undress. The film intercuts between the room and the wardrobe to emphasise Jeffrey's voyeuristic look. Dorothy's body is not, however, presented to the spectator in any way enhanced by the usual conventions of cinematic eroticism. When she answers the telephone and speaks to her son she is stamped as mother, and as vulnerable. But when she discovers Jeffrey's illicit presence in his hiding place, she threatens him with a knife, suddenly shifting from the vulnerable to the castrating mother. She infantilises him by forcing him to undress and then seduces him. Dorothy moves through contradictory iconographies of motherhood: from vulnerability to the father's aggression, to castrating threat to the helpless boy, to absolute incestuous desirability. Furthermore, the eroticism to which she initiates Jeffrey is perverse; she teaches him the sadistic sexuality that is associated with Frank. This scene, in all its permutations, is acted out with such extraordinary and shocking violence and eroticism that it is truly suffused with horror and the attraction of a fantasy scenario. The scene oscillates. Dorothy represents the 'monstrous maternal', the female villain of the old monster myths who threatens the small child and must be overcome in the name of autonomy and rational subjectivity. At the same time she is the vulnerable mother, threatened by the 'monstrous paternal', the male villain who confronts the child in Oedipal rivalry.

These psychoanalytic references place Dorothy and Frank within the realm of the unconscious, as the 'father' and 'mother' of the Oedipal child. *Blue Velvet* sends Jeffrey, not on the folk-tale's adventure into the liminal space away from home or outside the city, but on a journey into the Oedipal unconscious, to confront incestuous desire and the villainous father figure. In this sense, Frank represents the 'pre-Oedipal father'. The lifelessness of life in the small-town home contrasts with Dorothy's shockingly direct sexuality, her immediate seduction of Jeffrey, and Frank's horrific restless energy, always torn by violent emotion. But Frank is also, in a way, impotent. He is as dependent on his amyl nitrate fix for potency as Mr Beaumont is dependent on his oxygen apparatus for breathing. His rape of Dorothy is closer to Freud's vision of polymorphously perverse infantile sexuality than to adult genital sexuality, even at its most violent. He is far from a figure of mature masculinity. This is emphasised by his 'regression' to babyhood (wants to 'go back home'), his orality, voyeurism, sadism, acting out of the child's understanding of the female body as castrated and finally, and most significantly, his fetishistic fixation on the blue velvet. He is incapable of coherent speech and almost completely inarticulate in his repetition of obscenities. He is simultaneously an infant and the monstrous paternal.

In my 1987 article on the myth of Oedipus,[6] I was reminded of Frank Booth while writing about Laius. In the pre-story of Oedipus, which Freud has been accused of repressing, Laius had been exiled temporarily from Thebes and had taken refuge in the court of King Pelops in Sparta. There he had fallen in love with the king's young son Chrysippos, raped him and attempted to kidnap him. In revenge for this act of brutal violence, the king pronounced the curse that Laius would be killed by his son who would then incestuously marry his own mother, Laius's wife Jocasta. It was in order to escape this fate that Laius, in another act of brutality, ordered that his baby son Oedipus be killed. The joy-ride scene in *Blue Velvet* uncannily echoes these themes. Frank seems to recognise some affinity with Jeffrey when he says: 'You're like me' and before beating him up he puts on lipstick and kisses Jeffrey passionately on the lips. The brutal father seems to threaten the son with not only violence but a sexualised violence that approximates to rape. There is a sense in which Frank, like Laius, is pre-Oedipal. Laius in literal, generational chronology predates the Oedipal trajectory lived out by his son. Frank stands in polarised opposition to the Law, culture, the Symbolic order and, to all intents and purposes, verbal language.

Raymond Bellour puts the argument like this:

The bad father must die, in the final confrontation, so that the couple can be formed; he even has his double, his reverse image, the good father, who makes possible the entry into the geneaology, the continuity between generations. ... It is the movement from the adventurer, *sans foi ni loi* as we say in French (lawless and faithless) to the husband, the future father and the good citizen. ... The American cinema thus finds itself enacting the most classic paradigms elaborated for the subject of Western culture by Freudian psychoanalysis. ... My constant surprise was to discover to what degree everything was organised according to a classic Oedipal scenario which inscribed the subject, the hero of the film, in a precise relation to parricide and incest and to observe that his itinerary, his trajectory corresponded to a strict psychic progression which engaged the hero in the symbolic paths of Oedipus and of castration.[7]

Although Bellour draws attention to the persistence of the Oedipal narrative, he also describes how the Western erases the threat of the unconscious as the villain is erased from the story. The conclusion suggests that the traces of Oedipal desire are overcome and left behind in the story's lawless, liminal phase. The hero's erasure of the monstrous paternal allows the story to come to rest under the aegis of a new moral order. *Blue Velvet*, on the contrary, implies that the Symbolic order is imbricated with the monstrous paternal. The story records Jeffrey's transition into maturity, but at the same time the Oedipal figures of fear and desire have inscribed themselves into his psyche. When the camera emerges from Jeffrey's ear at the end of the film, the implication that everything else has been 'only a dream' is undercut by his new darkness of mood. It is clear that Frank Booth and Dorothy Vallens will live on in his unconscious, erupting into the symptomatic behaviour that characterises, and is repressed by, the patriarchal psyche.

The terrible violence and irrationality of the father/villain lie at the heart of the Gothic genre. The founding novel of the genre, Horace Walpole's *The Castle of Otranto* (1764), is a story of three failed fathers, but its narrative development is centred on Manfred's autocratic power. At the untimely death of his son, Manfred decides to marry his future daughter-in-law himself and the novel then unfolds in the aftermath of his monstrous fixation. Isabella's escape takes her into a 'netherworld', the characteristic Gothic *mise en scène* of underground passages, through which Manfred pursues her. Theodore, the young peasant whom Manfred also persecutes, rescues Isabella and it turns out that Manfred had usurped the estate to which Theodore is the rightful heir. Here again, a young man reaches maturity through a confrontation with a figure of the monstrous paternal, whose autocratic, irrational and instinctual tyranny belongs to a pre-Enlightenment age. In Mrs Radcliffe's *A Sicilian Romance* (1790), the Count imprisons his daughters' mother in an underground cave, directly under the deserted wing of his castle. The civilised surface life of the castle carries dark secrets beneath it and the father's behaviour oscillates between the darkness of the pre-Oedipal villain and Oedipalised patriarch.

Jane Austen's famous comment on the fashion for the Gothic, *Northanger Abbey*, written during the late 1790s at the height of Mrs Radcliffe fever, focuses both on the *mise en scène* of the Abbey and the heroine's semi-erotic terror of General Tilney, who, for her, becomes a figure of the villainous paternal. Breaking into a sudden parody of the Gothic's syntax, punctuation and use of the 'free indirect', Jane Austen suggests that the genre played on a state of mind, a propensity to fantasy in its young women readers:

> Catherine's blood ran cold with the horrid suggestions which naturally sprang from these words. Could it be possible? – Could Henry's father? – And yet how many were the examples to justify even the blackest suspicions! – And, when she saw him in the evening, while she worked

with her friend, slowly pacing the drawing-room for an hour together in downcast thoughtfulness, with downcast eyes and contracted brow, she felt secure from all possibility of wronging him. It was the air and attitude of a Montoni! – ... Unhappy man![8]

Jane Austen makes fun of the Gothic, but she takes seriously her heroine's desire to believe in the irrational evil conjured up by the genre. This rational, psychological portrait internalises Catherine's fears and renders them as figments of her imagination. The tensions between the exterior and the interior, the rational and the irrational, bring back the figure of Oedipus, to mark his status in the thought of the Enlightenment period.

II. The Enlightenment's Unconscious

It was with the publication of Horace Walpole's dream novel, *The Castle of Otranto* (1764) that the demonic found a literary form in the midst of Augustinian ideals of classical harmony, public decorum and restraint. Unreason, silenced through the Enlightenment period, erupts into the fantastic art of Sade, Goya and horror fiction.[9]

Jean-Joseph Goux emphasises that Oedipus defeats the Sphinx purely 'on his own', that is without the help from the gods essential to the other heroes' victories. Oedipus makes use of his own intelligence rather than magical objects donated by supernatural beings. He is thus poised on another threshold. He stands between a world inhabited by fabulous impossible creatures and gods and goddesses who intervene in the lives of men, and a world in which Man is at the centre and the 'marvellous' is equated with superstition. Oedipus does not deign to do battle with the Sphinx. She self-destructs when the riddle is answered, signifying that the epoch of credulity that had conjured up such creatures had come to an end.

When Oedipus was confronted with the riddle of the Sphinx: 'What speaks with one voice, walks on four legs in the morning, on two legs at noon and on three legs in the evening and is weakest when it has the most?' he answered, as everyone knows, with one word: 'Man.' This moment was adopted by Hegel as the founding moment of a subjectivity that is centred on human consciousness, that is on man's awareness of his own rationality. The relation between the question and its answer is not simply that of riddle and solution. The two terms are separated by the vast conceptual gap that represents the difference between meanings that are coded and obscure and those produced by man's ability to think philosophically.

Hegel uses the moment in the myth when Oedipus answers the riddle as a point of transition between two cultures: one is characterised by the philosophical abstraction of Greece, the other by 'Egyptian' symbolism. On this imaginary threshold the Sphinx epitomises the pre-rational. She is archaic and monstrous, a creature composed out of three different parts, human, animal and bird. She is a riddle and she poses a riddle. With a slight manipulation of geography and myth, Hegel conflates the Greek with the Egyptian Sphinx, thus enabling her to represent a culture of symbols, in which meaning is concealed in allusion. He wrote: 'In Egypt, on the whole, almost every shape is a symbol and a hieroglyph not signifying itself but hinting at another thing with which it has an affinity and thus a relationship.' Meaning has to be deciphered out of enigma. For Hegel, Oedipus is the prototypical philosopher, for whom thought can be expressed without mediation and obscurity. It is the anthropocentric answer 'Man' that causes the Sphinx to throw herself from the rock and kill herself.

Goux points out that the Cartesian revolution is itself Oedipal in its insistence on the autonomy of the individual subject, its insistence on the inherent ability of man to achieve rational thought without tradition or teaching:

> Descartes's patricidal gesture is incommensurable, in its import and its radicality, with any individual killing of any individual father. Descartes is a principal and abstract Oedipus. He denies the ontological dimension of paternity. He attempts to establish truth in the absence of that dimension, taking on himself, as an 'I' the function it purported to fulfil.[10]

The spirit of the Enlightenment attempts to elevate the subject's pure power of reason, and Oedipus is made to stand for its mythical origin. The traditional power of the priesthood, which held people in fear, ignorance and ritualised belief, could be swept away by the spirit of self-sufficient knowledge. The gods and goddesses, spirits and fairies, the saints and superstitions of Catholicism, even the purified, post-Reformation God himself, could all be dismissed as emanations of the human mind, simply figments of the imagination. From this perspective, Freud's theory of the unconscious appears on the intellectual scene as a final act of the Enlightenment. And psychoanalysis, from this perspective, constitutes a rational theory of the irrational, which could bring human fears, anxieties and credulities into a framework of articulate explanation. Even dreams could be translated out of their enigmatic language, interpreted and revealed to 'make sense'.

There is, of course, a further dimension to Freudian theory which is encapsulated in the next phase of the Oedipal trajectory. The effect of the presence of an unconscious in the human psyche is not dissolved or even mitigated by the fact that Freud formulated a theory and a vocabulary which describe and analyse it. The unconscious continues to haunt 'Man' even at his most rational. For Hegel, Oedipus stands on a threshold, an emblem of transition between the world of supernatural belief and rational understanding; for Freud, on the other hand, he stands on a threshold where the conscious mind meets the intractable presence of the unconscious. The Sphinx commits suicide, but Oedipus marries his mother. No longer the emblem of rational individualism, he becomes the emblem of the human psyche subject to 'the return of the repressed'.

Freud uses the Sophocles play *Oedipus the King* as his source material and his interest focuses on the events that take place within the spatial and temporal rules of the Greek tragedy, rather that in the wandering structure of the Proppian folk-tale type of story. These events come long after Oedipus's encounter with the Sphinx, his marriage and ascension to the throne, and concentrates on the return of the repressed which was of such interest to Freud. Freud transforms Oedipus from a figuration of human reason into a figuration of the human subordination to unreason. The Oedipal intelligence is, as the play progresses, at first clouded by resistance and then, through determined investigation and analysis, finally confronted with the real monster in the story: his own unconscious and his acts of parricide and incest.

To summarise in Jean-Joseph Goux's words:

> It is not surprising that Freud discovers the unconscious and the two Oedipal drives at the same time. The modern subject's self-consciousness is constituted as 'Oedipus's response', which leaves in obscurity, as a counterpart, the two never-extinguished drives that shape Oedipus's destiny. It is not just self-consciousness, reflective ego-centring that is Oedipean, as Hegel masterfully noted; it is also the unconscious and desiring counterpart that this response engenders, as Freud discovered. If consciousness is constituted 'in response to the Sphinx', the unconscious is the obscure, pulsional side of that response: patricide, incest.[11]

Oedipus thus becomes a double, Janus-faced, figure. He represents simultaneously humanity's utopian aspiration to the rational and to transcendent knowledge and its impossibility, the necessary failure, even the tragedy-laden fate, accompanying such arrogance. It is important to emphasise that, although Freud's discovery is, indeed, one of the essential intractability of the unconscious, it is still formulated and articulated within an Enlightenment aspiration. He not only notes that figures of fear and desire are strictly emanations of the human mind, but provides a language and a conceptual framework within which their meanings can be analysed.

In *Blue Velvet*, Jeffrey's rite of passage into maturity is also simultaneously a journey into the Oedipal unconscious. David Lynch does not allow the story to exorcise its demonic forces and return to the surface as a natural and normal site of being. The shots of the trees with the camera tracking into darkness, a candle flame, or a curtain blowing in the wind, suggest that the exorcised psychic forces live on in Jeffrey's unconscious mind. The hero's rite of passage into patriarchal maturity is built on his internalisation of the forces he overcame in the course of the story. And the last shot of the film shows mother and son, happily reunited in their ideal dyad, waiting for the whole process to begin all over again.

III. The Return of the Sphinx

Lacan's emphasis on the abstract, signifying nature of the father's symbolic authority links to both Propp's and Hegel's conception of the Oedipus story. Propp saw the Oedipus story as a transition to patrilineal inheritance, and Hegel 'Europeanised' the story by setting up a polarised distinction between an abstract and a symbolic system of representation. But it is essential to remember that, for Lacan as for Freud, language cannot escape from the effects of unconsciousness. His use of semiotics, his concept of the instability of meaning and its slippage from signifier to signifier, is a reminder that the Law is always fraught with unconscious effects. If the disposal of the Sphinx is, at one and the same time, the disposal of the 'monstrous maternal' and of 'Africa', her suicide acts as a metaphor for the repression of both the mother and the cultural other under the patriarchal Symbolic order. But the repressed returns, in disguised forms which are necessarily outside immediate transparent understanding, and demand interpretation which Freud compared to the deciphering of a rebus.

Hegel's beautiful characterisation of the Egyptian signifying system alters in the light of later psychoanalytic theory. He points out that the symbol and the hieroglyph are 'not signifying but hinting at another thing' and thus evokes the 'disguised' language of the Freudian unconscious, which makes use of condensation and displacement to find ways of articulating meanings unacceptable to the conscious mind. And when Hegel goes on to say: 'Egypt is the country of symbols, the country which sets itself the spiritual task of the self-deciphering of the spirit, without actually attaining to the decipherment',[12] he could be evoking the psychoanalytic project, in which the process of analysis deciphers signs, for instance the language of dreams, attempting to restore them to their original point of unconscious reference. But Hegel foresees the Lacanian warning of the ultimate impossibility of the task of decipherment; while signifiers form links sustaining slippages of meaning, pure reference constantly gets lost under an excess of signification.

The Sphinx belongs to the world of the marvellous, beyond the natural, in which disbelief is suspended in the face of supernatural phenomena. While Oedipus represents the unconscious, those elements in the human psyche that the Enlightenment did not acknowledge, the Sphinx represents a propensity to credulity and the persistent fascination with the marvellous and the supernatural that the Enlightenment, equally, failed to exorcise. Her image and the story of her fate can provide an appropriate metaphor for the culture of phantasmagoria that has always, technology permitting, fascinated credulous spectators. The story of projected phantasmagorias emerges as an accompaniment to the story of tension between rationality, superstition and the unconscious. It leads towards its twentieth-century apotheosis in the projected images of cinema which could also tell stories as well as simply amaze.

An important accompaniment to the culture of the Gothic was a fashion for ghosts, summoned up by phantasmagoric projections. The Enlightenment, illuminating the dark relics of religious belief with science and reason, banished ghosts and other terrifying manifestations only to have them crowd back through the culture of the Gothic. So, just as the old beliefs of the spirit world were swept away, their forms materialised onto magic lantern screens. The Gothic is closely tied to the proto-cinematic. Just after Matthew Lewis had become a best-selling author with the publication of *The Monk* in 1795, the Belgian showman Etienne Robertson was entertaining Paris with his phantasmagorias. Set in the labyrinthine underground vaults of the former Capuchin convent, Robertson put on a ghost show in mechanical projection. While the show overtly demystified superstitious belief, it used every trick of *mise en scène* to fill the audience with a sense of the 'horrid'. Terry Castle has argued that these phantasmagoric effects acted as a bridge between the spirits that people, once upon a time, believed existed in the world around them, and their relocation into the interiority of the human mind as symptoms of mental disorder. The phantasmagorias showed, she says, 'that although one knew ghosts did not exist, one saw them all the same, without precisely knowing how'. She continues: 'The rationalists did not so much negate the traditional spirit world but displace it into a realm of psychology. Ghosts were not exorcised but only internalised and reinterpreted as hallucinatory thoughts.'[13]

And thoughts could take on the haunting reality of ghosts. The supernatural marvellous is relocated in the mechanical uncanny which can then become a metaphor for the persistence of human belief in the irrational. Tom Gunning's article 'Phantom Images and Modern Manifestations' traces a line of descent, almost like a genealogy, across the latter half of the 19th century, that links the key role of women in spiritualist manifestations to ghost photography and to popular spectacle:

> While photographing manifestations played the more conventionally scientific role of capturing in a hopefully incontrovertible manner the evidence of the senses, the increasingly spectacular nature of Spiritualism mined a deep fascination in visual events that amazed spectators by defying conventional belief. The potential entertainment value of such visual attractions was immediately recognised.[14]

The lineage then leads to the London showman, John Maskeleyne, who understood the public taste for such spectacles and opened the Egyptian Hall in London as a permanent magic theatre. Gunning points out that: 'The fascination in visual entertainments and modern technology made the Egyptian Hall a natural place for one of the first permanent English film programmes.'[15] And it was Georges Méliès's visit to the Egyptian Hall that led him to bring together the different strands in his trick films. Christian Metz identified the fascination with illusion as specific to cinema. Suspension of disbelief, he says, is a similar mental mechanism to that of fetishism: 'I know these images are not real, but all the same ...'. And it was as Freud was working on *The Interpretation of Dreams* that the first film projections took place in 1895. Just as Freud extended rational investigation to the world of dreams, they returned on the movie screen, with the phantasmatic stories and scenarios that can recreate the marvellous and make any hybrid monster come to life.

However, the cultural impact of Freud's unveiling of the human unconscious and its language can be seen in its appeal to the Surrealists, who were totally opposed to Enlightenment rationality (even though they professed great admiration for psychoanalysis) and used the cinema as a way of materialising the dream life. André Breton was himself an admirer of both the English Gothic and cinema. In his introduction to the catalogue of the 1930 Surrealist exhibition, he commented on Walpole's account of the origins of *The Castle of Otranto* in a dream, in which a hand of an enormous scale appeared inside a house. Breton describes cinema in dream terms: 'From the instant he takes his seat to the moment he slips into a fiction evolving before his eyes the spectator passes through a critical point as captivating and imperceptible as that uniting waking and sleeping.'[16] And Brunius describes cinema as 'an involuntary simulation of a dream. The darkness of the auditorium, tantamount to closing the eyelids on the retina, and, for thought, *to the darkness of the unconscious*' (my emphasis).[17] Fragmented words and images appear on a screen:

> Neither chronological order nor relative values of duration are real. Contrary to the theatre, film, like thought, like the dream, chooses some gestures, defers or enlarges them, eliminates others, travels many hours, centuries, kilometers in a few seconds, speeds up, slows down, goes backwards.[18]

The Surrealists' passionate invocation of the irrational creates a link between the Gothic aesthetic, Freudian theory and the dream-like qualities of the cinema. They are also an acknowledged influence on David Lynch. *Blue Velvet* manifests these links through its narrative structure, and in its organisation of narrative into a topographical system. The Oedipal narrative unfolds in a *mise en scène* of the uncanny. In his 1919 essay,[19] Freud analysed the uncanny as the *unheimlich*, the unhomely, and located the strangeness of its effect within the home itself, ultimately locating it in the womb, the first home, and the tomb, the last. The power of cinematic language juxtaposes spaces and images which disturb the familiar with strangeness and the uneasy intimations of fear and desire. The uncanny is closely associated with place, or with the projection of unconscious unease into a fantastic topography. The Gothic is, quite obviously, a genre of uncanny *mise en scènes*: ruins, tombs, labyrinthine underground passages give material visibility to the presence of the past, doubling up the way that the stories are actually set in past historical time. The uncanny also occupies the underworld of the nineteenth-century city, celebrated in the detective genre that investigates its enigmas. The uncanny topography extends to the 'underworld' of crime, the nether side of law and order. All these spatial representations, the ruins of the past, the criminal milieu, make use of the division between surface and netherworld. Dorothy's apartment is, however, on a higher rather than a lower plane. As an apartment block rather than a self-contained 'home', the building introduces the architecture of the city into the topography of the small town. The ethos of the city at night and its underworld, associated with Dorothy and Frank, is thus carried by the polarisation between small town and urban space, and the spatial opposition is also strongly ideological. The high-rise building carries connotations of the 'nether'world. This 'nether' theme is confirmed by Jeffrey's disguise as the 'bug man'. The simple displacement of bug imagery links Dorothy's apartment to the bugs in the undergrowth in the film's opening sequence and the reappearance of the bug to blight the happy ending announced by the robin's return in the film's closing moments.[20]

Blue Velvet's opening sequence is designed around these intricate topographical metaphors, but in such a way as to make its implications as apparent as possible. The binary opposition between the everyday and netherworlds is there for all to see and to grasp. The sequence begins with a sunlit, leafy, small-town street, inhabited by school children and the benign authority of the fire brigade. The sequence ends in the darkness of the undergrowth, where, invisible to the normal eye, hideous insects are locked in mortal combat. This opposition is easy to understand and foreshadows the topographical organisation of the story that is to come, between light/day and dark/night, the institutions of law and the criminal underworld, conscious perception and unconscious experience, and between hero and villain. However, the surface world is depicted as 'surface'. It has the immaterial, itself uncanny, quality of the cliché which speaks of appearance and nothing else and the impermanent, almost comic, quality of the postcard which has no substance other than connotation. On the other hand, unlike the flatness and colour saturation of the opening images, the darkness draws in the camera with the force of fascinated curiosity.

The sequence sets up a spatial configuration around the home itself, that is suspended between the opposition surface/underworld. First, there is a shot of a house, the small-town home, white, with a picket fence. This image of the homely is quickly rendered uncanny. Mother and father are located one on the inside and one on the outside, the father waters the garden and the mother watches television. Suddenly a knot forms in the garden hose, and the father collapses with a heart attack. As he lies on the ground, the hose spurts water in a phallic stream and a toddler appears walking towards him, like a manifestation of the Oedipal death threat.

Small drops of water are reduced to slow motion as a little dog snaps at them over the man's prone body. Inside, a gun appears in close-up on the television screen, as the mother sips her tea. The collapse of the homeliness of the scene is accentuated by the cinematic effects, the slow motion in particular, and the sound effects which, as the camera follows the line of the hose pipe towards the undergrowth, drown out the strange, melancholic 'Blue Velvet' song, which prefigures the erotic element in the story, with noise of an indecipherable nature.

In *Blue Velvet*, the story buries a narrative of the unconscious within a frame that belongs to a world of normality. This latter world is, in fact, deeply implicated with its other, and exists as a fragile bulwark set up to keep out the forces of darkness. Given that *Blue Velvet*'s setting is small-town America, the film has to construct its 'Gothic' iconographies and *mise en scènes* out of generic and psychoanalytic references. The film excavates a topography of the fantastic, of an underworld, out of a social setting which appears to repress its very possibility. A vocabulary of visual and rhetorical devices and a syntax of story telling appear on the screen like phantasmagoric shapes whose immanent, misty, smoky, material congeals gradually into visibility. David Lynch uses this vocabulary and syntax in such a way that it should be readable to anyone in the audience who is prepared to think about it.

These images make a particular demand on the audience to figure out their relationship, to register the patterns set up between the opposing motifs that appear on the screen, while noting the imbrications between them as enigmatic and mysterious, as material that will have to be deciphered by the plot. In this way, as, during the main line of the story, Jeffrey will have to pursue and investigate the clues to the mystery of Dorothy Vallens and Frank Booth, so the audience will have to follow a parallel process of decipherment which cannot find full resolution within the consciousness of the protagonists themselves. For Freud, the topograpical metaphor that he used, in his early formulation of his theories, to evoke the relation between the conscious and unconscious aspects of the psyche was only the beginning of the story. There was no simple movement between the two. The unconscious manifested repressed desires into the conscious mind through a translation, or disguising of ideas, by means of the processes of condensation and displacement. The displacements activated by the images of the uncanny set up the more complicated displacements activated by the Oedipal narrative.

The specific formal properties of cinema play a crucial part in creating this further textual level in the film. They reverberate resonances across images, setting up links, which tie together into a chain of significance, rather as Frank's obsession with the blue velvet leaves fragments of the material scattered across the development of the drama. This is a point where the mechanisms of the dream work (condensation and displacement) find an equivalence in the cinema. In cinema, shifts in scale or repeated camera movements can tie together images to create linked meanings, either opposing the two in a binary opposition or carrying the significance of one image over and onto another. The language of cinema can set up meanings that inform each other not only through the nature of their content but through the rhetoric of their visualisation.

David Lynch uses psychoanalytic theory quite blatantly, almost a 'dollar-book Freud', as Orson Welles said of *Citizen Kane* (1941), to bring a Gothic uncanny home to roost in the mythology of small-town America and its amorphous temporality, a 1950s 'once upon a time'. Traditionally and innovatively, with a camp wit, he suggests that the cinema screen has been the site of phantasmagoric projection, which reached its supremacy in Hollywood. With its stars, its genres and its technological perfection, Hollywood recreated the marvellous, in its glamour, in its supernatural effects, and in the sutured surface world of its story telling. It is only with the decline of the Hollywood system, perhaps, that the cinema, once upon a time the guarantee of modernity and the progressive orientation of the New World, can become the archaic for American popular culture. The cinema always had something of the android in its fascination; its beauty and naturalism were only a mechanical effect, the animation of still frames, that could grind only too easily into stasis. And as the great stars grew old and died, their images continued to shine from television screens in a perpetual state of animation from beyond the grave.

Blue Velvet was released in 1986, the high point in the reign of the United States' first movie star President, whose own formation and self-image were grounded in the last moments of the Hollywood studio system, as well as the political paranoia and white suburban spread of the 50s. The year 1986 also saw a small plane shot down over Nicaragua, leading to the disclosure of the labyrinthine underworld known as 'covert operations'. The topographies implied in the metaphors suggest an uncanny underside to the surface presented by the President, himself an image of the uncanny: made-up, artificial and amnesiac. *Blue Velvet* restores an uncanny to American culture that the uncanny President disavows. In Freud's definition the uncanny is simultaneously located in homeliness and is the eruption of something that should remain hidden. *Blue Velvet* uses the cinema's own rhetoric to portray the uncanny as, for instance, when Sandy first appears on the screen in a long fade up from black and accompanied by a swelling score. The film also depicts the forces of the unconscious through a repeated topography which is decipherable to any spectator while at the same time evoking shades of the Gothic. The hidden is brought to the surface to trace its persistence rather than its erasure.

For Hegel, the passage from an unconscious symbolics (the Egyptians) to a conscious symbolics and to pure concept (the Greeks) leaves no residue. ... For Freud, on the contrary, there is an irreducible residue. The unconscious symbolics, that archaic mode of speaking based on the affinity of images, their tropological power of evocation and correspondence, is never completely supplanted. If that symbolisation has ceased to be collectively dominant, has stopped structuring the mode of communication of subjects in a society where conceptual thought reigns, it lingers in the subject's unconscious as the unrecognised counterpoint to the collective chorus that has submerged it; it persists as an effect of the split it has instituted in each individual soul. The primary processes of psychic activity and dreams continue to operate according to the logic of the archaic writings. Egypt (figuration in aspective) did not fade away in the face of perspective without leaving any remainder. It has become internal and individual.[21]

Or, perhaps, a collectivity that projected symbolisation across conceptual thought, and maintained the primary processes of psychic activity and dreams, might describe the cinema.

Postscript

Changing Objects, Preserving Time

I was actually taught opposites in school ... The teacher said that black was the opposite of white, sweet was the opposite of sour and that up was the opposite of down. I began to make my own list of opposites: the number one must be the opposite of the number ten, ice was the opposite of water and birds were the opposite of snakes.

But soon I had real problems, because if snakes and birds were opposites, where could I put the flying rattlesnake that we saw every night in the sky as the rattlesnake star? I theorized that in certain circumstances things could act like their opposites. If grey is the blending of the opposites black and white then the flying rattle snake could be seen as a grey bird.

Jimmie Durham, 'The Search for Virginity'

I believe that the acts and perceptions of combining, of making constant connections on many levels, are the driving motivation of our aesthetic ... So it is a system that attempts to break down separations, and is therefore an integral part of all other systems and activities. European culture has evolved into one of separations, of classifications and of hierarchies. I do not mean to imply that one culture is totally positive and the other totally negative, just that they are truly different. With that remarkable difference we find ourselves invaded by European culture. That directly involves artistic work with political work: two necessities that are inextricably bound to each other.

Jimmie Durham, 'Ni' Go Tlunh A Do Ka'[1]

These two quotations from Jimmie Durham's essays draw attention to his interest in the forms in which concepts are materialised. Abstract concepts, both philosophical and commonsense, latch onto modes of representation in a way that is both inevitable and questionable. Durham's art questions and makes visible the forms that inflect thought and, in these two quotations, he also draws attention to the way concepts congeal into patterns or configurations. The configurations formed by 'opposites' and 'hierarchies'

155

suddenly begin to lose their obviousness and appear as means of clothing complex issues according to a system of patterning. The polar metaphor that governs opposites creates an unbridgeable gap that is fixed and naturalised by its spatial patterning. Hierarchy also implies a spatial, or topographical, ordering around the metaphors of high and low. Jimmie Durham is a political artist, from the point of view of both the content of his work and its formal implications. But his politics also extends to exploring the relation between forms and concepts, including the ability of words to conjure up images and of images to convey ideas.

His 'acts and perceptions of combining' and 'breaking down of separations' form a conceptual point of departure for his art but also evoke the blurring of 'categories' that marks all aspects of his creative work, from poetry to politics to art. To begin with, his art evades boundaries of genre. It is easiest to describe him as a sculptor, but only because so many of his objects are constructions that stand free in space and can be approached from every angle. Even the sculptural constructions break out of formal unity. They are often decorated with a heterogeneous collection of extraneous things, such as written messages, a photograph, words, drawings and particularly found objects of various kinds. Titles are often an intrinsic element, emphasising the importance of words, while the materials themselves might range from wood to paper to PVC piping to metal from cars, screens from TVs, antlers from animals (to name a few). Such a variety of material generates, almost incidentally, a variety in the ways in which the works create meaning. So, from a semiotic point of view, written messages, sometimes in English and sometimes in Cherokee, are only comprehensible to those who understand the linguistic system and are within a symbolic code; wood can be whittled into the likeness of a figure, recognisable through an iconic code; and found objects, included in their own right, maintain an indexical link with their origins. But once again, these categories of sign overflow into and across each other to include many other kinds of materials and meanings.

It might well be possible to locate the blurring of boundaries that characterises Durham's work within the negative aesthetics of the contemporary avant-garde. From this point of view, his ideas and motivations would converge and overlap with other challenges to homogeneous aesthetics. But the concept of negativity, with its dependence on a binary opposition, is not an important origin or motivation for Durham's thought. Negation depends on opposition and polarisation, and thus suggests a conceptual terrain in which ideas materialise into a spatial relation, outside the mobility of contradiction. In Durham's work, ideas continually aspire to movement, breaking out of the purely visible into displacement, so that meanings are able to leap across objects with the agility of wordplay and, above all, irony. Irony assumes an awareness of the implied, the unsaid, as a basis for its wit and thus necessarily activates the viewer's own train of thought, tracing the twists and turns of ideas hidden in a simple juxtaposition of objects or word and object. To take an obvious example: 'Pocahontas'

Underwear' (a detail from *On Loan from the Museum of the American Indian*) in which a pair of feathered knickers sets up resonances between different kinds of fetishistic display (the museum and the erotic), while the reference to Raleigh and Astor evoke two 'robber barons' of different epochs, one travelling from England to the Americas, the other from the United States to England. The displacement of ideas and the displacement of journeys bounce off each other, while the reference to Pocahontas remains an ironic, empty sign. The work demands thought by means of wit and amusement, then turns to the seriousness of the politics and history.

Jimmie Durham's art objects emerge from a radicalism in which links between things are more important than demarcations between them. In keeping with the blurring of boundaries, his objects cannot be framed, either actually or in imagination. None of his works have the appearance of finish or completeness that would give them a privileged autonomy in time and space. His early sculptures, dating from 1972, are the result of a negotiation between artist and material which has continued to be central to his work throughout his career. His material does not lose its own nature as object. Durham makes explicit, or visible, his chosen objects' own, inherent, formal properties and intrinsic beauty, be it, in the 1972 work, the facets of a piece of polished wood or a more specifically anthropomorphic shape emerging out of oak. Some of these sculptures juxtapose two elements, such as a piece of black granite suspended on steel or black granite with iron, and the different materials are given a formal, unified pattern. In his later works, for instance those of the mid-80s, his sculptures are no longer organised around an aesthetic of formal unity. By this time Durham had begun to use assorted materials and ideas in discontinuity and dialogue. The sculptures still manifest an almost hedonistic pleasure in their materials and a confidence in their potential to evoke meaning and feeling. At first sight, these sculptures might often seem to be the product of 'bricolage', but in fact they are works of 'montage', in that the idea behind them is an essential part of their function. Although this emphasis on material could also be understood within Modernist terms, Durham foregrounds material politically and intellectually as well as aesthetically. He draws attention not only to the material signifiers of art but to the forms, the conceptual equivalent of material signifiers, in which thought itself materialises.

Given that thought, in addition to being moulded and shaped by metaphor, tends to be patterned by formal systems of conceptualisation, its content, and the materialisation of its content, is affected by its form. A 'poetics of thought' would draw attention to these patterns which materialise thought and would analyse the way in which abstract ideas attract certain spatial shapes and organising figurations. In Durham's art, ideas work through the juxtaposition and modification of one thing by another. It is a system that creates a conceptual space through displacement, with continuous shifts of meaning and resonance. Words, and the titles of the works themselves, are an intrinsic part of the process. This system involves, implicitly, a polemical indictment of binary thought. It is in this sense that his work, while being the product of a history and a culture that stands in confrontation with the mainstream of American history and culture, stands outside the concept of negation.

Durham is a political artist. His work is the product of an aesthetic stance and mode of thought that have their own political integrity, and, at the same time, it is a critique of the world and its view that he rejects. His culture and the kind of art he produces do not invoke a simple continuity with the history, culture and art of the native American people; Durham's art is the end-product of a very deep reflection on the Indian people's losses of culture, art, history and world view. Confrontation supersedes negation. Almost like the witnesses to a disaster that evades articulate expression, Durham's objects 'give evidence' through symptomatic appearance; they fill the vacuum left by a history of denial and misunderstanding. As a native American artist and intellectual, he represents the history that reduced his culture to traces and tatters, not iconically through an imagery of resemblances, but conceptually and aesthetically. Once again, his work collapses the boundary that demarcates the 'once upon a time' of nostalgia and invokes a potential mobility and flexibility of social being and a potential mediation and exchange of culture.

Native American history and culture fell victim to a binary mode of thought that had increasingly important legal and social implications for the political development of the United States. Although this mode of thought was inscribed into the first encounters between European and native people (revolving around the familiar oppositions of nature/culture, wilderness/cultivation, savagery/civilisation), this kind of binarism acquired an extra and disastrous significance during the 19th century, as the United States attempted to assimilate different waves of mass European, mainly peasant, migration. Christian thought has always tended to revolve around a broad antinomy between good and evil, even though adherence to this belief in an extreme form was rejected by the Church as the Manichaean heresy in the very early days of Christianity. The term 'Manichaean' may be used nowadays to describe any conceptual outlook which revolves around moral binary oppositions and which can, of course, extend beyond the theological. The theological good/evil opposition links to a cultural hero/villain opposition which has flourished from folk-tale to modern popular culture. The 'logic of the excluded middle' acts as an intellectual template and provides easy means of categorising the unfamiliar or the threatening, and avoids the need to negotiate with 'foreign' patterns of thought or ways of living. In the native American subjection to the 'excluded middle', many aspects of indigenous culture were erased. For instance, although the products of Indian cultivation had supported early settlers in times of need, this aspect of their economy was forgotten and lost under the image of an essentially nomadic, hunting-dependent society.

Frantz Fanon invokes the term 'Manichaean' to characterise the world of colonialism as 'a world cut in two':

> The colonial world is a Manichaean world. It is not enough for the settler to delimit physically, that is with the help of the army and the police force, the place of the native. As if to show the totalitarian character of colonial exploitation the settler paints the native as a sort of quintessence of evil. Native society is not simply described as a society lacking in values. It is not enough for the colonialist to affirm that those values have disappeared from, or still better, never existed in, the colonials' world. The native is declared insensible to ethics; he represents not only the absence of values but the negation of values.[2]

As critics have so often commented, the mythology of the United States, while disavowing its colonial heritage, depends on Manichaean modes of thought, particularly as represented in its privileged manifestation, Hollywood cinema. In Ronald Reagan's political demonologies, the Christian, racial, Hollywood and cold war forms of binary thought flourished to the point of absurdity, most obviously erupting in the Evil Empire rhetoric. Jimmie Durham's work confronts the rhetoric of binarism in two ways. First, his objects create meaning and emotion through gradual, delicate modifications, displacements and ironies. On the other hand, he also addresses the chasm between native and colonising Americans as a site of political dispossession, repression in image and representation and the fetishisation of a false history. The 'us/them' shifter of separation turns into the 'I/you' shifter of address.

I would like to expand this rather abstract opening section by considering Jimmie Durham's actual art works in greater detail, starting with my reactions and responses to his exhibition Original Re-Runs, held at the Institute of Contemporary Arts in London in 1994. The name, Original Re-Runs, with its Dadaist connotations, already implied a threat to familiar logic and usual ways of seeing and understanding.

Although all interesting art challenges the familiar and the usual, Durham uses his art, as I have argued above, to force an intellectual and political re-evaluation of the relation between seeing, the primacy of the visual, and understanding. But, looking at Original Re-Runs, these kinds of considerations only emerged very gradually through the slow process of working through the objects on display. And the theoretical impact of the work, and the thoughts I have outlined so far, could only come into focus in the aftermath of the exhibition's first surprising, disorientating, impact.

The first impact came from the sheer physical presence of the sculptures. They flaunt the rawness of their raw material whatever it might be, from wood with many forms and finishes, to plastic piping, to identifiable things which still preserve their original autonomy. And then, eventually, they became simultaneously a source of intuitive and intellectual reverie.

They seemed to stimulate thoughts that combined free-floating responses to the visual wit of the works and their curious beauty with a more concentrated, insistent, intellectual questioning. Looking at the surrounding objects, I felt immediately addressed but also asked to stand back and think again. This is the sensation that I want to evoke while trying to write about Jimmie Durham's work. My response is personal. However, I hope it might reflect the way that his objects possess the power to force thought and challenge sight, almost imperceptibly, with a kind of careless, throwaway style. Standing back at the time, questions began to take shape in my mind which have influenced the broad outlines of this chapter. First and foremost, how did this work come to be what it is, especially its mapping out of time and transformation of time into space? The gallery hand-out indicated the artist's origins, and anyway most people visiting the gallery would have some idea about Jimmie Durham's Cherokee descent and considerable involvement in the American Indian Movement. I would like to focus my curiosity on the objects' political reflection on time, space and colonisation and their insistence on a mode of understanding which derives neither from polarities nor from the immediate impressions of vision. To decipher Durham's work it is necessary to observe closely and to stand back and wonder.

I want to use the lay-out of Original Re-Runs as a way into this discussion. The exhibition created, in the first instance, an encounter with its space, so that one became aware of the space as a consciously produced environment before encountering the individual objects within it. Durham gave the ICA site a life of its own and it took on a momentum which carried one through a gallery space which had been transformed into a customised and vitalised place. The exhibition had several ropes stretching down from the very top of the walls to coil around on the floor. As the ropes dissected the empty areas of the gallery, dead or invisible spaces acquired an extra dimension. A visual and physical topography materialised that made itself felt and then had to be negotiated on the ground. The gallery had to be manoeuvred with consideration and an awareness that was implicit rather than directed. Empty areas were drawn into a general spatial relation and the works were encountered, almost stumbled across, in a casual mapping with its own hidden agenda.

While the organisation of the gallery integrated the sculptures and their surrounding space, it was also broken up by a series of signs that suggested confrontation rather than negotiation. Red, white and blue, freestanding, like street directions that would either bar or allow access, they jumped out at the eye, punctuating the implicit moulded and mobile space towards an expectation of command. But a second glance showed that a complex spatial system was at work which contrasted two ways of looking. One system could only be taken in properly from the top of the steps at the entrance to the gallery. From this position, the signs could be seen all at once and their high-impact visibility dominated the rest of the exhibition, like an overlay, or surface layer running across it. Looking from sign to sign, one series, in red and white, ran from the front, VERACITY, through the middle, VERACRUZ, to the very back wall, VORACITY. The words linked together through series and displacement of meaning, in a manner that undercut their immediate visual impact. These signs drew attention to two others, blue based with white lettering, VIRGIN and VIRGINIA, which linked back obliquely into the system. Later, I came across this quotation from Paolo Freire in an early essay of Durham's, which seemed to throw further light on the critical implication of the signs:

> In mass societies where everything is prefabricated and behaviour is al-most automized, people are lost because they do not have 'to risk them-selves'. They do not have to think about even the smallest things; there is always some manual which says what to do in situation A or B. Rarely do people have to pause at a street corner to think what direc-tion to follow. There's always an arrow which deproblematizes the situ-ation. Although street signs are not evil in themselves and are necessary in cosmopolitan cities, they are among the thousands of directional sig-nals which, introjected by people, hinder their capacity for critical thinking.[3]

The system set up by the metal signs inscribed a correct position for taking in and reading the words at a glance. Willy-nilly, one was placed at a domi-nant position, able to survey the space in which the sign system mapped across the rest of the exhibited works. From this initial perspective, the two, the signs and the sculptures, were in opposition. The signs were like signs of colonial presence, literally inscribed across and over the gallery space. The metallic material, the industrially produced objects, the words themselves, the viewer's perspective, contrasted with the rest of the ob-jects, which could not be accurately taken in from this position and which had, from a distance, a rough, organic resonance. Thus, at first glance, the exhibition's actual lay-out rendered visible the binary oppositions nature/culture, industrial/organic, word/object, above/beneath, modern/archaic, civilised/ primitive, city/country, and so on. And the subsequent journey into the gallery and through the work would be one in which this first impression would be modified and finally transformed. However, the signs' highly visual network across the room, shining with the red, white and blue of the US and British national flags, was already, at this first glance, open to transformation and modification that challenged the bi-nary assumption.

The word VIRGIN carries the concept of the 'virgin land', evoking European disavowal of any cultural, or perhaps even human, presence in the New World.[4] Such a disavowal, of course, not only stemmed from the logic of binary thinking, but also allowed the question of occupation and the establishment of ownership to be conveniently avoided. And the word VIRGINIA supplies a specific historical reference. The English colony of Virginia was only established in the mid-17th century, after various false starts in the late 16th, and has not been easily integrated into the myths of American ontology. Peter Hulme quotes from Perry Miller's attempt to construct an 'American Genesis' as dating from the Puritan migration ('I recognize ... the priority of Virginia, but what I wanted was a coherence from which I could coherently begin'). Hulme then comments:

> There is little in Virginia's early history to give a satisfying sense of an 'innermost propulsion' at work. Even worse, perhaps, Virginia had difficulty in maintaining the coherence and integrity that its name had hopefully suggested, the proper boundary between the 'self' and 'other' that is necessary to any establishment of national identity.[5]

And then, as every English school child knows, the colony was named in honour of Queen Elizabeth I, whose virginity was as mythic as that of the 'virgin land'.

The other series (VERACITY, VERA CRUZ, VORACITY) sets in motion another concatenation of ideas associated with colonialism. Ironically sited between religion and greed, 'Vera Cruz' evoked the Atlantic port in Mexico, named by the Spaniards with the unconscious accuracy of the pathological symptom. The name irresistibly conjured up the fetishistic aspect of contemporary Catholic belief in the True Cross (little bits of which were sold in forest-like proportions before the Reformation) and thus also the phantasmagorias that fuelled the Spanish conquest and colonisation process. Any truth that is upheld with utter certainty implies an element of irrational belief and the pathological sense of rectitude that justifies intolerance. It was this pathological certainty that justified the colonisation of Mexico in the eyes of the Catholic Kings (Ferdinand and Isabella) as a continuation of the expulsions and forced conversions of Muslims and Jews that 'unified' the Spanish nation after 1492. VERACITY and VORACITY then bear witness to the inextricable imbrication of political and personal greed with religious convictions. The literal displacement of the letters, and the use of CITY as a shifting signifier, celebrate the displacement of meaning with the simple gesture of a joke. But the shifting signifiers, condensation and displacement, allow the viewer to consider the signs as 'signs' within a psychoanalytic and semiotic intellectual framework, and thus bring to mind the intellectual disciplines which have particularly attempted to challenge inherited political and religious certainties. Encountering the signs from the vantage point of the gallery steps, the viewer was introduced to the vision of perspective and then warned against trusting in its truth. Tzvetan Todorov brings a number of these themes together in the following point:

> European linear perspective may not have originated from a concern to validate a single and individual viewpoint, but it becomes its symbol, adding itself to the objects represented. It may seem bold to link the introduction of perspective to the discovery and conquest of America,

yet the relation is there, not because Toscanelli, inspirer of Columbus, was a friend of Brunelleschi and Alberti, pioneers of perspective (or because Piero della Francesca, another founder of perspective, died on October 12, 1492) but by reason of the transformation that both facts simultaneously reveal and produce in human consciousness.[6]

Just as the dead space of the gallery had been materialised into a place with rhythm and presence, so the rigid truth of the word/name dissolved into wit, allusion and uncertainty. In this way, the gallery gained two extra dimensions in addition to the usual relation between viewer and art object in a gallery setting. First, the look that understands 'at a glance' was invoked and then discomforted. Interconnections between the signs had to be mapped by looks, and the looks took time, even if a short time, to read, to get the point, to be amused, and then to think about what it meant as a first step into the show as a whole. And once the show is stepped into, the signs will continue to reverberate as the visitor negotiates the other topography shaped by the hanging and coiling ropes. Before even thinking about the individual works on display, the scene is set for curiosity and encounter and the actual sculptures and other works on display had to be approached without recourse to immediate assumptions or a unified perspective. They had to be viewed and understood from different positions and with various approaches. For instance, written messages had to be read close to, but may also be integral to work that, as an aesthetic whole, could only be taken in from a distance that renders the words illegible. After the initial experience of word displacement seen from a single position, the rest of the exhibition became a journey of subtle displacements through material and ideas.

For instance, 'Red Turtle' (1991) places the turtle shell at the meeting point between two straight sticks forming a large X and two winding ones forming a horizontal snake across it. The snake sticks and the turtle shell are composed of the primary colours, red, yellow and blue. Between the two lower sides of the X, a piece of paper is attached. 'Red Turtle' caught my glance in the exhibition as a juxtaposition of shapes, emphasised with colour, that was extremely simple in design but held my visual attention and imagination. After looking at it from a distance for a time, I went over to read the words on the paper, watching it change from pure shape into legible message. Written in rough capital letters, it spelt out the colonial educator's classic *cri de cœur*: 'We have tried to train them; to teach them to speak properly and to fill out forms. We have no way of knowing whether they truly perceive and comprehend or whether they simply imitate our actions.' The message affected the work as a whole, so that the straight lines of the X to which it was attached took on the significance of a cross, a mark, a substitute signature, an error sign, which stood in tension with the indeterminate, organic shape of the snake, caught but still slipping away. The message knows not only that appearance is no guarantee of certainty but that appearance can defend something secret, invisible and elusive. It is the paper message that comes across as exposed and fragile in juxtaposition to the turtle shell, with its ability to defend its inside from outside investigation. The fact that the Cherokee turtle dance involves rattles made from turtle shells is not, perhaps, immediately relevant, but the shell is a reminder of a system of relating to the world that was invisible to the coloniser's uncertain certainty and could not be reduced to the bureaucrat's paper, pen and ink.[7] At the same time the snake shape could act as a reference to the Crazy Snake Movement, the last ditch resistance of the so-called Five Civilized Tribes to the Congressional Act which imposed private property on the Indian people. While these thoughts and reflections are inseparable from the object that produces them, they also travel beyond it, towards the misunderstandings that are central to the confrontation between colonised and coloniser. Reading the message, it was impossible not to smile and think of the despair experienced by Dominicans in Mexico, who, having built their altars on indigenous sacred sites, suddenly realised that the people might not, after all, be truly worshipping the cross.

Walking around Original Re-Runs, I was struck by the way that Jimmie Durham's art work grows out of two 'dialogues' or 'negotiations', first with his materials and second with his audience. In a sense, he addresses his materials and materialises his audience. His materials preserve their own presence as objects, so that the original shapes and textures enter into new configurations in his sculptures. A completed Jimmie Durham sculpture remains 'unfinished'. The raw material is not transformed into something born out of the artist's creative endeavour, into an original work of art whose previous existence is erased under the perfect finish of the new object. The creative process changes and affects the material but also treats it as 'found object'. The 'found object' has a tradition in twentieth-century radical art that dates back to Marcel Duchamp's move away from Cubism, which had incorporated bits of real things into art, to his readymades. When, in 1913, Duchamp placed a bicycle wheel on a kitchen stool to make a sculpture, both objects still preserved a continuity with their previous existence but had undergone a radical transformation. The artist chose the objects and, by putting them on show, placed them in a limbo in which their use value disappeared and a new aesthetic value was asserted. However, the aesthetic value would only really come into its own as an address, albeit a Dadaist one, to the preconceptions and receptivities of its potential audience. The address was theoretical as well as aesthetic, while presenting itself overtly in a negative relationship to the tradition of authorship it contested. Although any work of art demands that its audience negotiates with its presence and potential significance, the Duchamp readymade satirises the enigmatic moment of artistic creativity, which is then left exposed for reverie and critical examination.

Jimmie Durham puts these points together in a piece he wrote in June 1983, 'Creativity and the Social Process':

In one of my more famous theories about sculpture (famous, that is, among the voices inside my head; it has never been made public except in some bars), I explain that what a sculptor does is change objects. We take a stone or pieces of metal or plastic and rearrange them to make some order, or non-order, that satisfies us in some way. After Duchamp, this re-arranging can often be simply a matter of placing an object in a different way or in a different place than we would normally expect to see it, or by consecrating it with a signature. ... From this perspective we could substitute 'he created a new piece' for 'she changed another object'. The implied question would always be, 'Why did she change that object and what does it have to do with me?'[8]

The process then becomes a social process and one that puts the object into dialogue with its audience. Durham's pieces create openings for thought and possibilities for the viewer to ask the question 'why?' These openings and possibilities are offered in the first instance by the sculptures' 'montage' effect. The different elements fail to fit into an immediately perceptible aesthetic unity, preserving their own presence as object, albeit an 'object' that has been thoughtfully 'changed' through arrangement, decoration and exhibition. And the viewer, standing in half intuitive, half intellectual reverie is brought to consider the way these objects exist in time, and then, more generally, the temporal dimension of art and its process of creation.

Duchamp challenged a concept of creativity that valued an artist's ability to transform raw material to the point where it became something utterly new. In its mythic apotheosis, this tradition merged the creation of the art object with creation itself, as, for instance, in the story of Pygmalion or in its reverse, Edgar Allen Poe's 'The Oval Portrait'. Throughout the 20th century, radical art came to acknowledge the presence of its material, with the well-known Modernist emphasis on the specificity of the medium and pleasure in the presence of the signifier. However, the found object carries with it aesthetic factors that go beyond specificity into another kind of materialism. An object that maintains its own presence and significance within a sculptural work also maintains its dimension in time. For instance, 'Untitled '(1992) is a found object, a stick with the residual traces of its branches forming an asymmetrical pattern, painted red. It maintains its original beauty, its particular line and form that have been shaped by the process of growing and then by the process of decaying. It then acquires the beauty of its colour, a dense but luminous scarlet. The work has no chance of seeming to emerge out of the artist's mind and skill alone. Rather, the artist's skill seems directed towards recognising qualities and properties belonging to certain objects, while the artist's mind seems directed towards changing and arranging them for exhibition. The social process stretches backwards into the past and forwards into the future and the two materialisms, object and address, acquire a history. In the case of 'Untitled' (1992), which bears the appearance

165

of a red stick, history is invoked beyond the history of the object itself: *Red Sticks* was the name adopted by native people who attempted an armed resistance against Andrew Jackson's removal policy during the 1830s.

Time is a relatively contingent concept and one that is supremely subject to metaphorical representation and ideological investment. Durham's work raises questions about time itself and its relation to history. Perhaps the viewer is most immediately struck by Durham's use of animal skulls to create a temporal continuity between his objects' own history and their existence in the present tense of art work. In 'Ritual and Rhythm', a detail from the installation *Manhattan Festival of the Dead* (Kenkeleba Gallery, New York, 1982), he incorporated a variety of animal skulls decorated with brightly coloured paint, shells and pieces of wood. While the piece clearly refers to the Mexican Festival of the Dead, which celebrates the continued presence of the dead among living people, these sculptures also vividly inscribe the presence of the dead into the living art work. Once again, this is not the 'life' that an artist breathes into his raw material; it is rather an image in which hard and fast boundaries collapse, so that the gap closes between the dead and their presence as living memory and the art work's presence and its material past. Furthermore, the difference between Indian and settler attitudes to memory are evoked here. Durham is also drawing attention to the way that the past as presence was a central aspect of Indian culture.

During the late 80s and early 90s, Durham made maximum use of recognisable objects in his work and continued to use animal skulls, decorated and adorned with the addition of colour, and mounted on wood. At this point, the animal presence is modified by their combination with other kinds of material. As a political artist, addressing the non-history of the United States from an Indian perspective, Durham's use of found objects is polemical from both an aesthetic and an intellectual point of view. On the one hand, he presents the artist as negotiator in the creative process, on the other, he challenges a concept of history that is built on an invention of tradition. It is easy to make a metaphorical connection between an idea of art that invests in the absolute novelty of the creative process and a colonial history that invests in the absolute novelty of the New World. Or, to put it the other way round, insisting on the presence of the past in the work of art can make a metaphorical connection with an insistence on the past of the people who had lived for so long on the American continent prior to the arrival of European history.

From this point of view, the refusal of the moment of artistic creation as a zero point at which a new object comes into being from nowhere, combines with a rejection of the moment when America was created, as a zero date in the history of the continent. Such a disavowal of the past dragged itself forward in time. While the culture of the Indian people disappeared behind the binary and the linear, the reality of the Indian people disappeared into a teleological concept of history. Durham's depiction of time counters the linear narration that goes with historical time. He juxtaposes a biological passing of time that can be represented by objects that have lost their living presence but still carry its memory with a heterogeneous concept of time. On the other hand, his consideration of time is conceptual. A skull carries the memory of its living creature as trace and continues to exist like a fossil, holding its past and carrying it into the future. The present tense collapses. The materials are, in semiotic terms, indexical. Reference is not made through an iconic image, but through the real trace now transformed into image through adaptation and presentation. The indexical sign is particularly relevant here, because it breaks down the antinomy between nature and culture. Whereas both iconic and symbolic signs make present an absent referent through image or emblem, the indexical sign bears the imprint of its referent, creating a link or continuity with its presence. It exists therefore in both camps, in culture and in history, or rather, it collapses the dichotomy between them. The 'Cathedral of St John the Divine' (1989) consists of a moose skull painted blue and black and decorated with delicate yellow dots mounted on a rough wooden plinth; it has one antler and on its other side metal pipes supply a substitute. The moose skull plays its part in a montage of elements, in which a pure homogeneity of the natural world has no more place than the purely iconic image. On another level, Durham's use of animal imagery, in whatever form, pays tribute to a culture which blurred, in mythology (particularly myths of origins) and custom, the hard and fast demarcation line between animals and humans.

Durham's sculptures that primarily use wood as their raw material further complicate a nature/culture opposition. Wood ceases to be a single raw material. Pieces are arranged to form the main body of the sculpture, making formal patterns through the relationship between machine-finished shapes, sometimes juxtaposed to organic ones. The main body, in this set of works, is like a plinth growing out of a wooden stand and evolving, sometimes across a photograph or written message, to a crowning figurehead. One, for instance, contrasts industrial and organic shapes. Two planks, industrially produced by a sawmill perhaps for floor boards and sawn off with straight, abrupt, diagonal lines, are juxtaposed to a piece of wood that retains its original shape, like a branch or perhaps the trunk of a small tree, with a slight curve that merges into the shape of the animal skull that crowns it. The easy flow of the line is broken up by the rough addition of small bits of wood that jut out at right angles, and seemed, to my imagination at least, to give a material shape to the animal's sad cry. The pieces of wood contrast not only through the juxtaposition of the industrial with the non-industrial but through the curving roundness of the one with the square of the other. However, other sculptures make use of round lengths of wood which are machine produced, perhaps for broomsticks, and there are contrasts between the smooth surfaces produced by machines and the roughness of wood weathered by time. All these elements add to the sculptures' varied emotional impact, and the expressive relation between the figurehead and the main body of a work.

Durham's use of different kinds of wood, in different relations to the organic and the industrial, leads to his use of other materials, particularly PVC piping. In his essays, Durham frequently mentions the ease with which native people took up and made use of such new materials and technologies that arrived in their country, thus challenging the before/after, technical/non-technical divide:

There is a nefarious tendency to consider material manifestations as traditions. If we accept such absurd criteria, then horses among the Plains Indians and Indian beadwork must be seen as untraditional. Traditions exist and are guarded by Indian communities. One of the most important of these is dynamism. Constant change – adaptability, the inclusion of new ways and new materials – it is a tradition that our artists have particularly celebrated and have used to move and strengthen our societies. That was most obvious in the eighteenth and nineteenth centuries. Every object, every material brought in from Europe was taken and transformed with great energy. A rifle in the hands of a soldier was not the same as a rifle that had undergone Duchampian changes in the hands of a defender, which often included changes in form by the employment of feathers, leather and beadwork. We six (artists) feel that by participating in whatever modern dialogues are pertinent we are maintaining this tradition.[9]

These principles are ironically presented through 'Bedia's Stirring Wheel' and 'Bedia's Muffler' (1985), which decorate the modern, utilitarian car parts into exhibits for a future in which their utility is forgotten. In a further irony this tribute to an artist comrade, Bedia, which displaces use into display, shifts between the verbal and the visual, decorating the objects with beads which also, of course, refer to Indian adoption of European materials.

The native American economy was characterised by flexibility in its relation to its environment, shifting seasonally, for instance, between hunting and agriculture. And the landscape/environment was also culture, a mapping of traditional knowledge and existence onto the country itself. The settlers' misunderstanding of these relationships was formed by their perception of a landscape as a 'wilderness' rather than a repository of meaning. In this way, mythic belief, and the modes of thought that went with it, made up a base line for the political strategies that led to the Indians' history of loss and oppression. There is an essential connection here between a mode of thought and the evolution of the actual politics which characterises American colonialism. Although there is the first and obvious level at which the Indian people were displaced as a result of European demand and greed for land, other factors are also significant. Michael Rogin argues that the ideology behind Andrew Jackson's determination to 'remove' the Indian people in the 1830s was based on a perception of their relation to the natural world.

He quotes from Francis Parkman: 'We look with deep interest on the face of this irreclaimable son of the wilderness, the child who will not be weaned from the breast of his rugged mother.'[10]

Such a perception generated a fantasy of the Indian as infant or, in perhaps anachronistic but suggestive Freudian terms, as 'pre-Oedipal'. This altered iconography allowed the state to evolve a policy of subordination and marginalisation within legal and constitutional confines. Andrew Jackson was able to cloak his policies in the guise of paternalism and embark on a systematic programme of ethnic cleansing, with its genocidal hidden agenda, in the name of precipitating 'my red children' into a condition of maturity and individualistic independence. But even more significantly, the ideology revolves around an incompatible relationship to memory. An immigrant community is necessarily amnesiac. It is forced to cut off its ties with the past and even erase the political memory of conditions that may have given rise to its emigration. Thus, in a similar fashion, the Indians' ties to the land had to be broken. Two contrasting quotations illustrate the consciousness of these different cultural attitudes on both sides. In 1854, Seattle, a Dwarmish chief, said:

To us the ashes of our ancestors are sacred and their resting place is hallowed ground. You wander far from the graves of your ancestors and seemingly without regret. Your religion was written by the iron finger of your God so that you could not forget. ... Your dead cease to love the land of their nativity as soon as they pass into the portals of the tomb and wander away beyond the stars. They are soon forgotten and never return. Our dead never forget the beautiful world that gave them their being.[11]

Andrew Jackson had said in his 'Second Annual Address to Congress' in 1830:

Doubtless it will be painful to leave the graves of their fathers, but what do they do more than our ancestors did nor than our children are doing? To better their condition in an unknown land our forefathers left all that was dear in earthly objects. Our children by the thousands leave the land of their birth to seek new homes in distant regions. ... These removed hundreds and almost thousands of miles at their own expense, purchase the lands they occupy, and support themselves at their new homes from the moment of their arrival. Can it be cruel in the Government, when, by events which it cannot control, the Indian is made discontent in his ancient home, to purchase his lands, to give him a new and extensive territory, to pay the expense of his removal, to support him a year in his new abode? How many thousands of our own people would gladly embrace the opportunity of removal to the West on such conditions?[12]

Under this inappropriate symmetry is concealed one of the worst tragedies of the Indian people, who were rounded up by the army and moved with enormous suffering and loss of life. The Cherokee, for instance, lost a quarter of their people on their forced march and probably about 30,000 Indians died during the removal period. The historical details of these events became the subject of another wave of official amnesia, or rather lay neglected and forgotten under a growing mass of popular mythology and belief about Indian life.

Jimmie Durham's work needs to be understood in the context of these paradoxes. His works of art bear witness to a history of loss which, even in its most intense drama, passed into national obscurity to become a lost history, preserved only in Indian people's memory from generation to generation. However, the two aspects of loss then need to be understood within the context of a second paradox which also relates to Durham's work. Almost in proportion to the invisibility of Indian history, the image of 'the Indian' proliferated into visibility, first, in American popular culture, and then exported all over the world with the international economic dominance of American popular culture, particularly the movies. Given this history, Durham's work is necessarily wary of iconic representation. There is no other comparable case in which a devastated people has had its image appropriated and circulated by the perpetrators of devastation. The 'Negro' image had a certain kind of commercial exploitation but, almost totally repressed by Hollywood, it never achieved the visibility of the 'Indian'. Perhaps there is some parallel in the circulation of eroticised images of women, particularly within American commodity culture.

The iconography of the Western frontier gave new vitality to the American Manichaean mode of thought, transforming it out of generalised European origins into a substitute for historical understanding. In yet another bitter paradox, the mass circulation of Western frontier mythology, with its readymade Indian iconography, took place at the same time as another desperate moment in the history of the native Americans. During the 1870s and 80s, Congressional legislation denied the Indian nations' autonomy and independence from the United States. Finally, at the instigation of Senator Dawes, the Allotment Act of 1887 imposed private property on Indian people, decreeing that they could no longer hold land and possessions in common. 'The common field is the seat of barbarism', proclaimed an Indian agent. 'The separate farm is the door to civilization. ... The Indian must be imbued with the exalting egotism of American civilization so he will say "I" instead of "We" and "This is mine" instead of "This is ours".'[13]

The Dawes Act simultaneously overruled Indian social and constitutional traditions and, as individual 'lots' were fixed at 160 acres per head of household, it freed vast tracts of reservation land for white settlement or mining. It was during these decades that, with the industrial revolution in publishing, the 'dime novel' created the first mass-entertainment market, with a readership of millions whose preferred genre was the Western. This genre simplified even further the Indian iconographies that had been gradually taking shape in white culture, and circulated them to a vast readership of newly arrived immigrants. Henry Nash Smith comments:

> Orville Victor once said that when rival publishers entered the field the Beadle writers merely had to kill a few more Indians. But it went further than that. The outworn formulas had to be given zest by a constant search after novel sensations. Circus tricks of horsemanship, incredible feats of shooting, more and more elaborate costumes, masks and passwords were introduced, and even such ludicrous ornaments as worshippers of a Sun God devoted to human sacrifice in a vast underground cavern in the region of Yellowstone Park. Killing a few more Indians meant, in practice, exaggerating violence and bloodshed for their own sakes, to the point of an overt sadism.[14]

By 1882, the Wild West show had developed into marketable form, and the two strands of 'frontier entertainment', the novel and the spectacle, were ready to fuse into the Western film and then achieve worldwide consumption through Hollywood domination of the international entertainment market. The origin of this explosion of imagery, and the recycling of the Manichaean vision into mass circulation popular culture, was thus located precisely at the moment when the native people's actual survival was in doubt. It is as though the mythology had congealed into a huge smokescreen which concealed the United States government policies and their real effects on native people's lives.

Such a complete disjuncture between the Indian people's history in the 19th century and the fictions of the frontier has an important side-effect on imagery and iconography. The fetishistic image that emerges out of a disavowal of reality is characterised by self-sufficiency. Like an image projected onto a smoke screen, it must distract attention with its appearance of autonomy and verisimilitude from whatever it conceals from view. But as the fetishistic image attempts to hold the eye, its actual spectacular properties hint at and almost advertise its hidden secret. In this sense, an aesthetic that emphasises the reality of material rather than the realism of iconic appearance works against fetishistic belief. Jimmie Durham's works challenge aesthetic or artistic disavowal and the credibility invested in likeness as such, both the realist tradition of high art and the kitsch verisimilitudes of popular culture. His work is 'thing'-based rather than 'picture'-based, and it casually lacks finish or surface gloss. It is only with his work on historical 'go-between' figures, who moved across the European and the Indian worlds, that the human figure comes into particular focus. It seems as though Durham's figures acquire more iconic verisimilitude the closer they get to the European world, as though its culture bestowed outward visibility with its clothing.

'La Malinche' (1988–91), for instance, is composed of a white skirt, white stockings and a gold bra on a body reduced to only head and hands.

The gold bra condenses La Malinche's double association with desire, using the sexual metaphor of lust to combine the rape of woman with the rape of a people and their land. The bra's Western sexual connotations evoke La Malinche's relation to Cortes. As his mistress, she is an emblem of sexual oppression both actually, in her own story, and as the essential prefiguration of the sexual ravages of colonial domination. As Octavio Paz has pointed out, she is mother and whore, a traitor who bequeathed racial and cultural hybridity to Mexico. Through its colour, the bra links sexuality to lust for gold. As Cortes's interpreter, La Malinche smoothed his passage into Mexico and collaborated with the Conquest which was largely fuelled by the Europeans' desire for gold. At the same time, white and gold are the colours of the Spanish baroque and particularly the church altar pieces that both epitomise and disavow the true horror of Spanish colonial occupation. In Jimmie Durham's image of La Malinche, the tradition of her treachery is lost under her tragedy. The sculpture depicts a woman caught in events controlled by men and who had no power to affect the fate of her people. One side of her face is painted with an expression of dejection and defeat, the other is decorated with an intricate black pattern which is blank with illegible despair.

'Pocahontas' and 'The Little Carpenter' in London (Matt's Gallery, 1988) also centre on 'go-between' figures, and Durham's self-portrait, one of his few fully figurative works, may too. 'Caliban's Diary', on the other hand, records Caliban's wish to know what he looks like in the aftermath of Dr Prospero's arrival on the island. In his diary entries, Caliban confides his inability either to visualise or make his own image. There is a sense that European culture places a particular value on iconic representation; at the same time, to be at the other end of a Manichaean polarisation is to be deprived of self-image. But there is also an implication that the European need to represent connects with a need to categorise, which Durham caricatures in his series *On Loan From the Museum of the American Indian* (1991). All these works centre on issues of position, both in terms of an individual subjective position, a position of address, and a position as the place one occupies, or is assigned, in the world. Durham uses words, messages, quotations and direct address to highlight the misunderstandings and literal displacements in American colonial exchange. The placing of his address shifts, sometimes quoting from *The Pinkerton Men's Manual of Conduct*, sometimes from Frantz Fanon's *The Wretched of the Earth*, sometimes using the first person, sometimes the third person and always with irony. Meaning has to be considered; it never jumps directly out of the words as verbal discourse so easily can. And the irony often relates across word and object. For instance, 'I Forgot What I Was Going to Say' (1992) includes these words on a piece of paper sticking out from a piece of rounded wood that separates a revolver from its trigger. It becomes a speaking stick that has lost its voice. In a different mode 'Physickal Log' is made up of a very exquisite piece of birch wood; the central section has been whittled down to hold a message about paper. The paper referred to is apparently an academic paper, to be copied, but the viewer must also think about the origin of paper in wood and its endless waste.

Durham's ironies involve displacements of meaning across words and things. As everyone knows, the word 'Indian' is a displacement that resulted from a misunderstanding of geography, which was itself an attempt at a condensation of incompatible political and economic discourses in Columbian Europe. However, during the 19th century, the primal psychological, geographical and economic displacement of naming culminated in the Indian tribes being literally uprooted and 'removed'. At the same time, the people displaced by European economic and social upheavals and turmoil, vast masses of Irish, Italians, Germans, Russians and others, arrived in the New World to form the industrial and agricultural working class that would create the wealth and power of the United States. One of Durham's quotations from Fanon's *The Wretched of the Earth* is written across an animal skin: 'The settlers' town is a strongly built town, all made of stone and steel. It is a brightly lit town; the streets are covered with asphalt, and the garbage cans swallow all the leavings, unseen, unknown, and hardly thought about.' This relation between nature and culture urbanises the opposition between wilderness/agricultural cultivation and savagery/civilisation. It precisely evokes colonial settlement as something which is laid on top, on the surface, of the land. The Manichaean mode of thought has become topographical, but one side of the polarisation has become invisible, and written out, even, of the binary opposition. Durham's use of PVC piping brings back, ironically, the ironies of this way of thought. The piping is a conduit which connects the surface of the ground with its underneath. In Durham's way of thought, it condenses two main meanings. First, it acts as a means of disposal, of carrying the 'leavings' of civilisation to an unseen destination while also acting as a means of extracting the natural resources of the earth, such as oil, to the surface to be transformed into money. At the same time, Durham uses plastic piping as a conduit to the 'underneath' of memory, both as a metaphor for the 'burying' of memory under the flow of conscious daily existence, and as a modern metaphor for access to the actual buried history of the Indian people.

In 1993 the Wexner Center for the Arts in Columbus, Ohio, staged an exhibition Will Power, to counter-celebrate the quincentennial of Columbus's landing in the Americas. The exhibition included a piece by Jimmie Durham called 'On the Banks of the Ohio'. The piece was made of green pipes. The pipes start quite small, coming out of the wall of the museum and growing larger, with larger segments of pipe, to culminate in a huge head made of mud to suggest the shape of an enormous snake. It was difficult to see the snake as a whole. A small doorway opened a view of the head, rearing up and detached from any visible connection with its body. The body itself undulated along the gallery, set off by the white back wall which was painted with brown marks. Close by, the marks were shit-like in colour and smeared shapelessly across the surface. Seen from further back, the brown smears suddenly became elegant vegetal forms, like the growth of river plants, the tall, bending shapes of leaves. At the same time, the close-to effect remained and resonated with the presence of the pipes as cloaca, the transporters of contemporary shit through the landscape, usually invisible and underground but here monstrously visible and on display.

The serpent carried or condensed the representation of the hidden and underground transformed into the visible and overground, enacting Durham's intertwining metaphors. Just as, for instance, Bakhtin posited a relation between the impolite, lower parts of the body with their eruption in a carnivalesque mode, when the lower classes could assert a laughter of the socially repressed, so Freud used a metaphor of burying to evoke the unconscious and its repression which could erupt as symptom on the surface. For Freud, repression was historical and the buried was the past. And although he used images of known history, such as the eruption of Etna that buried Pompeii, to evoke the plight of the individual psyche, the metaphor can boomerang back to evoke the loss of a social and collective history.

'On the Banks of the Ohio' refers to the Serpent Mound, one of the most impressive of the Indian earthworks along the valley of the Ohio River; it winds along the top of a ridge, stretching 1,348 feet. It dates from the so-called Adena culture which lasted for about the last millennium BC, to be followed by successive cultures, which together formed a 'prehistory' for the native people of the area. The mounds are sometimes burial mounds, sometimes sacred gathering circles, sometimes, perhaps, lunar and solar observatories, and they bear witness to a people's commitment both to an agrarian way of life and to cultural continuity. Objects discovered in the burial mounds, such as freshwater pearls, obsidian and mica objects, grizzly bear teeth, hammered copper and gold, indicate that a complex trading network criss-crossed the northern part of the continent. Because these were locations of natural advantage, early European settlements tended to form on the same sites, and inevitably many were ploughed up, incorporated into towns or adapted into a variety of uses, from military encampments to present-day golf courses. Often only the word 'mound' incorporated into place names bears the trace of their loss. Some, like the Serpent, have survived and act as a sign inscribed into the landscape of the civilisations that existed in pre-Columbian America and a testimonial to the complexity of their history. They also stand as a testimonial to the way that the amnesia, imported by settler communities, was imposed, blanket-like, on the past of the country and on its landscape.

Jimmie Durham's tribute to the Serpent is symptomatic of his work. Although the presence of history and memory runs like a thread through his themes and materials, the past is not recovered 'in virginity'. It is always subject to the movement of time and history. But even more significantly, the Serpent can represent the multifaceted aspect of his work; there is never a concentration on a single meaning or a simple polemic. Materials act as conduits for ideas from level to level, exploring different topographies of time in space and space in time. While his rejection of binarism and the negative/positive opposition suggests a move towards a dialectic, his aesthetic position is one that stands back from the production of a conceptual innovation or progress through history as such. As he stands back, he examines the interstices of things, so that while the dialectic is still one of confrontation and struggle, it is illuminated by 'acts and perceptions of combining' and 'breaking down of separations'.

Object

It must have been an odd object to begin with.
Now the ghosts of its uses
Whisper around my head, tickle the tips
Of my fingers. Weeds
Reclaim with quick silence the beams, pillars
Doorways. Places change, and a small object
Stands defiant in its placelessness.
Durable because it contains intensely meanings
Which it can no longer pour out.

Jimmie Durham, 1964

Notes

Preface

1. I have not engaged with issues to do with the feminised fetish as discussed by Emily Apter, *Feminising the Fetish* (Ithaca: Cornell University Press, 1991).
2. Karl Marx, *The Poverty of Philosophy* (New York: International Publishers, 1963).
3. Christopher Norris sums up Baudrillard's argument: '[The Gulf War] is a conflict waged – for all that we can know – entirely at a level of strategic simulation, a mode of vicarious spectator involvement that extends all the way from fictive war-games to saturation coverage of the "real world" event and which thus leaves us perfectly incapable of distinguishing one from the other.' Christopher Norris, *Uncritical Theory. Postmodernism, Intellectuals and the Gulf War* (London: Lawrence & Wishart, 1992), p. 15.

Introduction

1. Slavoj Zizek, *The Sublime Object of Ideology* (London: Verso, 1989), p. 24.
2. Thomas Richards, *The Commodity Culture of Victorian England: Advertising and Spectacle 1851–1914* (London: Verso, 1991). See especially pp. 66–9 for a discussion of the changing language used to describe the commodity and Marx's use of metaphor.
3. Karl Marx, *Capital*, vol. 1 (Moscow: Foreign Languages Publishing House, 1961), p. 72.
4. Susan Buck-Morss, *The Dialectics of Seeing* (Cambridge, Mass.: MIT Press, 1989), pp. 81–2.
5. S. Freud, 'Fetishism', *Standard Edition of the Complete Psychological Works*, vol. 21 (London: Hogarth Press, 1961).
6. Thomas Richards, *The Commodity Culture of Victorian England*, pp. 60–1.
7. Rachel Bowlby, *Just Looking* (London: Methuen, 1985), p. 6.
8. Keith Thomas, *Religion and the Decline of Magic* (Harmondsworth: Penguin, 1971).
9. Karl Marx, *Capital*, vol. 3, p. 809.
10. Christian Metz, *Psychoanalysis and Cinema. The Imaginary Signifier* (London: Macmillan, 1982), p. 72.
11. See Kaja Silverman, 'Lost Objects and Mistaken Subjects', in *The Acoustic Mirror* (Bloomington: Indiana University Press, 1987), pp. 1–43, particularly for her critique of the assumptions behind Freud's theory of castration.
12. My thinking on this theme has been particularly influenced by Mary Ann Doane, *The Desire to Desire* (London: Macmillan, 1987), pp. 22–3, notably her comment that 'it is as though there were a condensation of the eroticism of the image onto the figure of woman – the female star proffered to the female spectator for imitation. The process underlines the tautological nature of the woman's role as consumer: she is the subject of

a transaction in which her own commodification is the object. The ideological effect of commodity logic on a large scale is therefore the deflection of any dissatisfaction with one's life or any critique of the social system onto an intensified concern with a body which is in some way guaranteed to be at fault. The body becomes increasingly the stake in late capitalism. Having the commodified object – and the initial distance and distinction it presupposes – is displaced onto appearing, producing a strange constriction of the gap between consumer and commodity.'

13. In Frank Baum's novel the *Wizard of Oz*, first published in 1900, the emphasis on spectacle and seeing is more important than in the film. In addition to the Wizard's skill as an illusionist and ventriloquist, all his subjects wear special spectacles: 'But isn't everything here green?' asked Dorothy. 'No more than in any other city', replied Oz, 'but when you wear the spectacles, why of course everything you see looks green to you.' It is hard not to see a metaphor for both cinema and ideology here.

14. D. N. Rodowick, *The Crisis of Political Modernism*: *Criticism and Ideology in Contemporary Film Theory* (Urbana, Ill.: University of Illinois Press, 1988).

15. Fredric Jameson, *The Political Unconscious* (London: Routledge, 1981), p. 35.

16. S. Freud, 'An Outline of Psychoanalysis', in *Standard Edition*, vol. 23, pp. 203–4.

17. Dana Polan, 'Stock Responses: the Spectacle of the Symbolic in *Summer Stock*', in *Discourse*, vol. 10, no. 1, Fall/Winter 1987–8, p. 124.

18. S. Freud, 'The Uncanny', in *Standard Edition*, vol. 27.

19. Barbara Creed, *The Monstrous Feminine* (London: Routledge, 1993), p. 54.

Chapter 1

1. Lev Kuleshov, *Kuleshov on Film: Writings of Lev Kuleshov*, ed. Ron Levaco (Berkeley: University of California Press, 1974), p. 127.

2. Robin Wood, *Hitchcock's Films* (London: Zwemmer, 1965), p. 9.

3. Thomas Elsaesser, 'Two Decades in Another Country: Hollywood and the Cinéphiles', in C.W.E. Bigsby (ed.), *Superculture* (London: Elek, 1975).

4. The *politique des auteurs* was translated into English by the American critic Andrew Sarris (whose ultimately successful attempt to return Hollywood to its own country also received at least a decade of bitter resistance) as the 'auteur theory', in the early 60s, and was first published in *Film Culture,* primarily a magazine of underground cinema and the emergent American avant-garde. I mention this to highlight the 'underground' and anti-establishment nature of a critical allegiance to Hollywood cinema at the time. The term was first used in stucturalist criticism by Geoffrey Nowell-Smith in his study *Visconti* (London: Secker & Warburg, 1969).

5. All published in the British Film Institute and Secker & Warburg's *Cinema One* series except for *Sam Fuller* and *Roger Corman*, which were published by the Edinburgh International Film Festival.

6. Quoted in T. Elsaesser, 'Two Decades in Another Country', p. 216.

7. Pam Cook and Claire Johnston, 'The Place of Woman in the Cinema of Raoul Walsh' (1974), reprinted in C. Penley (ed.), *Feminism and Film Theory* (London: BFI, 1988), pp. 25–35.

8. See, for instance, Peter Wollen, '*North by Northwest.* A Morphological Analysis' (1976), in *Readings and Writings* (London: Verso, 1982), pp. 18–33.

9. Barbara Creed, '*Alien* and the Monstrous Feminine', in A. Kuhn (ed.), *Alien Zone: Cultural Theory and Contemporary Science Fiction Cinema* (London: Verso, 1990); Teresa de Lauretis, 'Desire in Narrative', in *Alice Doesn't: Feminism, Semiotics, Cinema* (Bloomington: Indiana University Press, 1984).

10. bell hooks, *Black Looks* (Boston: South End Press, 1992), p. 126.

11. Jon Halliday, *Sirk on Sirk* (London: BFI and Secker & Warburg, 1972), p. 134.

Chapter 2

1. Joan Rivière, 'Womanliness as Masquerade', in V. Burgin, J. Donald and C. Kaplan (eds), *Formations of Fantasy* (London: Methuen, 1986), p. 38.

2. See, for instance, Claire Johnston's essay on *Anne of the Indies* in her and Paul Wille-men's *Jacques Tourneur* (Edinburgh: Edinburgh International Film Festival, 1975).

3. Lucy Fischer (ed.), *Imitation of Life* (New Brunswick, NJ: Rutgers University Press, 1991), p. 53.

4. Ibid., p. 64.

5. Lauren Berlant, 'National Brands/National Body', in Hortense J. Spillers (ed.), *Comparative American Identities* (New York and London: Routledge, 1991), p. 119.

6. In his obituary of Fredi Washington in the *Guardian* (9 July 1994), Ronald Bergen wrote: 'In the lunatic logic of pigmentocracy, Washington was too beautiful and not dark enough to act maids, but rather too light to act in all-black movies. This dilemma was illustrated in *The Emperor Jones* (1933) starring the great actor/singer Paul Robeson, making his screen debut. Washington was cast as Ondine, but when the producers saw the rushes they were scared that audiences might think Robeson was making love to a white woman. So they darkened her with heavy pancake and re-shot the scenes. ... After helping to found the Negro Actors Guild, she continued to perform spasmodically on the stage. ... However, this lovely actress was born too soon and neither Hollywood nor Broadway offered her challenging roles. ... As with so many other black actors and actresses of the past there hovers the nagging question of what might have been.'

Chapter 3

1. Jean-Luc Godard, 'Defence and Illustration of Classical Cinema', in Tom Milne (ed.), *Godard on Godard* (New York: The Viking Press, 1968), p. 28.

2. Eileen Bowser, *The Transformation of Cinema* (New York: Charles Scribner's Sons, 1990), p. 117.

3. Thomas Richards establishes the condensation between pretty girls and commodity promotion/consumption in late Victorian England through a reading of the Nausicaa episode in James Joyce's *Ulysses* (1922). See 'Those Lovely Seaside Girls' in *The Commodity Culture of Victorian England: Advertising and Spectacle 1851–1914* (London: Verso, 1991).

4. See the contrasting styles of Billy Bitzer and Henrik Sartov as discussed in Lillian Gish's *The Movies, Mr Griffith and Me* (New York: Avon Books, 1969), pp. 207–8; Karl Brown, *Adventures with D.W. Griffith* (London: Secker & Warburg, 1973), pp. 204–6 on Sartov's lens.

5. David Bordwell, Janet Staiger and Kristin Thompson, *The Classic Hollywood Cinema* (London: Routledge, 1985), pp. 287–93, for a thorough discussion of the soft-focus or glamour phenomenon all through the 20s. As a corrective to my perhaps overly binary argument, K. Thompson points out that 'Women usually got heavier gauzing, but certain men were associated with glamour as well.'

6. Lary May, *Screening out the Past* (Oxford: Oxford University Press, 1980), p. 218.

7. Lauren Rabinovitz, 'Temptations of Pleasure. Nickelodeons, Amusement Parks and the Sights of Female Sexuality', *Camera Obscura*, no. 23, May 1990, p. 85.

8. Gaylyn Studlar, 'The Perils of Pleasure? Fan Magazine Discourse as Women's Commodified Culture in the 1920s', *Wide Angle*, vol. 13, no. 1, January 1991, p. 15.

9. See for instance the contrasting iconography in *Love Em and Leave Em* (Frank Tuttle, 1926) in which Louise Brooks plays a liberated, entrancing and irresponsible 'flapper' to her older sister's (Evelyn Brent) responsible, talented, but sexually conventional, 'new woman'. Peter Wollen has analysed the modernity of the Brooks iconography and her ultimate move to Europe in *Sight and Sound* (February 1994). It is also important to remember Miriam Hansen's analysis of the Rudolph Valentino phenomenon in *Babel and Babylon: Spectatorship in American Silent Cinema* (Cambridge, Mass.: Harvard University Press, 1990). She argues that it was only in the Hollywood of this period, but with difficulty, that the iconography of a male star could appear on the screen overtly eroticised for female visual pleasure.

10. L. May, *Screening out the Past*, p. 236.

11. See Charles Eckert, 'Carole Lombard in Macey's Window', in Jane Gaines and Charlotte Herzog (eds), *Fabrications* (London: Routledge, 1991), p. 104; see also Kristin Thompson, *Exporting Entertainment: America in the World Film Market 1907–34* (London: BFI, 1985).
12. L. May, *Screening out the Past*, p. 205.
13. Jean-Luc Godard, 'Defence and Illustration of Classical Cinema', p. 28.
14. Mary Ann Doane, *Femmes Fatales* (London: Routledge, 1991), p. 1.
15. Eve Arnold, *Marilyn* (London: Heinemann, 1992), 2nd edition, pp. 27, 137.
16. Jean Baudrillard, *For a Critique of the Political Economy of the Sign* (St Louis, Mo.: Telos Press, 1981), p. 91.
17. Anita Loos, *Gentlemen Prefer Blondes* (London: Jonathan Cape, 1926), p. 121.

Chapter 4

1. Gaston Bachelard, *The Poetics of Space* (New York: Orion Press, 1964), pp. 85 and 211.
2. Marina Warner has demonstrated the role played by feminine figurations in allegory: 'Allegory means "other speech" (*alia oratio*). ... It signifies an open declamatory speech which contains another layer of meaning. It thus possesses a double intention: to tell something which conveys one thing but which also says something else.' Marina Warner, *Monuments and Maidens: The Allegory of the Female Form* (London: Picador, 1985), p. xix.
3. Hesiod, *Works and Days* (London: William Heinemann, Loeb Classical Library, 1954), pp. 7–9.
4. M. Warner, *Monuments and Maidens*, pp. 214 and 239; she also quotes Froma I. Zeitlin's evocative description of Pandora as 'Artefact and artifice herself. Pandora installs the woman as the eidelon in the frame of human culture, equipped by her unnatural nature to delight and to deceive.'
5. Annette Michelson, 'On the Eve of the Future: The Reasonable Facsimile and the Philosophical Toy', *October*, no. 29, 1984.
6. Dora and Erwin Panofsky, *Pandora's Box: Changing Aspects of a Mythical Symbol* (London: Routledge & Kegan Paul, 1956).
7. Ludmilla Jordanova, *Sexual Visions: Images of Gender in Science and Medicine Between the Eighteenth and the Twentieth Centuries* (London: Harvester Press, 1989), pp. 92–3.
8. S. Freud, 'Fragment of an Analysis of a Case of Hysteria' in *Standard Edition*, vol. 7 (London: The Hogarth Press, 1953), p. 69.
9. Dora and Erwin Panofsky, *Pandora's Box: Changing Aspects of a Mythical Symbol*, p. 77.
10. Ibid., p. 113.
11. Barbara Spackman, *Decadent Genealogies* (Ithaca: Cornell University Press, 1989), pp. 152–201.
12. N. Hawthorne, 'The Paradise of Children', in *Tanglewood Tales* (1853) (London: Blackie & Sons, 1905), p. 46.
13. Angela Carter, *The Bloody Chamber* (Harmondsworth: Penguin Books, 1979).
14. Mary Ann Doane, *The Desire to Desire* (London: Macmillan, 1987), p. 134.
15. Laura Mulvey, 'Visual Pleasure and Narrative Cinema', in *Visual and Other Pleasures* (London: Macmillan, 1989).
16. Julia Kristeva, *The Powers of Horror* (New York: Columbia University Press, 1982).
17. Barbara Creed, '*Alien* and the Monstrous Feminine', in Annette Kuhn (ed.), *Alien Zone* (London: Verso, 1990), p. 135.

Chapter 5

1. Cindy Sherman quoted in Sandy Nairne, *The State of the Art: Ideas and Images in the 1980s* (London: Chatto & Windus, 1967), p. 132.

2. Peter Gidal in Teresa de Lauretis and Stephen Heath (eds), *The Cinematic Apparatus* (New York: St Martin's Press, 1980), p. 169.
3. Fredric Jameson, *Postmodernism or The Logic of Late Capitalism* (London: Verso, 1991), p. 19.
4. S. Nairne, *The State of the Art*, p. 136.
5. Julia Kristeva, *The Powers of Horror: An Essay on Abjection* (New York: Columbia University Press, 1982).
6. Barbara Creed, *The Monstrous Feminine* (London: Routledge, 1993).

Chapter 6
1. Jean-Luc Godard, 'Defence and Illustration of the Cinema's Classical Construction', in Tom Milne (ed.), *Godard on Godard* (London: BFI and Secker & Warburg, 1972), p. 28.
2. Links between the spectacle and commodity fetishism had been made by Guy Debord in his pamphlet *The Society of the Spectacle* which had widespread influence in the late 60s culminating in May '68. He wrote: 'The spectacle is the moment when the commodity has attained total occupation in social life.' In *Une femme mariée* and *Deux ou trois choses que je sais d'elle* Godard shows the female body to be the signifier of commodity fetishism, linking it to the society of the spectacle through the discourse of sexuality in advertising.
3. Robert Stam, 'Jean-Luc Godard's *Sauve qui peut (la vie)*', *Millennium Film Journal*, nos 10–11, Fall/Winter 1981–2.
4. Raymond Bellour, 'I Am an Image', *Camera Obscura*, nos 8–10, l989, pp. 120–1.
5. F. Nietzsche, *The Gay Science* (New York: Vintage Books, 1974), p. 317.
6. Ibid., p. 316.
7. See P. Wollen, 'Godard and Counter Cinema: Vent d'Est', in *Readings and Writings* (London: Verso, 1982), pp. 89–90.
8. T. Milne, *Godard on Godard*, pp. 180–1.
9. André Bazin, *What is Cinema?* (Berkeley: University of California Press, 1967), p. 12.
10. Peter Wollen, *Signs and Meaning in the Cinema* (London: BFI and Secker & Warburg 1969), p. 134.
11. Ibid., p. 132.
12. I would like to thank Michael Chanan for confirming and developing this point for me.
13. Constance Penley, 'Pornography, Eroticism', in Raymond Bellour and Mary Lea Bandy (eds), *Jean-Luc Godard: Son–Image 1974–1991* (New York: Museum of Modern Art, 1992), p. 47.
14. Gayatri Chakravorty Spivak, 'Displacement and the Discourse of Woman', in Mark Krupnick (ed.), *Displacement, Derrida and After* (Bloomington: Indiana University Press, 1983).

Chapter 7
1. Frank Brady, *Citizen Welles: A Biography of Orson Welles* (New York: Charles Scribner's Sons, 1989), p. 285.
2. Miriam Hansen, *Babel and Babylon: Spectatorship in American Silent Film* (Cambridge, Mass.: Harvard University Press, 1991), p. 191.
3. Bernard Herrmann, 'Score for a Film', in R. Gottesman (ed.), *Focus on Citizen Kane* (Englewood Cliffs, NJ: Prentice Hall, 1971,) p. 70.
4. Robert Carringer, *The Making of Citizen Kane* (Berkeley: University of California Press, 1985), p. 11.
5. Pauline Kael, *The Citizen Kane Book* (London: Secker & Warburg, 1971), pp. 373–4.
6. Ibid., pp. 374–5.
7. Ibid., p. 340.
8. Ibid., p. 332.
9. Ibid., p. 330.

10. Ibid., pp. 363–4.

11. William M. Thayer, *From Log Cabin to White House: Life of James A. Garfield, Boyhood, Youth, Manhood, Assassination, Death, Funeral* (New York: J.B. Alden, 1883).

12. S. Freud, 'The Relation of the Poet to Daydreaming' in *Standard Edition*, vol. 9 (London: The Hogarth Press, 1953).

13. P. Kael, *The Citizen Kane Book*, p. 355.

14. Ibid., p. 340.

15. Freud often discusses the displacement of childhood memories onto things, particularly in 'Screen Memories' (1899), *Standard Edition*, vol. 3, and Chapter 4, *The Psychopathology of Everyday Life, Standard Edition,* vol. 6.

16. *Time*, 27 January 1941.

17. F. Brady, *Citizen Welles*, pp. 292–3.

18. Orson Welles's 'Introduction' to Marion Davies, *The Times We Had* (London: Angus & Robertson, 1975).

19. John Houseman, *Unfinished Business* (London: Chatto & Windus, 1986), p. 223.

20. W.A. Swanberg, *Citizen Hearst* (London: Longman's, 1965), p. 477.

21. William Stott, *Documentary Expression in America* (London: Oxford University Press, 1973), p. 79.

22. P. Kael, *The Citizen Kane Book*, p. 317.

23. Ibid., p. 337.

24. Quoted in Dudley Andrew, *André Bazin* (New York: Columbia University Press, 1990).

Chapter 8

1. Teshome H. Gabriel, '*Xala*: Cinema of Wax and Gold', in Peter Stevens (ed.), *Jump Cut: Hollywood, Politics and Counter Culture* (Toronto: Between the Lines, 1985), p. 335.

2. Noureddine Ghai says: 'The concept of "negritude" was developed by a group of French-speaking black intellectuals studying in Paris in the 1930s and 1940s, among them Leopold Senghor, later to be the first president of Senegal after … colonial rule. It denoted a view of black people as particularly gifted in the art of immediate living, of sensual experience, of physical skill and prowess, all of which belonged to them by birthright. It was an attempt at the time to combat the racist view of African civilisation as a null quantity, and the ideology that French colonial rule was providing otherwise worthless, culture-less beings with the opportunity to assimilate themselves to French culture. … Sembene is one of the many later African writers who have criticised the concept vigorously, among other things for underpinning the view that the European contribution to global culture is technological and rational, while Africa can remain in acute economic disarray because it is happy just "being".' 'An Interview with Ousmane Sembene', in J. Downing (ed.), *Film and Politics in the Third World* (Brooklyn: Autonomedia, 1987).

3. Ibid., p. 46.

4. Marcel Mauss, *Oeuvres 2* (Paris: Editions de Minuit, 1969), p. 245 (my translation).

5. William Pietz, 'The Problem of the Fetish', Part 1, *Res,* no. 9, Spring 1985, pp. 5–17; Part 2, *Res,* no. 13, Spring 1987, pp. 23–46; Part 3a, *Res,* no. 16, Autumn 1988, pp. 105–24 (Peabody Museum, Harvard University, Cambridge, Mass.).

6. W. Pietz, 'The Problem of the Fetish', Part 1, p. 6.

7. W. Pietz, 'The Problem of the Fetish', Part 2, p. 21.

8. Ibid., p. 23.

9. Karl Marx, *Capital*, vol. 1 (Moscow: Foreign Language Publishing House, 1965), pp. 272–3.

10. W. Pietz, 'The Problem of the Fetish'.

11. 'Du culte des dieux fétiches', in Jean-Baptiste Pontalis (ed.), *Objets du fétichisme, Nouvelle Revue de Psychanalyse,* no. 2, Autumn 1970, p. 132.

12. W. Pietz, 'The Problem of the Fetish', Part 2, p. 44.

13. From Auguste Comte, *Cours de philosophie positive*, extracted in J. Pontalis (ed.), *Objets du fétichisme.*

14. 'Fetishism leads nowhere and the colonisers may have a clear conscience.' Jean Pouillon, *Fétiches sans Fétichisme*, in J. Pontalis (ed.), *Objets du fétichisme*.
15. W. Pietz, 'The Problem of the Fetish', Part 1, p. 7.
16. W.J. Mitchell, *Iconology: Image, Text, Ideology* (Chicago: Chicago University Press, 1986).
17. Ibid., p. 200.
18. K. Marx, *Capital*, vol. 1, p. 72.
19. Ibid., pp. 74–5.
20. T. Gabriel, '*Xala*: Cinema of Wax and Gold', p. 340.
21. Ibid.

Chapter 9

1. Stuart Hall, Introduction to Allon White, *Carnival Writing Hysteria: The Essays and Autobiography of Allon White* (Oxford: Clarendon Press, 1933), p. 1.
2. In Lowell Edmunds and Allan Dundas (eds), *Oedipus. A Folklore Casebook* (New York: Garland Publishing, 1984).
3. Jean-Joseph Goux, *Oedipus, Philosopher* (Stanford, Calif.: Stanford University Press, 1993).
4. Teresa de Lauretis, 'The Desire for Narrative', in *Alice Doesn't: Feminism, Semiotics, Cinema* (Bloomington: Indiana University Press, 1982).
5. Barbara Creed, *The Monstrous Feminine* (London: Routledge, 1993).
6. Laura Mulvey, 'The Oedipus Myth: Beyond the Riddles of the Sphinx', in *Visual and Other Pleasures* (London: Macmillan, 1989).
7. Janet Bergstrom, 'Interview with Raymond Bellour', *Camera Obscura*, nos 3–4, p. 92.
8. Jane Austen, *Northanger Abbey* (Harmondsworth: Penguin Classics, 1972), p. 190.
9. Rosemary Jackson, *Fantasy: The Literature of Subversion* (London: Methuen, 1981), p. 95.
10. J. J. Goux, *Oedipus, Philosopher*, p. 161.
11. Ibid., p. 179.
12. Ibid., p. 164.
13. Terry Castle, 'Phantasmagoria: Spectral Technology and the Metaphorics of Modern Reverie', *Critical Inquiry*, vol. 15, Autumn 1988, p. 52.
14. Tom Gunning, 'Phantom Images and Modern Manifestations: Spirit Photography, Magic Theater, Trick Films and Photography's Uncanny', in Patrice Petro (ed.), *Fugitive Images* (Bloomington: Indiana University Press, 1995), p. 60.
15. Ibid., p. 61.
16. A. Breton, 'As in a Wood', in Paul Hammond (ed.), *The Shadow and its Shadows* (London: BFI, 1978), p. 43.
17. J. Brunius, 'Crossing the Bridge', in Paul Hammond (ed.), *The Shadow and its Shadows* (London: BFI, 1978), p. 61.
18. Ibid.
19. Sigmund Freud, 'The Uncanny', in *The Standard Edition of the Complete Works of Sigmund Freud*, vol. 17 (London: The Hogarth Press, 1955).
20. Thank you to Ann Banfield for pointing out these connections to me.
21. J. J. Goux, *Oedipus, Philosopher,* p. 177.

Postscript

1. Jimmie Durham, 'The Search for Virginity', p. 154; and 'Ni' Go Tlunh A Do Ka', p. 109, in *A Certain Lack of Coherence* (London: Kala Press, 1993).
2. Frantz Fanon, *The Wretched of the Earth* (London: Penguin Books, 1967), pp. 31–2.
3. Jimmie Durham, 'American Indian Culture: Traditionalism and Spiritualism in a Revolutionary Struggle', in *A Certain Lack of Coherence*, p. 2.
4. In his *Memoirs*, Chateaubriand tells the following anecdote about his first encounter with the virgin wilderness: 'When, after crossing the Mohawk, I entered some woods

where no trees had been felled, I was seized with a sort of intoxication and independence: I went from tree to tree, left to right, saying to myself, "Here are no roads, no cities, no monarchies, no republics, no presidents, no kings, no men." Alas, I imagined that I was alone in that forest in which I held my head so high! But suddenly I almost ran into the side of a shelter. Under the roof of that shelter, my astonished eyes beheld the first savages I had ever seen. There were a score of them, men and women, all daubed with paint, with half naked bodies, slit ears, crows' feathers on their heads and rings in their noses. A little Frenchman, his hair all curled and powdered ... was scraping a pocket fiddle and making the Iroquois dance the Madelon Friquet. M. Violet was the savages' dancing master. They paid him for lessons in beaver skins and bears' hams. ... Speaking for the Indians he always said, "These savage ladies and gentlemen". It was a terrible experience for a disciple of Rousseau, this introduction to savage life through a dancing lesson given to some Iroquois by General Rochambeau's sometime scullion. I was tempted to laugh but I felt cruelly humiliated'. *The Memoirs of Chateaubriand* (London: Penguin Classics, 1965), p. 164.

5. Peter Hulme, *Colonial Encounters* (London: Methuen, 1986), p. 139.
6. Tzvetan Todorov, *The Conquest of America* (London: Harper & Row, 1985), p. 121.
7. See J. Durham, 'American Indian Culture', in *A Certain Lack of Coherence*, pp. 16–17.
8. Jimmie Durham, 'Creativity and the Social Process', in *A Certain Lack of Coherence*, pp. 69–70.
9. J. Durham, 'Ni' Go Tlunh A Do Ka', in *A Certain Lack of Coherence*, p. 108.
10. Quoted in Michael Rogin, 'Liberal Society and the Indian Question', in *Ronald Reagan, the Movie* (Berkeley and Los Angeles: California University Press, 1987), p. 142.
11. Frederick Turner (ed.), *North American Indian Reader* (New York: Viking Books, 1974), p. 252.
12. Quoted in M. Rogin, *Ronald Reagan, the Movie*, pp. 154–5.
13. Peter Nabokov (ed.), *Native American Testimony* (New York and London: Penguin Books, 1991), p. 233.
14. Henry Nash Smith, *The Virgin Land* (Cambridge, Mass.: Harvard University Press, 1970), p. 92.

Index of Names and Titles

Titles (of films, books, etc.) are given in *italic*.
Character names in films have *not* been indexed.